Culture and Economy

Changes in Turkish Villages

Culture and Economy

Changes in Turkish Villages

Edited by Paul Stirling

THE EOTHEN PRESS

British Library Cataloguing-in-Publication Data
A catalogue record for this book is available from the British Library

First published by The Eothen Press, 1993

Published by The Eothen Press, 10 Manor Road, Hemingford, Grey, Huntingdon, Cambridgeshire, England, PE18 9BX

ISBN 0 906719 19 4

The publication of this book has been greatly facilitated by a loan made by the British Institute of Archaeology at Ankara.

Contents

Contributors

Dr Lale Yalçın-Heckman studied social anthropology at the London School of Economics and Political Science. She learnt Kurdish and worked in villages in Hakkari in S.E. Turkey. She is currently doing research on Turks in Germany, and is attached to Oriental Studies in the Otto-Friedrich University, Bamberg.

Dr Martin Stokes, after a first degree in Music at Oxford, moved to Social Anthropology, and did field work, now published as a book, on music, in Istanbul and in the rural Black Sea region. He is now teaching anthropology and ethnomusicology at the Queen's University, Belfast.

Dr David Shankland studied social anthropology at Edinburgh and Cambridge. He has done field work on Alevi and Sunni villages in central Anatolia. He is now Assistant Director of the British Institute of Archaeology at Ankara, and is working on a major comparison of 'modernisation' in rural Turkey.

Professor Werner Schiffauer studied social anthopology at the Freie Universität, Berlin, and conducted research both in a village of northern Turkey, and among its migrants in Germany. He is currently teaching and conducting research at the Institut für Europäische Ethnologie at Humboldt University, Berlin.

Dr Behrooz Morvaridi did field research on villages, in eastern Turkey, from Interdisciplinary Studies at the University of Kent. He is now teaching and conducting several projects at the Development and Project Planning Centre, Bradford University.

Dr Gabriele Paleczek studied anthropology at the Institut für Völkerkunde of the University of Vienna, where she now teaches and researches. After her research in a Laz 'forest' village near Bursa, she is now working on kinship and politics among Uzbeks in north-east Afghanistan.

Dr Ermine Onaran İncirlioğlu, after qualifying as a professional architect at METU, Ankara, studied anthropology at the University of Florida, Gainesville. She worked as Research Collaborator with Paul Stirling on his second study of two villages near Kayseri in 1986 and 1989. She is currently teaching Anthropology in the University of Kent at Canterbury.

Professor Chris Hann, after publishing his field work in Hungary and in Poland, studied tea production in north-east Turkey, and is currently working on the Laz in the same area. He has recently moved from Cambridge to Kent.

Dr Carol Delaney moved to anthropology, following up an interest in the relation between gender and cosmology. She has recently published her field research in a village near Ankara. She currently teaches in the Anthropology Department at Stanford.

Professor Bahattin Akşit studied sociology in the Middle East Technical University, Ankara, and then in Chicago. He has conducted several studies of Turkish villages and towns, is currently Professor of Sociology at METU, and is actively involved in a number of research projects.

Dr Çağlar Keyder studied economics at Yale and the University of California, Berkeley. He taught at METU, Ankara, and is currently Associate Professor of Sociology at the State University of New York, Binghampton. He is currently working on the decline of the nation-state.

Dr Belma Akşit studied sociology at METU. She is currently Associate Professor at Hacettepe University, Ankara, in the Department of Community Medicine, conducting research, advising, and teaching Medical Sociology and Anthropology in the Medical Faculty and the Schools of Social Work and Nutrition.

Professor Nermin Abadan-Unat after a long career, which includes Chairs of Political Science in Ankara and Istanbul, membership of the Turkish Senate, and many years of research, especially on Turks in Europe, is currently teaching political science at Boğaziçi University, and still conducting research.

Professor Paul Stirling studied Social Anthropology at Oxford; he is conducting research on rural change and labour migration. He has been working on Turkey since 1948, and now holds active honorary positions at the University of Kent at Canterbury and at the School of Oriental and African Studies, University of London.

[illegible]

The title 'Culture and Economy' was an afterthought to the invitation to run a conference, but one which reflected ideas and puzzles which have worried me for a long time. In the first invitation to potential readers of papers, I wrote, in a page on these ideas: 'An old commonplace in anthropology is that the economy of a people is embedded in their social structure ... more fashionably ... in their culture ... we could reverse the metaphor, and say that social structure and culture are embedded in a people's economy.' I make another attempt [illegible] these remarks in my opening contribution.

As with almost all conferences, the way the authors take seriously, interpret or ignore the announced theme is far from unifying. Obviously, my colleagues the authors do not share my puzzles in any simple way. I have not [illegible] to impose my own [illegible]. So reviewers may [illegible] that this volume, like most edited sets of conference papers, lacks unity.

Three replies. First, all the papers are about changes related to demographic and economic growth, and they are all concerned with villages in [illegible]. Second, by thinking of the articles not only as articles, but also as texts by informants, the multiple differences between the papers become fascinating in their own right and worth reading through as a single book. Third, in spite of the differences, we share disciplinary and intellectual common ground. [illegible]

This Book

Thanks and Comments

The essays in this book were first presented at a conference under the same title, organised at the invitation of Professor Clement Dodd of the Modern Turkish Studies Programme at SOAS, University of London, on June 6th and 7th 1990.[1] We had planned a small audience, to listen to a few papers for one day. We ended up with two crowded days and an astonishingly enthusiastic audience of over sixty people. By and large, the conference itself seemed to me, though I says it as shouldn't, an unmitigated success.

We would like to thank the British Academy, the British Council and the Nuffield Foundation as well as the Modern Turkish Studies Programme, the Centre for Near and Middle East Studies, and SOAS itself for generous support. The conference, and my contribution to this volume, arose from my research on two villages near Kayseri, S and E, from 1949 to 1990. I am grateful to the ESRC for two grants,[2] which financed my recent study. I thank also Dr Emine Onaran İncirlioğlu and others for collaboration in the research after 1983; and above all the villagers themselves, their children and grandchildren, for their unfailing Turkish hospitality over forty years, in the villages and in the towns of Turkey and Germany.

An edition of final versions of the papers cannot reflect the vivacity of a conference. It is not at all like the score to a symphony. Worse than that, my hopes and plans for a rapid edition of the papers, more or less as given, were aborted by realities, and I take the blame for hopes raised and not fulfilled, with profound apologies.

I originally intended an introduction in which I would conventionally and politely summarise each contribution. I rarely enjoy such introductions; and when I came to try to write one, I simply failed. So instead, I have aired some ideas which arise partly from two years of worrying about these papers; but even more from forty years grappling with insoluble problems as a teacher and researcher, but a highly constipated writer. In any case, the contributors are much better off, left to speak for themselves.

I decided not to try to group the papers by theme, but to print them in reverse alphabetical order. I then realised that this way, by coincidence, and with one major exception, all the papers which arise directly from empirical research come first, and the two last papers are general, with our senior contributor and perhaps most general paper in pride of place, as conclusion.The exception, Çağlar Keyder's article, fits best alongside Bahattin Akşit's paper, so I moved it out of alphabetical order.

The title, 'Culture and Economy' was an off-the-cuff reflex to the invitation to run a conference, but one which reflected ideas and puzzles which have worried me for a long time. In the first invitation to potential readers of papers, I wrote, in a page on these ideas: '.an old commonplace in anthropology is that the economy of a people is embedded in their social structure .... more fashionably ... in their culture ...; we could reverse the metaphor, and say that social structure and culture are embedded in a people's economy.' I make another attempt to explain these remarks in my opening contribution.

As with almost all conferences, the way the authors take seriously, interpret or ignore the announced theme is far from unifying. Obviously, my colleagues the authors do not share my puzzles in any simple way. I have not attempted to impose my own vision. So reviewers may well claim, with justification, that the volume, like most edited sets of conference papers, lacks unity.

Three replies. First, all the papers are about changes related to demographic and economic growth; and they are all concerned with villages in Turkey. Second, by thinking of the articles not only as articles, but also as texts by informants, the multiple differences between the papers become fascinating in their own right, and worth reading through as a single book. Third, in spite of the differences, we share disciplinary and intellectual common ground. Of the authors, eight are anthropologists, writing about field work in Turkish villages; three are sociologists with anthropological sympathies and anthropological style field work, of whom Behrooz Morvaridi now teaches development studies. Çağlar Keyder is a distinguished historian teaching in a historically minded sociology department. Finally, Nermin Abadan Unat is renowned as sociologist, political scientist, and politician, deeply committed to modernising Turkey. So not only do we have thirteen lively and serious papers; we have thirteen papers which relate to each other in all kinds of ways - complex ways!

The preparation of the typescript owes a lot to the help of Barbara Delaney, Margaret Stirling and Marc Arnold, but far and away the greatest efforts were by Joyce Hutchinson to whose incredible hard work and patience, well beyond the call of duty, in producing the final text I am deeply indebted.

Notes

1. Except for that of Werner Schiffauer, whom I invited to contribute.
2. Grants G 00 232121, 1985-6; and R000 321951, 1989-91.

| 1 |

Growth and Changes

Speed Scale Complexity

Paul Stirling

Turkey: Multiple Changes

Turkey became a nation state in 1923. From then on, it grew prodigiously. In round figures, by 1986, the population had multiplied by 4, from about 12.5 to over 50 million, and Gross National Product by about 20. So the GNP per cap., that is, in theory, the average wealth created annually by each separate citizen, grew five times - 500 per cent - in just over sixty years. True that this internationally established econometric construction is seriously misleading; that it ignores distribution, that it is a sieve of statistical loopholes, and that it in no way measures material welfare, let alone subjective sense of well being. But an increase of five times in the value of things produced on average by every individual, achieved within sixty odd years - one life time, two and a bit generations - is not just surprising, it is fabulous; what other superlatives can I use?[1]

Of course, this growth began from a trough. In 1923, eleven years of war had severely disrupted the traditional agricultural and craft production systems of an agrarian society, and almost destroyed its tiny modern industry. Wars and then the exchange of population with Greece had caused what Keyder (Chapter 12) calls a demographic catastrophe. But from 1923 on, the Second World War apart, the

Turkish economy grew by almost 7 per cent till 1978, and resumed growth at around 5 per cent in 1980.

Changes on this scale at this pace over decades are unprecedented in human history, and almost unparalleled even in recent times, except perhaps for Japan, one or two other contemporary nations, and countries with mineral windfalls. Certainly, both nationally and in local detail, they are breathtaking; and extremely complex. They are of course part of world capitalist industrialisation, which, for all the great minds, and billions of words, still defies description, let alone explanation. But even in the context of the 'world economy', they are exceptional; and a set of facts which virtually no one seems adequately to take into account.

Such a speed of economic growth imposes speed in numerous other changes. The movement and the uneven accumulation of old and new capital in dozens of different ways and thousands of different hands; uneven increases - and some decreases - in income, some very large; a new national occupational structure; the migration of millions from villages to towns and cities, and abroad; the introduction and invention of new ways of organising people, both in the private sector, economic and otherwise, and in a hugely increased state sector; masses of new legislation; vast new stocks of unevenly distributed 'social knowledge' - information, science and technology, alternative world views, political and religious ideas, familiarity with other societies. And so on and so on.

In the first years of this growth, when the economy was still recovering its former levels, Atatürk carried though his renowned and astonishing political reforms. The central provinces of the heterogeneous Islamic Ottoman Empire, legitimated by God, became a sovereign, national, secular Republic, formally legitimated by the Will of the People (Berkes, 1974). The pragmatic, now 'sacred', boundaries of this newly enacted people-nation enclosed a population, following exchanges and departures, almost wholly Islamic - the majority Sunni of the Hanefi rite. Over three-quarters spoke a form of Turkish as their mother tongue; the rest were conveniently decreed to be Turks also.[2] Ten per cent were literate, and about 80 per cent were villagers. The basic State services, and the formal basis of orderly social relations - law and the judiciary, education, the constitutional status of Islam, the script, even clothes, names, and the calendar - were transformed from the top down; in a European and secular direction, which explicitly rejected the

Ottoman and Islamic past.

It is one thing to pass laws, and impose conformity on the elites in the main cities. It is quite another to set up the institutions necessary to provide courts, lawyers, police, schools, teachers, medical services, government offices, all with adequately trained and loyal personnel. It is even more difficult to get people all over the country to change their personal habits, talk, thoughts, customs, moralities. The reforms took decades to put into effective practice. The interactions between the demographic and economic growth, the new ideas, and the new laws and institutions are immensely complex. One very general link; it was economic growth, and especially the migration of the villagers to towns and cities, that integrated the new nation, by gradually forcing people to apply the reforms in daily detail.

Theme and Contradiction

One theme is complexity. Almost all refutations of specific social science 'theories' amount to establishing that the theory or model is too simple. Usually rightly, because none of the models or theories discussed or proposed so far, measure up to the complexity of social processes, still less to the scale and speed of the changes in those processes. Not only the 'ordinary' people, the educated elite, and the politicians, professionals, and business men who make decisions for others, but we the accredited social science experts cannot do other than use models which are too simple.

The opposite is often claimed, and is highly plausible. Simplicity is the essence of scientific advance; atoms, viruses, the double helix. A major controversy. The great simplifiers in the social sciences are less precise, and less accepted; the hidden hand, the class struggle, false consciousness, reciprocity, segmentary structures, binary opposites, power and prestige, clientelism. And while simplifying is a necessary condition for working at all, we are not ready enough to recognise that simplifying also - inevitably - misrepresents.

In practice, all social scientists, even those who deny it, use the idea of a complex set of related processes which enable a society both recognisably to continue its existence and at the same time to change. I cannot see how to conceive of 'process' if not as a set, a tangled web, of interacting causes and effects. When the changes are rapid, the devising of adequate 'models' is prodigiously difficult.

The title of this book is a simplification. By setting 'culture' and 'the economy' side by side, I suggest, fallaciously, two entities between which causes and effects are possible. The same fallacy is implicit in distinguishing between culture and social structure, as I also did in my the first invitation to the Conference. I was restating the one time anthropological orthodoxy - 'substantivism' - that purely economic models of social processes grossly underestimate both 'culture', in the anthropological sense, and social structure, in the sense of the whole intricate pattern of social relations. But if culture is defined as everything learned, it cannot strictly be separate from, and opposed to, the economy or to the social structure; it must include them.

But the word is a chameleon, overused for convenience. It offers multiple escapes from precision. So let me make my point in more verbose rhetoric. The fund of cosmologies, myths, religious ideas, historical narratives, political models, private moralities, customs, rites, technologies, scientific ideas, which exists in any society at any given point in time must profoundly affect the way that economy functions and the way it changes; and economic growth must in turn have profound and multifarious consequences for that fund. A truism, but one largely ignored in practice; which is why economists and marxists get so many things so very wrong.

I used 'culture' because it is fashionable, and convenient. The notion of 'social structure' as a pattern of social relations - once called role relations - is less fashionable, but no less fundamental. It covers all social conduct, from minute by minute social encounters to the national and international distribution of power and resources. But who would allow '(Culture-and/or-Social Structure), and the Economy' as a title for anything?

The Two Theories

Let me caricature the two main 'economistic' ways of thinking about Turkey's experience. Modernisation theories implicitly assume that, with minor hiccoughs and accidents, all human societies, are being carried by unbuckable market forces towards a blessed, competitive state of advanced capitalist industrial prosperity, in a set of sovereign 'nation' states, each with, sooner or later, liberal elections. All humans will eventually enjoy human rights, and all will be comfortable and happy, if unequal. Except, of course, sadly, for the inevitable losers at the bottom (20 per cent?); the unfortunate, the incompetent, the undeserving, the unduly unselfish; and the 'individually' bad; or rather, the bad who are unsuccessful. These are taken care of by private charity, by public welfare, and by the police and the prisons.

Radicals - mainly (at the time of the conference) varieties of marxists and socialists - stress the appalling and cruel inequalities of modern capitalism, both within and between nations; the ways that the rich and powerful, deliberately or inadvertently, exploit the poor for their own advantage, and prevent them from catching up[3]; and, incidentally, are destroying the planet in the process. They advocate - or used to - an alternative road to universal happiness, based on rational, egalitarian and selfless co-operation and equality, organised by benign public control. Both sides treat 'culture' as a set of economically irrelevant pleasures and customs, and of traditional, even 'irrational', practices and 'attitudes', which may well inhibit progress. They do not allow for a set of autonomous 'cultural' factors in the social process; still less do they see themselves, their theories, and their political supporters as social and cultural phenomena to be analysed; phenomena which their own theories do not explain.

These theories, like most -all? - others, advocate or imply moralities, and purposes. People, including academics, see opponents as lost in culpable error, even as morally 'evil'. In spite of endless discussion of 'values' in the social sciences, the damage they do to clear thinking still seems to me seriously underestimated. If my own strongly held and often incompatible moralities confuse my own thinking, I find the same difficulties in much that I read.

Four Convictions

These papers then confirm four long-standing convictions. First, that the main task, and one which all of us take seriously, is modestly to establish specific causalities; that is, that a factor X has at least some influence on an outcome Y; or that an outcome Y is in part a result of a factor X. Yet authors avoid using the word 'cause' itself, using instead an endless variety of euphemisms.

Second, that both the 'facts' and the causal processes about which most of us express some confidence are far more difficult to establish than most of us admit.

Third, the central words, the major concepts, are virtually always shifting and fuzzy.

Fourth. We claim to study the 'mental maps', 'models' - large scale and small scale, culturally and personally constructed - which other people use. It is fashionable to stress, more than in the recent past, that we too have such mental maps and models, which are likewise constructed by our own cultures and personalities. Obviously true and important; implying a duty for 'reflexivity'.

But it does not follow that our work is invalid. These 'maps' are transmissible, discussable and in spite of losses, errors and misunderstandings, are by and large cumulative; they do get better as maps over time. To put the point differently, mankind has manifestly in the last 10,000 years, and especially in the last 200, accumulated by logic and evidence an immense store of 'truth', of effective maps of reality; social as well as physical. Yet it remains true (!) that every individual human lives, must live, in a cognitive universe, the main outlines of which rest not on logic, evidence and research, but on faith. And moreover even the myriad practical detailed maps of social reality which describe bits of that universe for daily use also rest more often on faith or on authority than on experience, direct evidence and logic. The ethnography of these 'maps' is both central to the changes in Turkey, and extremely difficult to record accurately.

Comments and Conclusions

Do I myself draw any conclusions about Turkey? Yes, with these reservations. Six generalisations, based on these thirteen excellent articles, and on over forty years of my own work in and on Turkey; with theoretical and, I regret, moral overtones. And a last comment on values.

(i) Demography

The population of Turkey, as I have said, has increased by a factor of over 4 since 1923; and since my arrival in 1950, by 2.5; from 20 million to well over 50 million. In S in 1950, 600 people resided in 100 households. In 1986, we estimated 840 people in the village in some 143 households, and 650 people outside the village in 165 households, all descended patrilineally from those six hundred.[4] These national and local increases are directly due to falling death rates, especially among children.

Two points. This growth is both proof and the direct result of a general rise in the standard of living. Second, in no way could these extra people have stayed alive without labour migration from the villages. Some migrants diversified and increased village household incomes by remitting urban earnings; some permanently removed whole households which the villages could neither feed nor employ, This huge increase in the numbers of both of urban cash earners, and of rural and urban consumers, must be an integral part of any causal model of social change. Without remittances and departures, rural death rates would have simply continued much as before.

Was this increase in people, with all its consequences, a good thing or a bad thing? That is quite another - unanswerable? - question. I would not know how to begin deciding, but it is not my job - our job - to do so.

(ii) Economic Growth

The real average standard of living has risen sharply. GNP per capita increased roughly threefold, 1950 - 1986. What I see among the villagers and their urban descendants makes these calculations a plausible index. Food, clothes, heating, housing, transport, health services, household durables and furniture, consumption for pleasure and for display, operating capital for farming, investments in agriculture, real estate and businesses are all incomparably more plentiful per person than in 1950; three times is not obviously wrong.

Agriculture alone nowhere near accounts for the increase. In the plateau villages which I know, with poor soils and a dry climate, the changes in agricultural techniques and crops have brought increases of around 50 per cent in production per hectare. Tractors and other machinery have greatly reduced the male labour required per hectare, and thus given a large increase in agricultural productivity per man day. As Morvaridi stresses, some agricultural changes actually increase the demand for, and burden of, some kinds of female labour, mostly unpaid; and many women suffer directly. But it does not follow that even their productivity has not risen; and when household income rises, as he says, women also get some benefit.

In other parts of Turkey, technical and crop changes, often combined with irrigation - cotton, citrus, vegetables, dairying, poultry, meat production, and so on - have increased both production per hectare and productivity per person, on a dramatic scale; in some cases agricultural labour demand has actually increased (Akşit, Chapter 13 and Sirman, 1988). These increases in turn depend on industrialisation; on tractors, fertilisers, transport, packaging, food processing; and on markets.

The growth of the urban economy - industry and services - has created a huge demand for this rural labour surplus. I now realise that till at least the late 1950s, Turkey had in fact a national labour shortage, greatly aggravated undoubtedly by local and seasonal under- and un-employment, by shortages of many much needed skills, and by geographical maldistribution. In hard fact, no one knows, or has ever known, real current unemployment rates.[5]

Wallerstein (Smith and Wallerstein, 1992) has recently classified household incomes into five sources; subsistence, profits, wages, investment income, and transfers. In 1950, most household income was mainly subsistence, with some profits, from land and animals; wages were already important for a minority. In 1986, all normal households had multiple incomes, of which that from land and animals made up on average a very much smaller part; in S, I estimate less than half the total village income.

Certainly, still in 1986, some were poor, and a few very poor. The most common causes of poverty were illness, handicap, or premature death. Where a household had no land, or very little, no adult man fit to work and earn, and no unmarried carpet-weaving daughters, life could be very hard indeed. In towns, unskilled or socially unsuccessful men might earn very little; the old might not earn at all. But in 1986, the handicapped apart, no one we met or heard about from the two villages seemed to be hungry, cold or in rags. In 1950/1, many were. In terms of material wealth and comfort, 1986 is, on average and for the vast majority, a totally different world from 1950.

(iii) Inequality

Successful capitalism creates wealth; a very large amount of it. It does nothing whatsoever to ensure that this wealth is 'fairly', let alone equally distributed; nor that the production of it is humane and environmentally harmless. On the contrary, wherever capitalism has prospered, it has led to major concentrations of wealth and power for some, destitution for others; and to all kinds of skulduggery, exploitation, suffering, social disruptions and political upheavals; not to mention ecological damage. All governments exercise a vast plethora of controls over market forces in the public interest, and by and large with considerable success. They must and do buck the market, and the market in turn depends on a minimal political guarantee of order

Overall, Turkey has currently one of the largest statistical skews between rich and poor reported in the World Development Report (World Bank, 1986). A few people - most had advantages to begin with - have got very rich; most are decidedly better off; some have remained poor; a few have even got poorer (Paleczek, Chapter 7). Some enjoy excellent amenities, even in so called *gecekondus*; others live and work in terrible conditions, often away from their families for long periods.

Could such a society, with different policies, have achieved this growth with less inequality, disruption, and suffering? Or could it have grown even faster? As a social scientist, I do not know; does anyone?

(iv) Occupational Change

The population not directly dependent on agriculture went up from around 4 million in 1950 to about 27 million in 1986, nearly seven times (İstatistik Yıllığı, 1951, 1986). Four-fifths of these extra 23 million must have been the children, children's children, or children's children's children of peasant families.

A 'peasant'[6] household is assumed - far too simply - to farm land and raise animals, which roughly employs all its collective labour, and produces enough in kind and in commodities to provide for all its collective needs. In a village of peasant households, the occupation of peasant is not an identity. A man is not what he does for a living, but the owner of a specific house and specific land, belonging in a specific way to a specific village. Men, women and children work as members of household teams. In 1950, in S and E, direct close links with townspeople were fairly rare (cf. Turhan, 1951, Keyder, Chapter 12).

Men who go to town, go to earn, that is, to find a job. In these villages, it was often a building skill; though I do have a list of about a hundred different occupations. Whatever the job, the new job holder has to develop an occupational network to get, keep or renew it, and to make it comfortable and lucrative. In the town a man is what he does. People learn all kinds of skills and find all kinds of jobs, and by doing so, they become new 'persons' with different identities. They now belong, both immediately and potentially, to a much more complex social structure, with many new kinds of social relations; and with different futures (Schiffauer, Chapter 5), as most contributors in this book make clear.

It is a commonplace that villages forge bridgeheads for finding urban jobs and urban housing. So sometimes people from a given area are concentrated in particular occupations, and sometimes in particular districts in cities. This is not by any means universal. S men migrants, for example, are nearly all connected to the building industry, (most of them are tilers), but they are residentially scattered. The detailed distribution of people in occupations - and also by residence - is not decided primarily by market forces, but by a whole set of interacting factors, among which the market is only one.

Millions of villagers are now distributed in urban Turkey in hundreds of new and different occupations, in a wide variety of residences and with a wide range of incomes, educations and statuses; they all live in social networks very different from those of full-time farming villagers, and often from each other. They do not constitute collectively a proletariat, still less an 'informal sector'.[7] Occupational change is central to economic growth; and that requires radical changes in identities, in social structure, in skill and knowledge, and *a fortiori* in 'culture'.

Because virtually all villages, and most village households, have now members earning in towns, or former members resident in town, village social networks and identities have also changed dramatically (cf. Schiffauer, Chapter 5, Abadan-Unat, Chapter 14). Their networks are far more dispersed, and integrated with the national and international society, and with Turks abroad; and far less homologous with those of fellow villagers. Villagers' village identities reflect the occupations, incomes, social statuses, and destinations of both their pendular and their household migrants.

(v) Organisational Change

The co-ordinated arrangements of people in groups to get things done are central to all activities in all societies. Unfortunately, in social science literature, 'organisation' often suggests modern management ; and 'social organisation', traditional kinship. Even in small groups, such arrangements virtually always involve some hierarchy. Organised groups have problems; control and delegation, legitimacy, privileges for some, internal competition, incompetence, and the use of organisational power and resources for private, even nefarious, purposes; larger groups have more problems. The most conspicuous form of large organisation is the State itself, - government - which was after all only invented about 6,000 years ago. My own hunch is that the progressive invention of more and more effective forms of co-ordinating people for an increasing variety of social purposes is one main factor in human social evolution. What sets the USA, Germany and Japan at the apex of the contemporary world is superior organisation. Likewise, the recent manifest political and economic failure of most of the world's socialist governments is organisational. The state has simply failed to run a modern economy efficiently and benignly.

Turkey's growth has involved the invention, reinvention and borrowing of dozens of new kinds of organisation; and the establishment or expansion of thousands of new and old organisations. Discovering and setting up effective rules, controls and arrangements, training personnel, building up experience and informal working practices takes decades. Since (almost?) all humans are primarily concerned with their personal power and prestige, controllers and members of organisations often put their private interests ahead of those of the organisation (Stirling, 1968). In all countries, 'better' organisation is an issue. In Turkey, from the organisation of the government itself down to the village midwife sunning herself in the garden of her government house, there is a vast amount to be learned - and applied - about effectiveness, commitment and supervision.[8]

The villagers of course always knew effectively about their own organisations; households, farming, marriages, villages, markets, and relations with their State.[9] But they have also learned an enormous amount about outside organisations of many kinds. They learn mainly *ad hoc* what it is in their interest to know, what helps them to solve the next problem. They can only do this within the limits of their existing knowledge, perceptions and experience; and of their own morality. Enriching their household, or doing favours for kin, friends and allies is a moral duty; far more important than observing specific laws or formal rules, or pursuing the planned purposes of other people's organisations.

By contrast, villagers who become entrepreneurs find themselves needing to organise and control others in new ways, and to establish new kinds of relations with other businessmen, professionals, and officials. Many villagers from S and E now act as building contractors, many run commercial undertakings, retail and wholesale, and a few have become manufacturers. A large number are building subcontractors in a given craft. All these have to learn to manage the internal and external relations of new organisations unlike villages and farming households.

A great many Turks, and not only villagers, seem to assume that if you want something from, or within, a large organisation, then to get it, what you most need is not a formally correct case, nor even manipulative knowledge of the working of the system, but a personal link to someone of power above or within the organisation who is prepared to use that power on your behalf. Thus personal networks, 'patron client relations', are thought to be the most crucial factor in the daily running of organisations (Güneş-Ayata, 1990). This perception, which is far too simple not to be false, closely matches the villagers' experience, assumptions and commitment to households and friends. Village and migrant morality fit cosily into this national culture of networking. Which raises interesting, if sensitive, questions for another occasion.[10]

(vi) Cognitive Change.

Nothing struck me more forcibly when I returned to the two villages in 1971 than what I then called the information explosion (Stirling, 1974). In order to earn, a farmer goes to town and learns a new skill; he may even go to a new country. Even to go to town, he needs information. When he gets there he needs to know how to survive. To earn, he needs to know not only what the job requires, but who gives jobs, how they can be persuaded to choose him; and so on. Those who enter new skilled occupations - the building trade, contracting, shopkeeping, manufacturing cement sewer pipes - need to know a lot more. Young men in the village learn to repair tractors, operate videos, mend refrigerators, wire houses. All who do not go and talk to those who do. Everyone watches television and listens to the radio. I was constantly asked about Thatcher and Liverpool (*futbol*). The State, through schools, colleges and universities, and through the Office of Religious Affairs is pumping out vast quantities of new knowledge and ideology. In short, the increase since 1950 in 'knowledge' in Turkey, in the sense of all the bits of information and disinformation, facts, ideas, theories, dogmas, stories, cannot be measured; but it is certainly huge, vast; and underestimated, under-researched and under-discussed.

Of course, everyone knows about the need for formal knowledge, for science and technology. What is not discussed is what I call social cognition (Fischer, 1991). Humans seldom stop talking. Out of this continuous conversation is created a shared world of ideas and beliefs built - now - round the multitude of new experiences and new learning and new purposes which arise from new social contexts. All this is linked to the new occupational structure, and to the growth of new organisations; greatly augmented by formal education, television in almost every home, and an active press. But it is also part of every social encounter in the land.[11]

The words 'information' or 'knowledge' imply feeding blocks of truth into a vacuum. But this new socially shared construction of reality is grounded in existing experience, and existing cognitive structures. People as they pass it on to others add home-made logic, plausible connections, misunderstandings, and that quintessential human gift, fantasy. This vast arena of possible ideas is flexible and kaleidoscopic. The people who are doing new jobs, operating in and manipulating new organisations and social networks, are also living in new cognitive worlds of their own shared constructions. These constructions are of course constantly trimmed by real - or imagined - experience. Some ideas, new and old, take a long time to change; some never do. Moreover, these cognitive processes are not homogeneous; they generate cognitive proliferation, and often fierce arguments, even violence. That is, in time, people, within the cultural unity derived from, imposed by the nation state, become, more or less fortuitously, more and more culturally distinct.[12]

A digression. Social cognition seems to me highly relevant to the 'Islamic Revival', and to the academic and political discussion about it. Islam provides most Turks with (among other things) a cosmos, a guarantee, an ultimate legitimation of social order, morality and purpose. But people's cognitive worlds are in complex flux, from science and Darwinian evolution in schools, and a secular, elected government which controls religion and pays all imams, to an international world, often seen mainly as hostile, dominated by Europe, the USA, Japan and the multinationals. Of course, not all Turks live in the same Islamic universe in the first place (Tapper, 1991; Shankland, Chapter 4). But making sense of their new worlds in terms of their old cosmos gives people a whole spectrum of different constructions of reality and of morality. I find it consistent (notice that I am covertly implying causal connection) with this generalising impressionistic description that some of these new constructions proclaim new fundamentalist certainties, which, though seen as grounded in the old unchangeable revelation, in fact provide a new social and political programme to cope with the new situations and new threats.

(vii) Causal Complexity

Each of these five headings is shorthand for a whole set of further points; and they are not independent. Isolating topics for research is essential. But it is both difficult, because of the seamless tangles which are social reality; and dangerous, because the simplifying essential to comprehensibility is likely also to mislead. This brings me back to the theme of complexity. Many models - for example, the argument for a distinguishable set of 'paths of transformation' (Keyder, Chapter 12; Akşit, Chapter 13) are not wrong. They are too simple. We need to work out more complex models; much more complex. I know that I am not able to do so. Others may be more confident.

Values Again

All these changes cause new, sometimes intense suffering, and a host of perceived injustices and grievances. So did similar changes in Europe and the USA; and have already (with worse to come?) in former socialist countries now attempting a market economy and democratic politics. For Turkey, the suffering apart, there are those who lament the Mercedes culture of the idle rich, the nationalisation of local 'folk' music, the transformation of the five days of village weddings into an evening in a hired hall with the bride in a white European dress, the arrival of western symphony orchestras, and *nouvelle vogue* films in Turkish elite 'culture'. Not to mention discussions of the 'peripheralisation' of the Turkish economy; its subordination to western based multinationals, international banks, and the interests of the G7; the 'forced' rural urban migration, consumerism, sharp and growing inequalities, and secularism, agnosticism and anti-secularism. Not surprising that some of Delaney's village informants share her suspicions of modernism and progress (Chapter 10).

But I do not want to reverse it all. I would not want my best village friend's *gelin*, who was saved by caesarian in the Kayseri University hospital, to have died with her child, as she would have in 1950. Nor do I want people to be walking in the snow without shoes, shivering because their supply of cattle dung cakes has run out before the end of winter, nor seeing their children weedy from malnutrition.

The extollers and the denouncers of modernisation, or capitalism, are both highly selective. How can anyone make an overall moral judgement on all these processes of change? They have happened: the results are there.

As an anthropologist, I am part of a collective effort to understand them. I find the complexity incredibly difficult to analyse. As a moral person, I have my own firm views and I hold that understanding social processes is relevant both to judgements, and to framing successful policies at all levels. But I also hold that understanding - achieving 'truth', that is, less misleading models of social processes - is a separate and morally neutral task.

Notes

1. I first realised the startling speed of growth in the first two decades from tables 3.2 (p.46) and 4.5 and 4.6 (pp.76-7), in Hale 1981, based on Bulutay *et al.* 1974. See also tables 5.10 (pp. 108) and 7.2, 7.3 (pp.132-3), based on DSİ 1973, and more recent official sources. See, e.g., *Turkey Economy,* Aug. 1992, p.47.
2. All school children in Turkey declare daily in unison how fortunate they are to be Turks; to the surprise of visiting foreign children - recent personal communication from foreign children.
3. 'The poor are not just living off the crumbs from the rich man's table, they are being asked to put the crumbs back', David Bryer, Oxfam director, Observer 11 October 1992.
4. Of course I am not claiming any demographic rigour. My reasons for not following up the households of married daughters, and daughters' daughters, as well as those of married sons and sons' sons, were largely pragmatic; but also related to the perceptions and knowledge of my largely male informants. The decision was taken in 1950, and irreversible.
5. All published numbers are calculated from economic models. Hard empirical evidence that unemployment is now serious and growing rests on widespread personal impressions. Certainly in 1986, the greater part of the village and migrant households which I knew had at last an adequate income, and many were comfortable. I knew of very few adult men who could be called 'unemployed', on a long term basis. The majority worked intermittently; and, except at harvest, most men present in the village at any one time had little to do. By contrast, David Shankland commenting on this note, reported personally a large amount of unemployment in the Alevi village which he studied, and among its migrants (Chapter 4).

6. Notice that Turkish has no word for 'peasant'; *köylü* - villager - is not 'peasant,' though most peasants are *köylü,* and most *köylü* peasants. cf. Keyder (Chapter 12).
7. The idea of two separate urban economies is nonsense, at least in Turkey.
8. Attempts to make this point in Turkey. even privately. normally arouse combative resentment. One 'objective', if foolish, public attempt cost me, in my view of reality, a year of research time. People see organisation, not as something which needs slow cultural learning, but as a natural national virtue. Even to raise it for discussion is insulting. But human societies do vary sharply in the style and effectiveness of their organisational culture. In 1923, notwithstanding the renowned Ottoman efficiency in earlier times, the Republic of Turkey began to 'modernise' with 80% peasants and 90% illiteracy; it did not have an easy road to modern efficiency.
9. It is difficult not to slip into writing about villagers as inferior. even as foolish, because they lack specific kinds of experience and information. Emphatically, they are not. But I fear there may be examples in my own writings; and certainly elsewhere in this book.
10. Have I got it wrong? If not, how does this affect public and private sector efficiency?
11. In a paper about our research delivered to the M.E.S.A. Conference, October, 1992, İncirlioğlu gives specific examples of the way reality is constructed, both by herself and me, and by the villagers.
12. Gellner, 1983.

| 2 |

Sheep and Money

Pastoral Production at the Frontiers

Lale Yalçın-Heckmann

Themes

Crossing frontiers is often risky. The frontiers of Hakkari are currently (in 1989) more than normally perilous; even in 1980, a measure of masculine bravado was involved. The patterns of internal and cross frontier trade are, obviously, related both to national policies, and to international patterns of exchange among the Kurds on each side of the border. This situation raises some interesting sociological questions. In this paper I examine the organisation of small scale 'illegal' animal trade in Hakkari, Turkey's most southeasterly province, describe the habitus of a smuggling community there, and evaluate the various aspects of this trade for those involved as actors. I also explore the particular ways in which the mode of pastoral production sets the conditions and limitations for this trade. The arguments here are based on fieldwork data from Hakkari, which I collected from 1980 to 1982. Due to the particular nature of this trade and its negative name (*kaçakcılı*, smuggling), exhaustive and systematic information on cross frontier trade was not available. Nevertheless, the tribal group and the tribal village which I know best lived from smuggling and pastoral trade. Hence my analysis is based on a certain degree of logical guesswork about the networks and relations of smuggling, and on evaluation based on post-fieldwork visits to, and on communications from, Hakkari.

The discussion here draws on at least two wider issues: firstly, it is related to the problem of identifying the national and the local levels of economy. The particular forms of penetration of the national into the village economy and the interaction between the two in the Turkish context have been discussed by several authors (Aydın, 1986, Keyder, 1983). These works provided models to explain structural transformations at macro and micro levels.

The pastoral economy in Hakkari is, in many ways, determined by both ecological and by historical factors. Yet national economy and state policies play a crucial role at all levels of the pastoral production and trade in Hakkari. I discuss this particular relationship from various aspects in this paper.

Secondly, the discussion here is concerned with the debate on the extent of an economy's embeddedness into culture. This issue, which has been much explored by anthropologists, is addressed to the level of moral meanings, symbols, and discourse Parry and Bloch (1989), for example, have recently argued for putting the analysis of money back 'into the cultural matrix into which money is incorporated' (p.21) and emphasized 'how an existing world view gives rise to particular ways of representing money' (p.19). In a similar fashion, I depict, on the one hand, the cultural background to a particular type of pastoral economy, and analyse how the value and means of exchange are produced and converted. More explicitly, I look at the organisation of semi-nomadic pastoral production in Hakkari's mountain villages, the conversion of sheep into money and vice versa, and discuss the effects of the political discourse and state policies under which certain economic activities are labelled 'legal' and others 'illegal'.

The Ethnographic Background

I begin with a brief outline of the organisation of semi-nomadic pastoral production in Hakkari. Mountains cover 88 per cent of the province, and 59 per cent of arable land is used as pastures. As a result, the village settlement pattern is extremely dispersed. Villages, which are really *mezraa* or *koma* rather than *köy,* have a mean population of about 600 people.[1] According to the 1980 census, 72 per cent of Hakkari's population was rural.

The semi-nomadic mode of life implies that the various village units are further divided seasonally and spatially according to the movement of flocks up and down the mountain pastures. The seasonal mobility and dispersion of the village population occurs between two extremes. From December until February, because of the climate, villagers and their animals are restricted to the village compound. The main pastoral productive activity during this time is the transfer of hay from the high mountain slopes on sleighs to the village, and feeding it to sheep and goats which stay within the household compound. At the other end of the cycle, the dispersion and mobility of both the people and animals are at their highest. This is the period between July and September. During these months villages are used as temporary residence, and pasture tents are the centre of all productive activity. Men and women daily travel between the village and the mountain slopes, for cutting and piling hay, for grazing the herds, or for milking the sheep and goats.

The seasonal cycle of pastoral production in the mountain villages determines not only the population mobility and the settlement pattern, but also the time and the ways of animal purchase and sale. Sheep and goats in Hakkari are the major source of capital.[2] In addition to the sheep and goats each household has at least a mule, sometimes a horse; and some households have cattle and oxen, used for milk and meat as well as for draught. Cattle, however, are rare in mountain villages. For those villages without proper roads, mules are the major means of transport, hence the market for mules is very active. The prices reflect the supply and demand not only in Hakkari but also in villages across the borders in Iran and Iraq.

Sheep and goats provide wool, hair, milk and skin for the household's own consumption and for sale. Like the Luri nomads described by Black-Michaud (1986:42), the semi-nomadic villagers in Hakkari keep fewer goats, which are for subsistence, than sheep, which are for sale and basically for accumulating wealth. Ewe's milk is used for making butter, cheese and yogurt; the latter two are the villagers' staple diet in the mountains. Butter is the main processed animal product. It is sold in large quantities to traders who come from town.

The Limits of Pastoral Production in Hakkari

The productivity of flocks, and the level of sales of products, are dependent on four sets of factors: geography and climate; demography; tribes and social organisation; markets and political organisation. First, Hakkari's rocky and mountainous landscape is not suitable for large-scale cattle raising. Sheep are also affected by climate fluctuations. Long winters are always feared. The amount of hay which has been piled up in autumn may not be enough. Hay bought in winter in town is about ten times more expensive than in summer, and large amounts of dried fodder are difficult to transport in winter conditions without proper roads. Short winters too are feared. Without enough snow it is difficult to bring the hay downhill on sleighs. Finally, other natural and physical events such as avalanches, landslides, and drought may all have a drastic effect on pastoral productivity and the price of sheep.

Second, demographic factors; the limitations set by the man/land/sheep ratio. Mountain villagers in Hakkari have little land on which to cultivate grain or maize. The crucial type of land is on the slopes of mountains on which grass can be cut. The mountain slopes around the villages are divided into strips of individually used meadow. The rights of usage for this land is mostly inherited, and occasionally sold as individual property. The pasture land, on the other hand, is almost always communally owned and used. The size of a household flock depends then on its rights to hay slopes, and to pasture; and on its male manpower for cutting and transporting grass. Alternative strategies, in cases of a shortage of manpower or land, involve the use of social capital (e.g. the support of kin), or of material capital such as land, cash, or hired labour.

Third, tribal and kinship relations. Tribe in the context of Hakkari and the Kurds is a group of people, who share the ideology of common patrilineal descent, even if the exact traces and links are unimportant and impossible to ascertain. The most important attribute of a tribe (*eşiret* in Kurdish) is that, it is the main population group which can claim, on the basis of traditional rights, the use of communal pastures. The term 'tribal' refers to attributes pertaining to, or thought to pertain, to tribes, and to their 'culture', norms, and values.[3]

Summer pastures 'belong' to tribes. So acknowledged member–ship of a tribe is a necessary condition for access to pastures. Even if a non-member can buy fields and a house in the village and the rights to cut grass on certain strips of mountain slopes, he cannot take his flock onto the summer grazing area without some form of kin or tribal connection. The most common way of forming such a contact and contract is through marriage. On the whole, there are three ways of obtaining access to pastures: (1) through inheritance within the patrilineal tribal group, (2) through affinal ties with a tribal member, (3) through 'buying' or 'renting' the rights of pasture usage. In fact, patrilineal inheritance first and foremost renders access to pastures possible. But kinship and tribal links are vital for the maintenance and the continued cultivation of pasture and land usage rights. It is kin and tribesmen who manage the herds, trade, and work together. Without their support the management of flocks becomes harder and one might be forced to employ extra-village social and economic resources and connections.

Fourth, market conditions and political organisation. The market for sheep and goats is of two kinds. Some of the sheep and goats are bought by traders to be sold in animal markets further west in Turkey. Some sheep are bought by the state owned meat factories (*kombina*).[4] The main market for the sheep and goats in Hakkari is, however, across the borders to Iran and Iraq. Selling in Turkish markets costs more in transport, and the prices offered are low, reflecting the generally low quality of sheep and goats in Hakkari. Villagers, therefore, prefer to sell their animals to Iran and Iraq, even if in small quantities.

The Organisation of Trade

The organisation of this international trade, that is, smuggling, has important implications for the moral economy and the meaning of money in Hakkari. Smuggling is not of course restricted to flocks. Goods ranging from guns to consumer goods such as tea are regularly smuggled. But smuggling is organised on different levels and scales. What I discuss here is the smuggling economy at the village level, which involves the purchase of consumer goods from Iraq and Iran, and the sale in return of sheep and goats and some agricultural or animal products. Smuggling of flocks is organised at various village and town levels. The trader who comes to buy the animals from the villagers is sometimes a co-tribesman, from another village or the town, but most significantly, he is someone who always has existing multiple relations with the villagers. He is never a stranger.

The next person involved in the organised smuggling is the shepherd. The villagers may make a contract with the trader to act themselves as the shepherds, especially if the animals are to be taken across the border near the village. The payment for the shepherds is set according to that season's standards, and to the size of the flock and number of days the journey takes. The price of purchase and sale of animals, therefore, has to take into consideration the average prices offered each year, the distance to be covered, the quality of the animals, the shepherds' fees, and the bribes to be paid on both sides of the border.

For a villager who wants to accumulate wealth, smuggling offers various possibilities. The villager may become a shepherd himself and if he is successful ends up with capital in cash and sheep. However, the shepherds for such smuggled flocks must have not only daring and courage, but also an exact knowledge of the whole area and all the routes, as well as official contacts and trustworthy allies in the area. Such a job, therefore requires a certain degree and type of knowledge, established networks, and personal qualities. Success depends first on power, on contacts, on relationships of trust; the wider a man's range, the more he can coerce or convince, by various means, those he is less sure of. Second, it depends on resources in cash or animals.

An alternative is to engage in the international trade oneself. Like shepherds, traders need wide contacts and relations; not only in their own local villages, which are interrelated through kinship and tribal ties, but also in those villages where they have no kin or tribal links. Such traders usually belong to the prominent families of the tribe, have a career of smuggling experience, as partners or shepherds, behind them, and own accumulated capital.

Sheep or Money: a Question of Meaning and Identity?

The situation I have described raises several issues. To what degree are sheep and money convertible? What kind of social meaning is attached to each? What are the moral and political implications of smuggling for this border community?

Sheep, as the main source of income for mountain villagers in Hakkari, are significant for the construction and maintenance of village identity and gender roles. Pastoral production, combined with cross frontier trade, marks the symbiotic relationship between villagers and flocks in a special way. The pastoral village life, with its cycle of seasonal dispersion and reunion, with its high spatial and cyclical mobility, demanding great physical effort, is a distinct way of life, articulated as a distinct village identity for both men and women. This village identity is visible especially in contrast to urban identity. Villagers who migrate and settle in the town of Yüksekova, for example, find their time and life cycle fundamentally changed. The dependency of human activities on pastoral production in the village is then either idealised, or remembered with disdain. The contrast between the pastoral village life and the urban life is especially remarkable for women. The mountain village woman's life is centered primarily around pastoral production. She learns the female chores from her childhood onwards. Her spatial mobility in and around the village, on mountain slopes and pastures are all related to pastoral production activities. Later in her married life, she competes with other women in her household to perform the more prestigious jobs like milking or churning butter, which are again connected to pastoral production. Raising sheep, therefore, plays a central role in the life of village women.

For major social events such as weddings and gift exchanges in a ritual context, the number of sheep is the measure to assess the amount of expenses and returns. For instance, a wedding or the settlement of a conflict after a wife-kidnapping (*kız kaçırma*) would be remembered by the number of sheep one sacrificed or gave away. Similarly, life cycle rituals, such as the pilgrimage (the hajj), are evaluated in terms of the number of animals one had to sell for the occasion.

Money, on the other hand, is an ambivalent category and does not enjoy the symbolic value accorded to sheep. Cash is an indispensable part of the capital for any household in the village, for buying consumer goods, durables and prestige goods in internal and international markets. Obligatory expenses for non-prestige purposes, such as for health, travel and military conscription are paid in cash, and counted as cash expenses. Cash is also a source of security; it has the power to obtain services and goods in emergencies. Where and when sheep cannot be sold or exchanged, cash is the medium for exchange. Hence, villagers hoard cash, especially for winter, for unexpected emergency expenses. For long-term and planned expenses, however, the household's strategies are reckoned in the number of animals to be sold and bought.

The convertibility between cash and sheep, therefore, depends on the type of transaction and the degree of ritualisation of the particular context. A gift of money is rarely acceptable; but sheep are the most highly valued form of gift. In situations where cash is given, for example, the money given by neighbours and relatives to a young man leaving to do his military service, it takes on a symbolic character, expressing more the bonds between the gift receiver and gift donor, than the monetary value of the gift. The money-gift is given in a ceremonial way, and the young man is expected to bring a present upon his return.

The two sides of the coin, sheep and money, reflect the dilemma of the symbolism of accumulating wealth. Sheep are seen as the real source of wealth and prosperity, but without being able to convert them to cash, one cannot act in a market economy. Cash, on the other hand, when received regularly, as in a salary, is a source of security. But for the mountain villager, cash is also the obvious link to the smuggling economy, clear evidence that one is involved in smuggling. Because cash has such connotations of illegality, villagers are cautious about having cash with them when travelling. Village men are worried about becoming a suspect smuggler if a large sum of money is found on them at some military check point. So they prefer to give the cash to women to carry, especially if it is foreign currency, as women are not regularly controlled by the gendarmerie. This is an irony in a way, as women in general possess no cash, and have no means of controlling the cash capital of their household.[5]

The Political Implications of the Economy of Smuggling

Smuggling involves everyone in Hakkari, either in a buyer-seller relationship, or as controllers and controlled. These relationships often overlap and get mixed. The gendarmerie officer may be chasing the shepherds of smuggled flocks on one occasion, but in the village he may be drinking smuggled tea and eating smuggled rice. I summarise the implications of such a 'smuggling' economy under six headings.

First, the economy is more than usually illegal. A person could be held responsible for possessing 'smuggled' goods when smoking tobacco, grown 'illegally' in his own garden and rolled in cigarette paper 'smuggled' from Iraq. This makes illegality a kind of everyday experience, which is learned through socialisation and by everyone.

Second, the economy in this context of smuggling is also even more than usually linked to social relations, social groups, and informal social sanctions. For the villagers social links are vital in order to participate in any and all phases of the pastoral economy. One cannot smuggle with everyone, and in order to participate in this economy, one needs to develop 'accomplice' relationships with fellow villagers and kinsmen.

Third, the principles of 'morality' within the smuggling economy reflect the arbitrariness of power. The state power is exercised arbitrarily, so that some of the rules and regulations are applied some of the time. Because of the insecurity inherent in this system, lying becomes a tactical usage, without necessarily impairing the morality of the people who lie. As with the Luri nomads, for whom 'lying is second only to physical violence as a means of getting the better of an adversary' for the villagers in Hakkari, lying is a legitimate tactic in an unstable and risky social and political environment. Lying does not, of course, have a positive moral value. If exposed, it is likely to be passed off as a 'joke'.

Fourth, the paradox that this economy is both widespread but 'illegal' affects the individual's and group's relationship with the state. From the villagers' point of view the state represents the traditional patrimonial type, '*devlet baba*'. It is powerful; and it both provides and punishes. The head of the state is personally attributed power and authority. The villagers often expressed their anger with the corrupt military officers and bureaucrats, adding that if General Evren, the head of the Military Security Council at that time, knew about the corruption, he would have stopped it.

Fifth, if the state as an abstract body is arbitrary and powerful, its agents are not necessarily all alike. Villagers were keen to get to know those military and administrative personnel who lived closest to them and had the most to do with them. This contact was forced on them sometimes because of winter conditions, when everyone was snowed in and cut off from other settlement units. But voluntary contact was important in order to find out how flexible an agent was. Depending on the flexibility of the agent, rules could also be manipulated. In other words, the formal rules of the state authority cannot be enforced at all times; nevertheless, the non-enforcement had to be tested on each military officer. Moreover, there were additional 'undercover' reasons for the non-enforcement of 'illegal border-crossings'. Crossing the border was 'normally' illegal, but it was allowed, even encouraged, when it was for tracing fugitives or 'subversive elements', that is, Kurdish guerillas.

Sixth, the economy of smuggling in Hakkari plays another significant role for the political socialisation of villagers. İsmail Beşikçi, the first sociologist to examine the significance of smuggling for the Kurds of southeastern Turkey, asserts that the relations across the frontiers are natural and economic at the same time (Beşikçi 1970, pp.436-7). According to Beşikçi, they are natural because the Kurds on both sides of the border are related to one another through kinship and tribal ties. They are also economic because the goods bought on the other side of the border are not available within Turkey, or the terms of trade are more favourable across the frontiers. Although it is true that the market conditions on each side of the border play a role in determining the type of trade, it does not follow from this that the villagers necessarily trade with kin or co-tribesmen. Trading relations are formed and sustained under much more complex conditions and social rules. A recent argument by Beşikçi (1990) emphasises the nationalist and separatist struggle of the Kurds along the border area in raising the political consciousness of the villagers of this region. I believe the economy of smuggling paved the way long ago for shaping the relations between the state and the village in this region. The military presence and the political conflict in the region since the beginning of armed attacks of the Kurdish guerillas in 1984 could be seen as new in scale, but not in quality.

Notes

1. *Mezraa* is often the high altitude mountain settlement with very few, primitive shelters for shepherds and animals jointly. *Kom* is a seasonal settlement unit smaller than *mezraa*. *Köy* is the colloquial term for village. Yalçin-Heckmann, 1991.
2. For other examples, see Beck, 1986, Black-Michaud, 1986, Tapper, 1979.
3. For more on tribes and the tribal system in Hakkari, see Yalçın-Heckmann 1991.
4. The meat factory in Hakkari, however, was not functioning fully during my fieldwork period and had bought very few sheep.
5. Compare also Black-Michaud's perceptive comment, 'If the victim of a lie gets wind of the trap in time and refuses to blunder into it, the liar will declare that the whole thing was a "joke" - which, in Luri parlance, is tantamount to a facesaving admission of failure in a game that the liar is invariably playing to win', Black-Michaud, 1986, pp.4-5, n.4; and see Beşikçi, 1970, pp.436-7.

3

Hazelnuts and Lutes

Perceptions of Change in a Black Sea Valley

Martin Stokes

Talking about changes in the performance of music in the Eastern Black Sea region of Turkey in 1975, the ethnomusicologist Laurence Picken wrote:

> In the coastal towns, the *kemençe* (box fiddle) is replaced among the settled urban population by the *saz* (long-necked lute) in its various sizes. A sailor from Akçaabat (Trabzon), for example, with a family shoe-making business to return to after his period of national service, is more likely to play the *bağlama* than the *kemençe* (Picken 1975, p.325).[1]

At the time of Picken's research this development was very much limited to the coastal towns, but the replacement of the indigenous *kemençe* by the now urban and Anatolian *saz* is still an issue among folklorists in Turkey, particularly in the East Black Sea provinces of Giresun, Trabzon, Rize and Artvin. Folk music research throughout Turkey is propelled by the belief that 'traditional culture' is swept aside in the process of modernization and development - a paradigm of development expressed most succinctly in Daniel Lerner's *The Passing of Traditional Society: Modernizing the Middle East* (1964), and replicated by a number of researchers working in Turkey (e.g.

Kolars, 1963, Szyliowicz, 1966). In this paradigm, traditional rural society is inexorably transformed by improving communications and the gradual absorbtion of the rural economy into the centralised national market system. Economic development brings in its wake cultural change, transmitted by television, radio, schooling and literacy. This in turn is a view of cultural change and development that has been endorsed by successive governments in Turkey committed to improving the lot (some might say superficially) of Turkish villagers, until recently their largest potential source of votes, and to presenting a positive image of change to the outside world. It is no wonder that cultural change and economic development in rural Turkey are still largely understood in terms of official ideologies and their statistical apparatus.

Picken's notion that the urban *bağlama* is slowly but surely eroding the indigenous *kemençe* culture of the Eastern Black Sea region owes much to this model, one which also provides a foundation for the research carried out by such state-run institutions as the Turkish Radio and Television (TRT), the National Folklore Research Bureau (MIFAD) and the state music conservatories in Ankara and Istanbul. I argue that this fundamentally misconstrues a more complex relationship between the *bağlama* and the *kemençe*, and that an analysis of this relationship raises wider issues of social change, development, and the power relation of centres to peripheries in 'developing' countries.

Social anthropologists have long been aware of the fact that in the economic development of tribal societies, change imposed from outside a community is immediately embedded in the symbolic and cultural practice of that community. Bloch and Parry (1989) have recently argued against the idea that economies involving money in the developing world always have the same emerging properties (as both neo-classical and Marxian theories of money would have it). Instead, the role that money assumes in the economic organisation of many tribal and developing societies reflects more fundamental cultural attitudes towards exchange - money is adopted only in as much as it can be embedded in pre-existing cultural forms.

In the argument presented by Picken, we can equate the role of the *bağlama* with that of money, in that it transforms the indigenous musical 'economy' for the fluid exchange medium of national cultural forms, and in so doing, draws the local network into the orbit of the national. If, however, we chose to ignore an 'official' view of musical change and concentrate on the way in which the *bağlama* has become embedded in pre-existing musical practice, a different picture emerges. In this picture, two distinct processes can be defined. In the upper valley the *bağlama* has been absorbed alongside the *kemençe* in a way that does not displace the latter. Their musical repertories are kept separate and distinct. In the lower valley however, the *bağlama* has absorbed the *kemençe* repertory in such a way that the latter has been rendered redundant. First let us put this argument in its context and describe what is typical and what is peculiar about the valley under discussion, the Ağasar valley on the western extremity of the province of Trabzon, in which I carried out fieldwork in 1987 and 1989.

Folklorists are inclined to validate and compound official understandings of change. The Eastern Black Sea area is often understood in terms of two opposed cultural zones: a spoilt and urbanised coastal culture and a highland area rich in folklore. The highland area is one of high 'event density', to use Ardener's expression for the construction from centres of peripherally 'remote' areas in terms of the frequency of experiences structurally registered as 'events'. It is the frequency and intensity of events such as high-pasture migration and its attendant festivities, fights, violence and feuds and their narration, music and dance occasioned by weddings and work parties (*meci*), intensified by 'local' dialect, custom and dress, which, for Black Sea lowlanders, marks the significant difference between lowland and highland areas. This division of the Black Sea area into a *sahil* (coastal) culture and a *yayla* (highland) culture was held to be particularly marked in the Ağasar valley. This bifurcation is marked by the division of the valley into an area of intense lowland hazelnut cultivation and highland semi-transhumant pastoralism and labour migration. The recent administrative division of the valley into the lowland ilçe of Beşikdüzü with a population, according to official statistics, of 23,896 (Aksoy, 1989), and the highland ilçe of Salpazarı, with a population of 21,205, in June 1987 has emphasised this bifurcation. For all those professionally and otherwise involved in the folk music and folklore of Trabzon, the lowland zone was held to be particularly lacking in any form of worthwhile cultural activity, whilst the highland area was considered to be particularly rich. This richness is clearly related to its perceived remoteness.

The 'remoteness' of the upper valley has two aspects. One is the political and historical marginality of this area known to outsiders and researchers. From the fourteenth century the highland area was dominated by Cepni Turkomans. Relations between the settled Turks of the area and these bellicose and highly mobile pastoralists were far from stable (see Bryer, 1971, Yücel, 1985). Whilst the inhabitants of the valley do not refer to themselves as Çepni, their neighbours do.

In common with many of the nomadic Turcoman groups pushed into Anatolia by Mongolian expansion in Central Asia, the Ağasarlı Çepni were Alevi and amongst the first followers of Haci Bektaş Veli. Quite when they converted to Sunni orthodoxy is not certain; the Ağasarlı are themselves unable to offer any clues. This fact is used by their neighbours to explain the cultural isolation and peculiar characteristics of the Ağasarlı - their dialect, their 'Asian' features, their foul language and quarrelsome nature. Amongst etymologies of the name Çepni offered to me in Tonya was that it came from *cebren*, 'by force', alluding to their forcible conversion to Sunni orthodoxy, and an etymology of the word Ağsar itself suggested that it came from the valley being 'surrounded with a net' (ağ, 'net', and *sar*, the verbal stem meaning to surround or enfold), again alluding to their forcible subjugation. In spite of this, their resistance to the settled Turks, to the Ottomans and to the *derebeys* and *ağas* who mediated their power in the late nineteenth and in the early twentieth century is well known. In May 1989, the fact that Şalpazarı voted for an independent mayor in the local elections rather than for a representative of the major political parties was the subject of amused comment in Trabzon later that year, indicating that this was only to be expected of such independently minded people.[2]

The other aspect of this perception is the self-ascription of remoteness by the Ağasarlı themselves. Their Alevi past and delicate relations with the settled Turks of the area have largely been forgotten. Their perception of their own identity revolves around strict endogamy, of an intensity unusual even in the Black Sea area, in which the marriage of the son and daughter of two brothers holds pride of place. This preference is however undermined, or complemented, by regular inter-valley elopement, *kız kaçırma*. Their dialect is held to be close to a pre-Islamized Central Asian Turkish on one the hand, and 'Istanbul Turkish' on the other. It is indeed true that the phonology of their dialect is closer (in its adherence to patterns of vowel harmony) to what is commonly understood as Istanbul Turkish than that of their neighbours in Tonya. The lack of vowel harmony and the consonantial mutations (in which voiced and unvoiced consonants are regularly inverted) makes the Turkish spoken in Tonya in many ways closer to Pontic Greek. In Ağasar the 'Greeks' of the neighbouring valleys are readily dismissed for their talkativeness and pretentions. The outside world for the Ağasarlı is then one of compromised Turkishness.

As a result of the construction of stabilised roads and the electrification of villages in the upper valley, which had been gaining momentum since 1985, this formerly 'remote' area was now in every sense closer to the vilayet center than ever before. This situation legitimated a great deal of intense research into the architecture, textiles and dance of the area by local academics and intellectuals. Their understanding of this situation owed much to Ziya Gökalp's distinction between an urban, Islamised culture (*medeniyet*) and a pure and uncorrupted Turkish culture with its roots in the experience of the Anatolian Turk's Central Asian forebears (*hars*) (1923, p.27). The complication of this situation lay in the fact that one of the principal agents of the urban *medeniyet* in the Black Sea area was precisely that instrument which had been deemed by ideologues to represent the quintessence of Central Asian Turkishness, the *bağlama*. This overlap has arisen from the association of the *bağlama* with the popular urban genre of Arabesk, in which the alienation of rural-urban migrants is expressed in a mystical fate-absorbed vocabulary strongly remniscent of Sufi hymnody. Arabesk is dismissed by most Kemalist intellectuals throughout Turkey as reactionary and Islamist. Elsewhere in Anatolia, where the *bağlama* is simply 'the' instrument (*saz*), this overlap does not apply. In the province of Trabzon however, where the indigenous rural instrument is the *kemençe*, the *bağlama* has become in official discourses the agent of a tainted and Islamised urban culture.

The upper and lower valley are then seen as two very different kinds of places and this difference is expressed in a spatial idiom, of remoteness and proximity to the coast. However the most striking feature of the social geography of the entire East Black Sea area is the migration to high summer pastures (*yaylacılık*), which immediately blurs the distinction between *sahil* and *yayla* zones. Nearly all of the residents of both the upper and lower valley had summer residences dispersed around the site of Kadırga *pazarı*, the location of one of the most important high pasture festivals (*dernek*). The village of Akkese, in which I spent much of my time in the lower valley was unique in having its *yayla* some five kilometres from Kadırga. The common experience is that highland pastures are shared by groups of people from villages which may be spatially distant in the valley. The *yayla* of Sis Dağ, to which a number of villages in the higher bowl of the Ağasar valley migrate (particularly Geyikli and Doğancıköy) brings together in relatively close proximity village groups not just from the province of Trabzon, but from the neighbouring Giresun.

Most families in the valley keep a few cattle, which they feed on maize, and whose milk products they consume. The entire economy has however been transformed by the cultivation of hazelnuts from the 1950s, and in the upper valley by labour migration to Germany and Istanbul. People no longer migrate to the high pastures as a matter of economic necessity. Migration continues because village (*köy*) and pasture (*yayla*) constitute a fundamental polarity of Black Sea social existence, and the ritual dimension of semi-transhumant pastoralism has an intensity which is striking even in the Black Sea context. The day on which the *göç* is carried out is anticipated eagerly. Cattle are decorated in multicoloured tasselled halters even though most are now taken up by individual households in lorries. The *dernek* festivals - not just those of Sis Dağ and Kadırga but those much further away from their *yayla* territories - are attended assiduously by the Ağasarlı. The opposition between the life they lead in the pastures and that which they lead lower in the valleys is clearly marked to the Ağasarlı, if not always to an outsider. In the valleys, business is dealt with, marriages contracted and celebrated, the dead buried, and social existence is articulated by the call to prayer from the mosque. At the *yayla*, all such matters are forgotten, religion left far behind, and time is given over to food, drink, music and guns. Whilst the *dernek* originally had a religious significance, being based on the burial sites of a number of local saints (*evliya*) - often on the very peaks of the mountains on which the festivals are held - today this is a fact known by few except local history teachers and village imams.

The *yayla* is not then in any sense a preserve of indigenous Black Sea culture as is often suggested. If anything it is exactly the opposite. The very fact that the *göç* provides such a focus for the inhabitants of the Black Sea valleys mean that inhabitants of the lower and higher valleys throughout the Black Sea are brought together into close proximity. In particular, music and dance bring together people from neighbouring valleys, migrant workers from Germany and Istanbul, and even representatives of Pontic Greeks displaced by the population exchanges folowing the treaty of Lausanne in 1923. In a sense then, the concentrated world of the village is left behind for a wider Black Sea context at the top of the valleys.

The conventional model does not allow for the intense seasonal mobility of the inhabitants of the valley, which is in many ways a more homogenous unit than this model would allow. However, there remain important differences between the upper and lower valley in the way in which urban instruments and urban musical forms have been absorbed and adopted. These differences, and the relation that they have with patterns of economic development, will occupy the rest of this paper. I will take two singers, one from the lower valley and one from the upper valley to illustrate the point.

Necmi Çınar was 17 years old in 1987, and at the time I knew him, had dropped out of school prior to doing his military service. His father had recently died in Germany, and he lived with his mother, younger brother and sister in Düzköy, Şalpazarı, in the upper valley. Throughout the summer wedding season and *yayla* period he was occupied fully as a singer. From this he earned a good income, although, as he was fond of pointing out, the money coming in from his father's insurance scheme in Germany meant that he could take on whatever work he liked. Such was the demand for his services that life in the summer was a riotous circuit of every event in the valley and on the *yayla*, weddings, *muhabbet* (social drinking), collective work parties, and a number of weddings in the neighbouring valley of Tonya as well.

Music in Ağasar shares many of the characteristics of Black Sea music elsewhere, differing principally in speed, pitch, vocal quality and dialect. Improvised couplets are sung to fixed melodic patterns known as *kayde*, which are accompanied on the *kemençe*, usually but not always played by another musician. *Kayde* consist of brief fragmental melodic phrases, in which the voice follows the *kemençe* closely. An element of polyphony is added by the instrument which plays in parallel 4ths, since the bow touches two and sometimes three strings at a time (the third functions as an unmoving drone in such cases).

Music is divided according to function, being either for seated entertainment purposes or for dancing. Most *kayde* are used for both purposes. What begins as a sitting down *kayde* might inspire those seated to get to their feet and dance. A total of twelve *kayde* appeared to me to be current in Ağasar in 1987, although some musicians claimed that there were many more. *Horon havaları* accompany the dance, the *horon*, of which perhaps the most interesting feature is the movement of the musician. When enough people are dancing to form a circle moving slowly to the right, the *kemençe* player and singer step into the middle of the circle and dance in the other direction, ostensibly to keep the dancers in time. The singer follows the *kemençeci* improvising couplets. The principal aesthetic force of the dance is then the relatively slow and gentle bobbing motion of the dancers, and the agitated stepping of the *kemençeci*, singer and attendant tape recorders around the inside of the circle, when it has formed.

There are two kinds of *horon* in Ağasar, in both of which the performance criteria outlined above apply. The *dik horon* (upright *horon*) is danced only by men, since its execution requires arms to be held up in the air as the dance approaches its final sequence (*aşağı inmesi*). This is considered immodest for women, although I have seen older women dancing this. The second kind is the *kız horonu* (girl's *horon*), which is so named only because women may dance in it - it is usually danced mixed. This consists of a slow bobbing stepping motion, moving to the right and paced over ten beats, whose distribution over the melody corresponds to the binary division of the basic pulse of the *kayde*.

These are contrasted with *muhabbet* or *oturak havaları* 'songs of friendly conversation'. These are again sung in the same manner to the accompaniment of the *kemençe*. Occasionally, the accompanist himself joins in. These are sung in the company of small groups of men at any convenient time, in which the emphasis is very much on spontaneity. Enough foresight is however required to bring the essential ingredients of a *muhabbet* - a bottle of *raki*, several packets of Marlboro 100s, a water melon and a supply of white cheese. Improvisations begin with a series of couplets which set the scene by referring to the location, the particular gathering of friends at the *muhabbet*, the particular combination of *rakı*, beer or cigarettes which happens to be uppermost in the speaker's mind. Even though the improvisations are highly formulaic, the event emhasises spontaneity through its insistent reference to a unique situation, albeit one that involves common and general sentiments. My first attendance at a *muhabbet* involved a protracted farewell between two close friends, one of whom was Necmi, the other of whom had recently been signed up to play for a league football team, over the mountains in Erzincan. The lyrics of this typically emphasised separation and loneliness. The texts are highly formulaic; the context provides the meaning. Couplets involving sentiments of love are always left anonymous, even though it is always known exactly who is being referred to. *Muhabbet* improvisations are very much the art of the unspoken.

A story told of one of my hosts in the upper valley illustrates what happens when this rule is broken in a dramatic manner. Ali was a generous and much respected man, the beauty of whose wife, before being crippled by TB, was highly praised, and often in song. One of these songs is known even today by the name of his wife. A version of this, recognizable only by its *kayde* and its words, was played on a cassette recorder within the earshot of her husband, which had been recorded at a *muhabbet* the previous day. Whilst drastic measures might have been taken by a man of less wit (since everybody is armed), the man reputedly took the cassette-recorder, an expensive ghetto-blaster bought in Germany, put it on a stone by a bridge, took the gun out of his pocket and calmly shot the machine to bits.[3]

Formally speaking the *kayde* has three elements, an opening motif, a repetitive pattern known as *sayma* which carries the bulk of the recitation, and a closing motif, which is frequently a descending sequential movement. If a singer gets out of breath or needs to pause for inspiration, he can take recourse to closing his improvisation with a finishing motif and letting the *kemençe* take over for a moment, or to allowing one repetition's gap between vocal lines. Alternatively, when inspiration runs out, the singer can sign off, and pass on to another singer.

My recording of the *muhabbet* described above began with a typical formula: '*Evlerinin önündel Direk geçıyu, geçi*' ('in front of the houses/ pass the telegraph poles'), repeated twice to music 'A' (see Appendix, Example 1, 'Evlerinin Önünde'). The 'B' pattern began with a couplet: '*Annenin verdiği kizl Seni istemedim*' ('girl provided by your mother/ I didn't want you') which introduces a narrative in which the singer, Necmi, sees himself due to wed a girl he does not love, and secretly loving another. He proposes elopement and escape to the mountains. Eleven couplets followed with a high degreee of redundancy and repetition. To the closing 'C' music, he imagines his tormentors calling out to him '*Gel de yemek yiyelim*', which he repeats, and in doing so invites those listening to him to dig into the cheese and melon provided in the cafe. The *kemençe* carried on whilst cigarettes were lit and drinks refilled. Necmi began again with an opening motif ('A'), again repeated, '*Rakıyı içelim, rakı oy/ Birayla karışık*' ('Let's drink *rakı* mixed with beer'), holding his glass in his hand, and turning to me, sang '*Gel otur konuşalım/ Canım sana alışık* ('Come, sit, let's talk/ I'm getting used to you'). The *sayma* followed this in the same manner, and the subject of the friends' departure to Erzincan was woven into the original narrative. In this way, themes of loneliness, separation and the friendly exchange of confidences were woven into a number of narratives - the elopement, the departure of the friend, the presence of a guest and the actual situation of the *muhabbet*, which in turn were recombined with consummate skill.

This describes in a skeletal form the kind of music commonly described as 'Ağasarlı' music. It does not however account for the totality of music now played at weddings, one of the main focuses for musical activity in the valley. At a number of weddings that I attended in 1987, the *kemençe* player and singer shared the evening festivities with an *elektrosaz* playing popular Anatolian folk songs and Arabesk dance music for people to dance the *çifte telli*. Necmi himself listened to radio and television, and was thoroughly conversant with both Arabesk and TRT music.

The profound difference between these two dances should be noted. In the *horon*, the dancers are relatively motionless, dancing in a line and facing the same way, whilst the musician dances round the dancers. To employ Rouget's useful verb, we could say that the musicians are 'musicated' by the dancers (Rouget, 1985). In the *çifte telli*, the musician is entirely motionless, and the dancers move around the dance space and around their own axes. The *elektrosaz* player is of course literally bound to his instrument, and in any case has to play the instrument seated. The dancers are in this case 'musicated' by the musician. The first is often explicitly described as a dance which emphasises group solidarity, whilst the second is an individual dance, even though the *horon* seemed to offer abundant opportunities for fights and displays of violence. An incident at Kadırga in 1987, when a man was shot as a result of a *dava* (feud) whilst dancing in a *horon* circle, attracted particular condemnation.

So both indigenous and non-indigenous cultural forms share the same functional spaces at weddings and pasture festivals. Both of these two different areas of musical experience are compartmentalised, and whilst they undoubtedly affect one another, the boundaries between genre are carefully maintained. One of the most important ways of maintaining this boundary lies in musical performance on the *kemençe* itself. The lack of frets, the irregular action of its bowing technique and the polyphony of its three closely positioned strings serve to maintain a clear division between indigenous Black Sea music and that of the Anatolian *bağlama*. However, the TRT has successfully imposed upon the population of Turkey a performance style which is tightly bound up with the construction, sound and playing technique of the long-necked lute (Stokes, 1992), and this style dominates performance lower in the valley. A singer from the lower valley, İbrahim Can from Akkese village, Beşikdüzü, has been employed by the TRT as a *mahalli sanatçı*, a 'local artist'. Currently 29 years old, İbrahim graduated from Trabzon *Erkek Lisesi* before doing his military service, won a TRT scholarship to study first in Ankara and then Istanbul, where he now works both for the TRT and as a freelance singer.

His task has been to render precisely the 'local' musical tradition of Ağasar and the valleys lying immediately to the west which share many of the characteristics of Ağasar music (in particular Görele) intelligible in terms of the performance styles propagated by the TRT orchestras. This constitutes his immediate responsibility. Currently in Istanbul, he is the only *mahalli sanatçı* from the Black Sea area, and is consequently obliged to sing in all programmes dealing with the Black Sea area in general. This requires him to sing in a patently made up (*uyduruk*) accent which only faintly resembles one that he never used in the first place. The irony, to him, is that during his early musical training in the village and Trabzon he was always encouraged as far as possible to sing in an Istanbul accent. As an employee of the TRT he is therefore required to 'translate' his local repertory into terms acceptable not only to the TRT, but to the urban Black Sea migrant community (largely in Istanbul). This community incidentally, consisting by now of several generations who have never seen the Black Sea, increasingly shares a sense of pan-Black Sea identity which is addressed and shaped by such singers as İbrahim Can, Süreyya Davulcuoğlu, Mustafa Topaloğlu, Erkan Ocaklı and others.

Firstly, the *kayde* of Ağasar are reorchestrated in such a way that the rhythmic and polyphonic peculiarities imbued by the *kemençe* are removed, and the melodies are performed on the orchestras of *saz* in various sizes (principally *divan, tambura* and *cura), kabak kemane, mey* and *def* or *koltuk davul* favoured by the TRT. It is striking that the *kemençe* is so inappropriate to this style that it seldom appears in the final mix of recorded folk music at all. TRT musicologists in Istanbul and Trabzon were quick to point out the difficulty in finding *kemençe* players who could read notation, and would thereby qualify for places in the TRT orchestras. This is indeed true, but not the point. The TRT prefers to pay a *kabak kemane* player (which shares the *kemençe*'s property of being a small musical instrument played with a bow) to learn the *kemençe*, by which process they provide themselves with two musicians for the price of one, and one who is moreover capable of reading music. The result was that in 1987, the Istanbul TRT had no *kemençe* players from the Eastern Black Sea at all, a fact that was bitterly resented by Black Sea musicians. Their claim that the *kemençe* is not regarded as a 'proper' musical instrument by the establishment certainly has some justification.

On the occasions in which the *kemençe* is included in the final mix of either a TRT or a commercial recording, the speed of the Black Sea music is so much slowed down to suit the longer necked *bağlama* that the rhythmic impulse of the music is fundamentally impeded, and the result is a tentative and unconvincing sound. Its scratchy, yet dense, polyphonic texture is considered by recording technicians and producers to fit badly with the other instruments. The presence of the electric bass, synthesisers, Western drums and percussion in commercial recordings only makes the task of the *kemençe* player more difficult. It is an instrument which distinctly lacks *uyum*, 'conformity'. So the occasions on which it does appear, it appears in inverted commas, so to speak, and makes brief appearences only. It is not surprising that established *kemençe* players will have nothing to do with the whole process. İbrahim is required to use a young and relatively inexperienced friend, who I frequently saw in tears of frustration at the end of long recording sessions in which unsympathetic producers were asking him to perform the impossible.

At a concert given by İbrahim in Trabzon in May 1987, İbrahim attempted to balance a chorus of four *bağlama* and rhythm with no less than two *kemençe* players. Co-ordination proved impossible, especially since there were not enough microphones to go around, and the *kemençe* required microphones to be placed extremely close for them to be heard at all. First one *kemençe* player was dispensed with in the rehearsal, and the second was dismissed a few hours later. So the impossibility of co-ordinating *kemençe* with *bağlama* has a practical as well as purely symbolic dimension. Furthermore, when he gave the same concert in his home town of Beşikdüzü, he did not even bother to bring along the *kemençe* players at all, a fact that did not go unnoticed by musicians from the upper valley who had come down to the coast for the occasion.

TRT performance therefore modifies sound texture and the speed of performance. The 'knock on' effects of this run deep into the very heart of the performance. A fluid but irregular binary division of the melody, which is so rapid that it cannot be reduced without ambiguity to the combinations of two and three beats required by the notational conventions of Turkish musicologists, is characteristic of Ağasar music. These binary units shift from relative proportions of 9:8, through 7:8 to 5:8 in such a way that to notate them as an Anatolian *usul* of 7/8 throughout, or 5/8 does little justice to the peculiarity of the music - and yet this is required for the purposes of TRT archival notation and performance.

Similarly, the fluidity of the improvisatory structure of the Ağasarlı verse is 'frozen', through careful editing and musical reorganisation at the TRT. The world described in the Ağasarlı song texts, a world of male concerns and conflicts, and dense nature symbolism rooted in the local landscape, is, in the TRT repertory, rendered meaningful to an urban audience which is not necessarily male and not necessarily from the Black Sea. An example of this is the song '*Atmacayı vurdular*', which was recorded for the TRT by İbrahim and enjoyed popularity throughout 1987 (see Appendix, Example 2). In this version of the song, references to the local landscape are confined to Kadırga and Sis Dağ, the site of high pasture festivals which would be known to most urban Black Sea migrants, and would not necessarily confuse those are not. Whilst the TRT '*Atmacayı vurdular*' does not strictly speaking tell a story, the couplets are organised in such a way that they give the sense of imparting a fairly simple narrative to a general audience. The text begins with the couplet 'They shot the hawk/for a handful of blood', goes on to address a lover and alludes to an impending separation ('They are taking my little rose away'). The second verse refers to the high pasture migration festivals and the intractable nature of the terrain; the steep, dark and misty roads separating the traveller from Kadırga and Sis Dağ becomes a metaphor for the separation of the lovers. The final verse alludes to a *kaçırma* (elopement), with the two lovers on the run.

This narrative sense is emphasised by the fact that the TRT song is divided into three verses of equal length, interspersed by musicial interludes (*arasaz*). Each verse in the TRT song has a repeated internal structure, matching text repetitions to the music. The transcription of this song in the Appendix shows how the words are fitted to these units. As with the upper valley *kayde* the opening unit (A) is repeated twice to the same words. The *sayma* (B) is however not freely extendable, but is repeated to three couplets in each strophe, and the closing unit (C) is again repeated twice to the same words. Perhaps the most significant change is that the sound of the *kemençe* no longer organises the TRT performance of the song.

İbrahim never played or sang to the *kemençe* whilst learning his trade in Beşikdüzü or Trabzon. He and his brothers, in common with many living in the lower valley, bought *bağlama* at an early age, listened to and admired the sound of urban Arabeskci Orhan Gencebay (one of the very few Black Sea Arabesk singers), and considered the *kemençe* a waste of time. In his youth, the last generation of lower valley *kemençe* players from the Beşikdüzü region, such as Katip Şadi and Sırrı Öztürk were at the peak of their popularity, but the younger generation of musicians from the lower valley had clearly set their sights on other targets.

Lower valley weddings conform to the urban pattern of an evening in a *düğün sarayı* (often a room put aside for such functions by the town council) in Beşikdüzü or Trabzon, rather than the three day village celebrations considered normal above Salpazarı. In these, the sound of the *kemençe* is conspicuously absent. The *kemençe* is not so much disliked as considered a difficult instrument. Many *bağlama* players expressed an interest in learning it, but put this low on their list of priorities. Non-musicians in the lower valley were more attracted by the idea of learning the *bağlama* than learning the *kemençe*. Singers such as İbrahim are both a product of the changed horizons in the lower valley, and as a result of their popularity and success outside the valley, have continued to shape and define musical practice in the lower valley itself.

Such is the power of the models of folk music performance

propagated by the TRT that today, young people at school and university in Trabzon (in particular those from the lower coastal regions) are consumed by a passion for the *bağlama* which has totally excluded the *kemençe*. Prizes in national competitions are regularly won by Folk music *dernekler* and *cemiyetler* from Trabzon. Such is this passion that throughout the coastal area the *kemençe* is entirely neglected. Even though the oppressive dampness of the region rapidly warps the necks of the cheap *bağlama* imported from Istanbul, music shops in Trabzon are full of these instruments. *Kemençe* players either make their own (as is invariably the case in Salpazarı), or order their instruments from Black Sea makers in Adapazarı or Istanbul. University folk dancing groups in Trabzon at the time of my fieldwork had great difficulty in finding anybody to play the *kemençe* for them at all.

The incompatibility of the *bağlama* and *kemençe* seen from the perspective of the upper valley is mirrored by a process of 'economic' development which has included the lower valley in its entirety but has left the upper valley untouched. The principal agent of this process has been the intensive cultivation of hazelnuts. Even though hazelnuts had been cultivated in the Eastern Black Sea region since Byzantine times, it was not until the late 1920s that cultivation began on a commercial scale, marked by the foundation of the hazelnut growers co-operative Fiskobirliği in Giresun in 1928. By the 1950s it had totally dominated the provincial economy. This allowed relatively small land owners such as İbrahim's father to accumulate enough capital to set up his restaurant in Trabzon. Intensive cash cropping has thus drawn the lower valley closer and closer into the national market network.

This option has not been available to the inhabitants of the upper valley, where a combination of cooler climate and altitude has only permitted the intensive cultivation of maize. Famine between 1946 and 1950 drove many Ağasarlı to migrate to Istanbul where they live today in characteristic aloofness and isolation in *gecekondus* on the slopes above the Bosphorous between Çamlıca and Beylerbeyi. Opportunities to work in Germany were quickly seized (as elsewhere on the Black Sea). Every household in the upper valley today derives the majority of its income from labour migration, *gürbet*. Maize and cattle provide only food for those who remain in the valley, the dairy at Sütpınar being the only commercial venture in the valley of any size. This uses surplus milk provided by villagers in the region lying above Şalpazarı which is bought for cash, and the cheese that is produced is marketed in Trabzon. Sütpınar is however an isolated exception. Consumer goods such as televisions, refrigerators, cassette recorders, cars, jeeps and guns (the last two being particularly important prestige goods) are bought in from Germany, or with money earned in Germany. Money earned in Germany also provides for one of the major expenses of Ağasarlı life, namely bridewealth *(başlık)*. In most ways, the Ağasarlı of Salpazarı and above neither benefit from, nor contribute directly to, the national economy.

In relating development and change to various aspects of musical change, I am not suggesting for a moment that it is possible to instantly reduce one to the other. Instead, I am looking at both as interdependent aspects of the same processes. In Ağasar there is a bifurcation of the valley into a lowland and highland area which owes something to the ecological peculiarities of the valley and the intensive cash cropping of hazelnuts, and something to the growing importance of the *kemençe*. This instrument figures in the self-definition of two groups of people. The first feels it has maintained its identity through compartmentalising its cultural experience by maintaining the *kemençe* alongside the *bağlama*. The second feels it has done the same through incorporating its musical repertory in conformity to TRT performance practice and replacing the instrument with the *bağlama*. The symbolic capital of the *kemençe* repertory has been converted into the national *bağlama* repertory in the lower valley, whilst in the upper valley the essential distance between the two spheres of exchange has been maintained. This has allowed the *bağlama* to coexist with the *kemençe* but has prohibited the process of conversion from one to the other. The change taking place has therefore been one in which the remoteness of the upper valley is becoming more and more accentuated rather than the reverse - the situation widely held to be the case outlined at the beginning of the paper. The opposite side of this coin is that lack of involvement in the national economy in the upper valley is replaced by an involvement in the international economy of labour migration. What is 'remoteness' from one perspective is of course exactly the opposite from another.

In conclusion, I would like to widen the perspective slightly. The importance of folk music for the state is obvious, creating and instilling a sense of shared cultural experience and history through the medium of something which can be presented, by those with the political clout to do so, as being politically disinterested and immaterial. Music in Turkey has however always been the vehicle for those 'inner' discourses of sentiment and affairs of the 'soul' (*gönül*) through which the fundamental injustices of power are expressed. In the Black Sea, music has long celebrated the exploits of the brigands who opposed the Ottomans, the *derebeys* and the modern state, those '*istoria*', to cite Michael Herzfeld, which 'treacherously reveal (the state's) internal fragmentation' (1987, p.43). The replacement of these *istoria* by 'History' with a capital 'H' has long been one of the first and most pressing tasks in processes of modernisation and the extension of state power. Music is often then a tacit battleground in which the 'real' issues of power are being thrashed out in the most bitterly contested terms, precisely because so little seems to be at stake.

The notion of music as 'disinterested' and reflecting the material world only in a distant and ephemeral way (if at all) must be dismissed as a fiction maintained by those who have been most successful in controlling and shaping it. It will be clear from this paper that music involves such 'material' issues as the properties and construction of musical instruments, perceptions of identity in relation to the state, and that most fundamental resource, the human body itself. The manipulation and control of music is thus impeded and compromised at every turn. We have seen the way in which the agent of centralised cultural authority, the *bağlama*, is diverted and made to serve entirely different ends which leave untouched exactly that which it engulfs lower in the valley. To understand change in rural Turkey only in terms of official models would exclude an understanding of not only this fact but the ways in which imposed change is refracted and subverted.

Appendix 1: Musical Examples

The examples illustrate the difference between lower and upper valley performance practice. In the upper valley (Example 1, *'Evlerinin Önünde'*), narratives are sung to repetitive melodies called '*kayde*'. These are divided into three parts (labelled A, B, and C). The distribution of text to melody in the upper valley example is discussed on page 35. The most significant feature of this organisation is the fact that the 'B' melody can be repeated endlessly as the narrative is developed.

In the lower valley (Example 2 '*Atmacayı vurdular*' see page 39), the narrative is organised into three distinct strophes each containing internal repetitions and a balanced number of lines. 'A' is sung to a repeated couplet, 'B' to two couplets, and 'C' to a repeated couplet, as indicated by the letters next to the song text. The editor and author decided not to include a translation of this song, since the Turkish is condensed and elliptical and a 'correct' translation would not be possible without a page of explanatory notes. The text is paraphrased and discussed on pages 39-40.

Example 1. '*Evlerinin Önünde*'. Upper valley *kayde.*

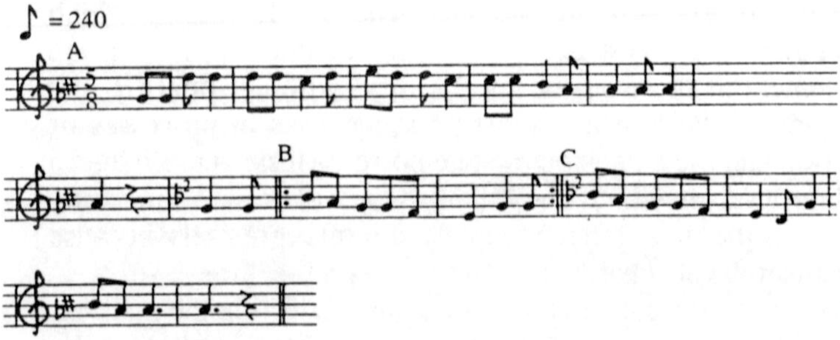

Example 2. '*Atmacayi vurdular*'. Lower valley *türkü.*

	Verse 1	Verse 2	Verse 3
A	*Atmacayi vurdular,*	*Kadirganin yolunu*	*Burasi derin orman*
	Bir avuç kani için	*Gidemiyum Karadan*	*Gorulmiyelim aman*
B	*Gel Edelim sevdalik*	*Sevdalik edenleri*	*Senin gibi guzele*
	Babanin Cani için	*Ayirmasin sevdadan*	*Canin yoluma gurban*
	Gadirga yok diyular	*Hadi gidelim Sis'e*	*Gadirganin basina*
	Nereye gidiyulur	*Sizin yollari çise*	*Dolu yagiyu dolu*
C	*Benim ufak gulumu*	*Ne dedim de darildim*	*Seni gavurun gizi*
	Ellere veriyular	*Niye gelmiyon bize*	*Dursak bile ne olur*

Notes

1. *Bağlama* is a form of *saz*. (ed.).
2. Beşikdüzü voted in a candidate from the left-of-centre SHP.
3. Guns and shooting imagery pervade musical performance in the Black Sea area. In large *muhabbets* pistols are held authoritatively in the air as a singer takes his turn, and are fired into the air by others throughout the singing, but particularly at the end. In performances taking place within earshot of the *jandarma*, I saw percussion caps being used, presumably not as an acceptable alternative, but to remind those present of what they were no longer officially allowed to do. *Muhabbets* are frequently recorded on ghetto-blasters. These cassettes are duplicated by friends and are played *ad nauseam* in cafes and in the minibuses connecting Salpazarı to the coast usually until the cheap cassette tapes disintegrate. The destruction of the machine by Ali was in this context particularly resonant.

| 4 |

Alevi and Sunni in Rural Anatolia

Diverse Paths of Change

David Shankland

The Sub-Province

From March 1988 until November 1989, I conducted fieldwork in a sub-province in the north-eastern part of central Anatolia and returned for a brief visit in August 1990. The population of the sub-province is approximately 70,000; about 12,000 live in the only town, the remainder dispersed among 96 villages. I lived in one village but made frequent visits to others, and to the town.

The people are Muslim, divided into two sects, *Alevi* and *Sunni.* seventy four villages are Sunni and twenty are Alevi. Two villages contain both Alevi and Sunni. The town I estimate to be 90 per cent Sunni.[1]

With the exception of three villages, the inhabitants regard themselves as indigenous Turks (*Türk*). These are a Circassian village (*Çerkez*), one of Yugoslavs *(göçmen*, immigrants), and one of Kurds. All three are Sunni. Also, the Sunni part of one of the mixed Alevi/Sunni villages is Kurdish. In this paper, I discuss only the Alevi and Sunni *Türk* villages.

The Research

The finding which I discuss here is that the Sunni villages are more successful than the Alevi villages at moving into the modern world. More specifically, though most Sunni villages are declining in size, some are growing larger, and even turning into small towns.[2] In striking and direct contrast to this, *all* the Alevi villages are losing population, so much so that the total Alevi population of the sub-province has diminished by more than half over the years 1980-1990. Similarly, whilst most Sunni men continue to affirm their faith, many Alevi men are becoming sceptical, some even doubting the existence of God.

The Model Stated

Modernisation is an extremely complex process. Here, I shall concentrate on only one - obvious - consequence of moving into the modern world, but one which provides a useful framework to begin discussing why the Alevi and Sunni villages should differ so. To take their place in the modern world, a people, or community, must become part of a nation-state. This movement is fuelled from both above and below; to rule successfully, a state wishes to keep order, to obtain people's loyalty, and to educate them. The people themselves gradually obtain an increasing part of their identity from their place as citizens, and transfer, or affirm, their allegiance to the nation, from which in turn they expect material and moral support. Thus there is a patrimonial relation between state and citizen; the state educates, guides, rules, enriches and protects in return for fidelity; in all but exceptional cases, a person can be a member of only one nation, and that nation has first claim on their loyalties.

I argue that this patrimonial relation between citizen and state is compatible with traditional Sunni village/state relations and that the social order within the Sunni villages is compatible with being absorbed gradually into the national, centralised administrative system. In contrast to this, traditional Alevi culture is based on the idea that they have offered submission to an authority which is not that of the central government, and which lies outside the jurisdiction of the central state. The Alevi cannot integrate into the modern Turkish State without relinquishing literal belief in their myths, rituals and ideals, because these undermine the legitimacy of the central government. Their mechanisms of social control must change far more radically than those of the Sunni villages because the right to solve disputes becomes transferred from indigenous mediators, whose position is supported by the traditional myths, to figures whose authority is sanctioned by central government. There is also a demographic problem; the Alevi settlements are much smaller than the Sunni; a number of them together are declared a village by the state, causing conflicts of loyalty, ownership and identity within their communities. In short, the dispersed nature of Alevi traditional settlement patterns and their uneasy relationship with central authority means that their communities cannot become part of modern Turkey without undergoing enormous disruption.

This model, parts of which I shall illustrate briefly below, is greatly influenced by the work of three researchers. Gellner's (1981) analysis of the different forms of social organisation which he finds representative of Islamic societies, Stirling's work over many years in Sunni Turkish villages, and Sirman's recent PhD. thesis (1988) and her articles (e.g.1990a) on the relationship between villager and state. I am equally indebted for the generosity with which they have given their time for discussions of this research, though I remain, of course, fully responsible.[3]

The Sunni Villages

In the sub-province, all the land and all the settlements are defined by the state as being part of one village or another, and the boundaries between one village and the next are noted and approved.[4] The state declares pasture, woods and scrub within the boundary a collective good. The villagers are not permitted to sell such land, fell trees growing on it, nor open fields within it, but only they may use it; and all villagers are given equal rights to do so. Services (co-operative bank, health centre or school) which the state awards to the village it expects to be constructed on land donated by the villagers. This land the state also defines as collective property, as it does the land on which the mosque and cemetery are built.[5]

All the Sunni villages I visited, heard of or saw at a distance, unless prevented by the lay of the land, consist of a single group of patrilineal, patrilocal households clustered together near the centre of the village territory, in the midst of which is a mosque.[6] I would estimate an average-sized village as having between 70 and 120 households, each usually containing two or three generations. Nearly all households own some fields on one side of the village and some on the other. All the villages I visited or enquired about have a single rotation cycle; the households sow wheat or barley collectively on one side of the territory owned by households from the village and the next year the other side. There are no sharp internal divisions within the village; villagers may regard themselves as belonging to different village quarters, but to come from a particular quarter gives no rights over land or other resources.

We can see immediately several ways in which the state's encroaching matches the indigenous organisation. The villagers themselves make a distinction between land which is owned by a household and land which is not. Ploughed land is regarded as being the property of individual households, land which is not yet ploughed up as being available for exploitation by any man (Stirling, 1965, pp.134-40). The state declares only unopened land collective property. Thus though it imposes a distinction between collective and individual property rights, it does not disrupt the existing pattern of ownership,[7] but merely discourages any further extension of individual holdings.

Further, the category 'village' is imposed on a single settlement with no internal divisions; the village boundary is at once the social, economic and territorial boundary of the community and the legal boundary given to it by the state.[8] The *muhtar,* headman, whom every village is compelled to elect, and whose main function is to act as a link between the authorities and the villagers, represents only one community. The services which the state gives the villagers may be shared by all without claims of priority by one part of the community or another.

The most important organisational principle in a Sunni village is *no man has the right to dominate any other by virtue of his birth, but all women are subordinate to all men.* Where practical, the household's head is the oldest male. Though the course taken by any one household may be subject to various degrees of negotiation between its members, ultimately he has the authority to sell the household fields and to decide the way the money of the household shall be channelled. This pattern of authority is reflected in the way the public spaces are used. If a man meets a woman on the path, then she stands back and lets him pass; likewise if they find themselves going through a door together. Women avoid the central areas of the village. Only if they are accompanied by a man is their presence in the open accepted as legitimate.

In this respect also, the Sunni villages are compatible with being integrated into the nation-state. A recent article by Sirman (1990a) shows that as the village opens out towards the outside world, men who already possess a monopoly of the public spaces of the village, can retain, and even strengthen their position (cf. Delaney, Chapter 10). In addition, because there are no indigenous mediators and no man is sanctioned to judge another, the state's gradual take-over of responsibility for dispute settling does not disturb an internal hierarchy. Rather, as Sirman shows, each man becomes a representative of the state within the household, the reflector and possessor of its authority, a process of integration from which women are cut off, and thereby remain without power.

Religion

It is a commonplace of anthropology that a coherent ideology subsumed under the rubric 'religion' normally supports the existing power relations within any group or community. The Sunni villages are no exception. The men I spoke to regarded it *günah* (sinful) for a woman not to wear a headscarf, *günah* for her to disobey her husband, and her body was *haram* (forbidden) to other men.[9] Islam functions in a different way with regard to relations between men. Whilst women are told they are inferior,[10] and their subordination is endorsed by religion, any man can be as holy as any other by fulfilling the ritual demands made on them by God.

The same pattern appears at the village level. Mosque-going is not held to be absolutely necessary except at the two religious festivals[11] of the year, but most men attend the Friday noon service and *iftar*, the prayers held after the break of fast during Ramazan. Women, however, are not permitted in the mosque except at Ramazan, and only then curtained off, out of sight of the men. The mosque ceremony, almost exclusively male, ensures those who hold authority and power in the community also dominate access to the ideal place of worship, whilst the exhilaration of worshipping together enforces ties but minimises the inequalities between them.[12]

There are above all two considerations which the state must take into account of when formulating a policy toward religion. The first is that a state must have men's loyalty. In Turkey, the only governments who have ever won a majority are those who have agreed to support Islam, in particular to allow mosque building, to train religious functionaries and to facilitate the practice of the 'five pillars' of Islam. Now, in 1991, all villages are entitled to an imam, who is a civil servant. He not only shows the villagers how to pray, reassures doubters, and teaches the children how to intone the Koran, he also passes on special announcements from the central religious authorities which arrive via the *müftü* office in the sub-province centre. For example, he explains to the villagers how to fill out the necessary forms and the arrangements they have to make in order to go on the pilgrimage to Mecca. His Friday sermon, *vaiz,* is sent to him already written, ready to read out to the congregation. The state broadcasting corporation transmits programmes on religion throughout the year, and during the Ramazan indicates province-by-province the time for the break of fast.

The second point which the state must consider is that as long as believers do not attempt to usurp the authority of the state, Islam is a support, not a hindrance to the social order. Islam encourages the nominal equality of all men, the collective rituals in the mosque and the subordination of women, all of which are vital to the Sunni village organisation. There is, therefore, a convergence between the desire of men that the state should support religion and the requirement of the state to rule in orderly fashion. This convergence means that the role of the state in the villages returns very slowly to one which is parallel, though not identical, with that of the traditional role of the state with regard to the Sunni villages in Ottoman times. The state must govern, men are prepared to let it do so through the teachings of Sunni Islam. Republican ideals have not faded away, but they must live uneasily alongside the moral teachings of Islam.

In sum, I have given several indications of the way in which the initial model, that the Sunni villages are compatible with becoming towns and the villagers citizens of the nation-state, may be enlarged upon. The state choses *one* settlement and turns it into a village, the villagers have no internal mediators or judges; they had already, before the modern state, given authority to rule over them to the central government; in return for loyalty to any government, they insist that the state support Islam; and the state is able to support Islam because this in turn helps maintain the social order.

I do not imply that these indications are exhaustive; I have not treated the way governments or villagers combine Kemalist principles with Islam (Tapper, R. and N., 1987) nor the role of the brotherhoods or saints, nor the reason that men continue to believe. Nor have I considered other equally significant changes which are taking place, and with which the existing order the Sunni villages can also cope, such as the rise in interaction with the outside world, the expansion of knowledge, variations of belief within the village community, or the shift from subsistence farming to cash-crops.[13] In spite of its brevity, however, this model is sufficiently concrete to contrast with the Alevi villages, to which I now turn.

The Alevi Villages [14]

The Alevi also live in nuclear settlements. Each consists of predominantly patrilineal, patrilocal households whose members till fields which they themselves own. Each settlement pursues its own rotation cycle and households of one settlement only rarely own fields in the territory of another. However, the number of households in each settlement is less than in the Sunni villages. I would estimate the average Alevi settlement to have between fifteen and twenty households, the largest I came across about fifty, the smallest, four.

An Alevi village, as defined by the state, comprises a number of these settlements, which the villagers refer to as *mahalle,* village quarter; no Alevi village in the sub-province has less than two distinct and separate *mahalles*. The village in which I lived had seven, the next village, ten. Only when the time comes to go to the summer pasture do the *mahalle* divisions dissolve. Then, all the households using a particular pasture group together around an enclosure (*oba*) in which they place their beasts at night .

That there are semi-independent units within each village, often several kilometres apart, each with its own agricultural cycle highlights the tension between the traditional life of the villagers and the identity, mores and laws which are imposed upon them by the state. Whereas in the Sunni village, one settlement equals one village, and therefore the more significant the weight of the state, the more the traditional boundary, cohesion and identity of the settlement is reinforced, the process is reversed among the Alevi. The state defines and protects a boundary for the village which embraces and ignores the indigenous *mahalle* divisions, imposes collective pasture which is at odds with the individual cycle practised by each *mahalle* and identifies people as coming from a settlement which has no basis in the traditional life of the Alevi.

'Aleviness', *Alevilik*

Among the Sunni, Islam is the most coherent and embracing of the various ideologies and concepts which serve to perpetuate the existing social order. This is also the case among the Alevi, but theirs is a different *type* of Islam, one which differs so much from the Sunni that it is not always clear, even to the Alevi themselves, that it is right to regard it as Muslim.

The Sunni define *Müslümanlık* mainly by literal belief in the Koran, praying in the mosque, and the 'five pillars'. The Alevi minimise the importance of these criteria, saying that they possess 'Alevi conditions' of Islam, *Alevinin Şartları.* These are *'Eline, diline, beline sahip ol!* ' 'Be master of your hands, tongue and loins!' These conditions are not exclusively Alevi; they are present throughout Turkish culture as a whole, in the mystical or Sufi side of Islam, where they are known as *edep.* But the Alevi have raised them to a jural level, so that they are the defining characteristic of their form of Islam, at the *expense* of, rather than as an accompaniment to, the 'five pillars'.

That the Alevi place the *edep* ideal at the heart of their form of Islam gives a clue to the way that they build up a separate identity from the Sunni. Though, of course, individual Alevi are articulate to varying degrees, many refer to their style of life (*Alevilik*) as *Tarikat,* and the Sunni style (*Sunnilik*) as *Şeriat.* By *Tarikat* the Alevi mean praying collectively in a 'reunion', *cem* (see below), respecting their 'three conditions', and paying heed to a great body of mystical lore which contains an assumption of allegiance to certain men (*dede* and *efendi*) who have been designated by God to keep order within the Alevi community and who are its guide to correct conduct. By *Şeriat,* which they contrast with *Tarikat* , and say is a quite different way of life to theirs, the Alevi do not mean the codified law of Islam, rather they mean praying in the mosque, interpreting the Koran literally, and following the 'five pillars'; that is, the daily round of religious life in a Sunni village. They also equate *Şeriat* with the power and exercise of authority by the central government.[15]

The Alevi Hierarchy

It is extremely difficult to be certain, but I estimate that about ten per cent of the population are accepted as belonging to a *dede* lineage. The every-day burden of perpetuating *Tarikat* tradition and mediating disputes within the framework of the religious authority falls on the *dede*, and no one who is not a *dede* may pronounce *Tarikat* prayers or lead *Tarikat* ceremonies.

Though each *dede* lineage regard themselves as descended from different founders, for example one *dede* lineage traces its descent to *Ibn Arabi*, nearly all acknowledge their subordination to *Haci Bektaş*, and men named *efendi*, whom they regard as descended from *Haci Bektaş* himself.

The *efendis* live at the town of *Haci Bektaş* (Norton, 1983) in the province of *Kırşehir*, about five-hours drive from the sub-province, and come perhaps once or twice a year to the village in which I lived, to collect dues and to reaffirm their contact with the villagers. They do not play a large part in the life of the village, though the villagers do say that the *efendis* are a type of higher court to whom they can appeal for judgement on points of ceremony or for mediation.

Every man, whether *dede* or not is a pupil, *talip*, to a particular *dede* lineage. A *cem*, the most important of the *Tarikat* rituals, can only be held if a *talip* lineage offers a sacrifice to their *dede*, and *dedes* may only mediate in a quarrel if they are invited to do so by a *talip* lineage. Also, once a year, before the winter sowing, the *dede* is supposed to visit all his *talip* lineages, ascertain from them any disputes which they have had during the year, reconcile them and leave them 'clean', *temiz*, for the coming planting season (see below).

The Alevi and Mystical Shi'ism

The Alevi also interweave the *Tarikat* ideals into their position *vis-à-vis* Islam as a whole, so that their religion might be summed up as 'mystical Shi'ism'. Briefly, they maintain the twelver Shi'ite tradition; that Hüseyin and Hasan were murdered at the Kerbala, that the rightly-guided caliphs succeeded them until the twelth, *mehti*, disappeared and will ultimately return. The *cem* celebrates the martyrdom of Hüseyin and Hasan in song and ritual. They say that they were taught how to perform the *cem* by Ali; and a slow stepping dance in the *cem*, the *sema* of the forty, *kırklar semahı*, commemorates the first men and women who gathered around Ali and learnt from him. Ali, they say, learnt his knowledge from Muhammad, who was commanded by Allah to impart his esoteric knowledge of religion to Ali and ultimately to the villagers.

This unusual combination of mystical *Tarikat* and Shi'ism is elucidated in a work named *Buyruk*, 'Decree'. The villagers claim that this work, which they read in a modern Turkish edition, is the collected sayings of *İmam Cafer, Sadık*, the sixth of the twelve imams. Most *dedes* possess a copy and consult it frequently. This book contains no codified law, but rather is a series of descriptions of different facets of the correct workings of the *Tarikat*, of religious anecdotes and of ritual prescriptions. I hope to cover it in more detail in a later publication.

Tarikat Rituals

Tarikat rituals are held in the main room (*ev*) of any house which is sufficiently large, always after dark. The whole of the *mahalle* in which the ceremony is taking place is expected to attend. They are forbidden to non-Alevi and I was permitted to enter only after the villagers had discussed the matter for some months.

A rug is laid in the centre of the room, Ali's space *Alinin meydanı.*

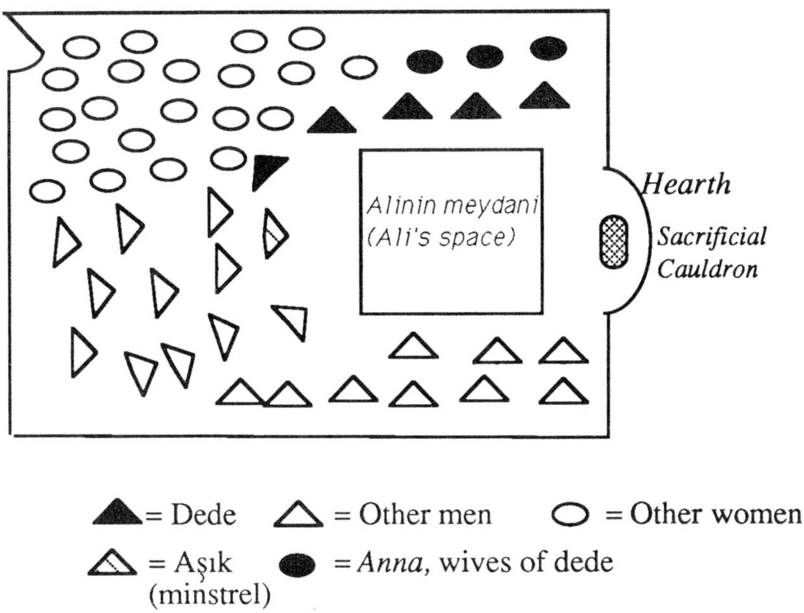

Before worship begins the dede asks the congregation, *cemaat*, whether any present have a dispute with each other. If any admit to a quarrel they must be reconciled, or the disputants must leave. Then the husband and wife who are offering a sacrifice come forward to Ali's space and confirm, in response to the *dede's* questioning that they have no quarrel with each other, nor with anyone in the room. This they call *ölmeden ölme,* to die before dying. They explain this expression by saying that the questioning, which they undergo from the *dede* is parallel to that which they shall receive from Allah after they have died, on the basis of which He shall judge whether to send them to heaven or hell.

In the Autumn, before the season of the *cem* may begin, a series of rituals called *görgü* are held.[16] They say that these mark their New Year and that until they have been conducted no field should be sown (though, in practice, this rule is frequently broken). In the village in which I stayed there are seven *mahalles*. On the first night the ceremony is held for the three smallest *mahalles*, on the second night for the fourth and fifth, on the third night for the last two. During the course of the three days a couple from *every* household in the village go through the questioning 'to die before dying'. That is, alongside other couples from their *mahalle*, they go forward to Ali's space to answer whether or not they have a quarrel with any one in the room. I quote a few lines of the ceremony here to illustrate their tenor.

The *dede* addresses those on the *meydan*:

Dede: 'Evveli baştan sizi sizden sorıyorlar, evinizinen, ocağınızınan, coluğunuzunan, cocuğunuzunan, feylinizinen, amelinizinen, gövdedinizen, nice belirsiniz? Dört camdinizden kendinize yarı garmı?'

Dede: 'Beginning from the first they ask of you, of your homes, of your hearths, of your wives, of your children, of your husbands, of your actions, of your bodies, what do you say? Are you happy within yourself?'

Those on the *meydan: 'Eyvallah, dede'*. 'By God, *dede* '. (yes)

Dede: 'Allah hepinizden razi olsun. Ellerinizinen koymadığınızı alman, gözünüzünen görmediginizi söylemen, ... komşu hakkında, yol darmında, verecekte, alacakta, bilenler bu kişilerden razımısınız?

'Let Allah be content with you all. Do not take what you have not yourself set down, do not say what you have not yourself seen....on the rights of neighbours, in the narrow part of the road, on that to be given, on that to be taken, you who know, are you content with these persons?'

When the existence and circumstances of a dispute have become clear, the *dede* suggests a reconciliation, based on whether the disputants have shown the correct degree of respect to each other (a young man must respect an older, a wife her husband), or abused one another's rights (*hakkı yemek*). The assembly, *cemaat,* then must agree with his decision, or else it is not valid. The *dede's* suggestions are supplemented by a '*görgü* committee', *görgü heyeti,* of which he is the head. The other members of the committee are not necessarily *dede,* but must be respected men of the village.

If the problem cannot be resolved, the person disagreeing with the majority must leave, and is said to be fallen, *düskün.* In this case, at best he or she will be forbidden entrance to religious ceremonies and at worst will not be spoken to or allowed to work with others on daily tasks, or may even be forced to leave the village. If one of a *dede* lineage fails to pass through the centre, then the whole of lineage is forbidden to practise until he or she has done so (see example below).

Some examples (from a *görgü* in 1989 which I witnessed)

(i) A man aggrieved with his neighbour because he had sold a field without giving him an opportunity to buy it.
Solution: the younger man was told to kiss the hand of the older, the older to kiss the younger's eyes, and the two not to argue in future.

(ii) A man failing to visit his sick brother.
Solution: it was wrong not to wish a sick person well. The brother still being sick, the offending brother shook hands with his wife, and was made to promise to visit the next day.

(iii) A woman losing her temper with her neighbour because she believed he had taken a piece of firewood from her door.
Solution: it was wrong for women to swear, and anyway he hadn't taken it. They shook hands.

(iv) A young man, whose father had died, throwing stones at a neighbour's sheep.
Solution: his mother said that she could not control him. It was decided to ask the village headman to speak to him, and all who saw him causing trouble to beat him.

(v) An enemy of the headman, *muhtar,* had reported to the sub-province governor that the *muhtar* was spending time in Istanbul and not in the village. The man who made the complaint came to the centre and said that there was no connection between events particular to the village and those to do with the state, that *Tarikat* could be separated from *Şeriat.* On this there was an outcry of protest. One man made a speech, saying, 'When *Şeriat* is separated from *Tarikat*, then Alevi life in this village is finished.'[17] The offending man withdrew. There was great consternation at this because the man was a *dede*, and as he had not been through the ceremony, the whole *dede* lineage would be unable to conduct the ceremony for their *talips* in the neighbouring village. He was persuaded to come back.

Solution: his brother's son spoke up, a man who commands great respect, and a member of the *görgü* committee. He explained that he had talked with the *muhtar* (who was not present through illness) and been appointed his representative. He promised he would reconcile the two's differences soon.

On hearing this promise the assembly allowed the man through without taking the matter further. When I went back to the village the next summer I found that, indeed, the two had resolved their quarrel.

Discussion

Alevi society is inherently hierarchical. It has men who are both empowered to lead and to teach the mores of the society to those who are their followers. Also, collective rituals, at which the norms of the society are reaffirmed, can only be conducted by activating the relationship between *dede* and follower, because of the rule which states that *cem* can only take place when a sacrifice is offered to a *dede*. It also possesses an extremely effective system of social control, using the authority of the *dede*, the *edep* philosophy, fear of the hereafter, and the approval of the collectivity to regulate disputes and impose conformity within the community.

In modern Turkey this way of life cannot survive. The snag is not so much the increased power of the central state over people's lives, though this is a constant factor in the demise of the *dede*, it is rather that the people themselves do not wish to remain independent of the nation-state; men increasingly internalise their membership of Turkey and they are equally anxious to enjoy the fruits of modernisation. Both these ambitions, which fuel each other, can only be realised by accepting the authority of the central state and therefore by breaking the relationship between follower and *dede* and abandoning the myths, embodied in the Shi'ite doctrine, which stress the inadequacy of the legitimacy of Sunni rule.

This inevitable shift has different and complicated implications for the community in which I lived. Though the overall effect is clear - the traditional life is fast disintegrating - it is difficult to disentangle the causal threads precisely. To give some indications, the *dedes* in the village are rapidly losing their power. Only those born into a *dede* lineage may become *dedes*, so that *dede* lineages depleted by migration cannot make up their number from non-*dedes* within the village. The remaining *dedes* are either old and not in contact with changing conditions, or younger, and not fluent in the necessary religious knowledge. Some villagers become openly derisive, others continue to show the *dedes* respect but avoid asking them to officiate in a *cem*. During the complete year I spent in the village only two were held.

As more of the village gains an income from the outside and more people migrate, life in the village becomes less based around the mutually intertwined interests of a tight-knit community. The problems - and disagreements - besetting those living in the village often involve negotiations with kin and friends living outside, sometimes as far afield as Germany, and are not likely to be solved simply by those remaining resolving their differences with each other. Sensing this, many doubt the relevance of a community-based sanction. Also, the most serious punishment is banishment. More than half the households have left, and most of those remaining spend much of their time trying to raise the money to move. Those still in the village are distressed that their neighbours have gone and are not inclined to make more people leave.

The villagers are acutely aware of the dichotomy between the chain of authority which leads through the *dede* to *Haci Bektaş* and *Ali* on the one hand, and the power of the state on the other. Now that the villagers want to become urban, *şehirleşme*, and develop, *gelişme*, the state, vastly more powerful than any means at the villagers' command for achieving this goal, is the sole acceptable authority. The *muhtar* is seen as representative of this authority. It is he who solves most of the petty quarrels which occur from day to day. Even if a very intelligent and charismatic *dede* emerged, able to justify his position solely by tales ever more difficult to believe, and with his authority continually undermined by the encroaching central authorities, he would but delay the decline.

I do not wish to put forward a picture of complete social disintegration. As the population of the village falls, so does pressure on resources. Fifteen years ago, when the village population was at its peak, the villagers say that there was a severe shortage of water and fields. Now there is more than ample bread and fresh vegetables and no shortage of land to plough and sufficient water for irrigation. That hunger is not a problem means that it is easier than before, at least from the material point of view, for an individual to fulfil the commandment 'be master of thy hands, loins, and tongue', and it is frequently quoted.

The *cem* and *görgü*, described above, are *ciddi*, serious. At them it is shameful, *ayıp*, to make jokes or chatter, or be drunk. During weddings, or *muhabbet* (drinking with companions) this stricture is removed. Men, and sometimes women, may be drunk without any shame at all, and the company is often riotously merry. There are parallels between the two types of ritual in that they both present an opportunity to relive Alevi ideals in a highly structured setting. When a group of men decide to spend an evening drinking, they group around a table and appoint one of their number *saki*, distributor of drinks. No man may begin before the *saki* has given a formal toast to open the proceedings, and thereafter all men at the table must obey *saki*'s command to drink. If a man leaves the table without permission from the *saki* he is open to punishment, *sitem*, from the *saki*. The standard punishment they term a *cabriel*, 'Angel Gabriel', and consists of a cockerel and a bottle of *rakı*.[18]

Such drinking sessions usually take place with a minstrel, *aşık*. I have been present at many gatherings at which the *aşık* began by singing a drinking song, then moved on to laments mourning Ali, then to a sequence of dance songs culminating in a *sema*. This *semah* is precisely the same one as, *gönüller semahı*, which brings the *cem* service to a close. At the sound of the *semah* it is usual for a man to call for his children, both boys and girls, and encourage them to dance to the accompaniment of cheers from the drinkers. Often women are present, either sitting with, or waiting on, the men. They usually dance in the *semah* with the men.

Thus the power of the *dede* is waning, and the religious ceremonies over which they preside are ever less popular. A few villagers still believe without question the teachings of the *dede* as the true form of Islam; more are sceptical as to the worth of religion. All I spoke with or witnessed remain attached to their dance and song, but practise them mainly in a secular setting. Here, the dance and song are seen not as religion but as a part of 'Aleviness'. I witnessed, therefore, a community in which for many individuals the trappings of religion are coming to be seen as 'culture'.[19]

There is one more shift I should mention. The integrity of each *mahalle* is declining. The *mahalle* is important primarily for subsistence farming, and as a base in which people experience their closest social ties. In both respects it is being eroded; the villagers rely increasingly on remittances from outside for their livelihood, and as such large numbers of people have migrated, those people remaining in the *mahalle* are, though neighbours, often not as closely related to each other as they are to migrant workers outside the village. This decline is matched by an equivalent shift in identity; the village unit is taking over as the most important residence unit by which people define themselves. This can be seen not just in the village, but also outside. When the villagers leave the sub-province and settle in Istanbul, they do not build or rent houses according to *mahalle* divisions, but according to village. There, men collect in a coffee-house as *Susesi* [20] migrants, and during weddings and *muhabbet* sing songs celebrating the fine water, women and landscape of *Susesi*, making no specific heed of the *mahalle* from which they come.

Conclusions

In this paper I have sketched how the increasing interchange between central government and village leads to quite different ethics of modern life. The Sunni's village organisation survives, the villagers retain their faith and they favour the parties, all of which are lenient toward Islam, who customarily win a majority in the National Assembly. The Alevi in contrast are unable to adapt; their village life is disrupted and their beliefs eroded.

Why is the Alevi village population declining so drastically? I think the answer is that the Alevi traditional communities cannot integrate into modern Turkey without the difficulties, contradictions and disorganisation that such a change in orientation requires appearing more painful than simply moving to a city and starting life again. Alevi villages are in a state of flux. Men cannot entirely abandon the traditional way of life in the separated *mahalle* communities and the network of reciprocal obligations and ties which this implies, yet nor do they accept the living conditions which life in such communities imposes on them. In addition, even when the separate *mahalle* co-operate as a village to exploit the services available from the state, and individuals embrace their identity as villagers, there is no obvious discourse with which shared rituals can be celebrated.[21] In the town, the difficulties and contradictions are less. Alevi 'culture' (traditional religion shorn of the Shi'ite myths and subservience to *dedes*) with its emphasis on correct conduct, responsibility to the community, and its collective music, poetry, dance and song, fuses well with the philosophy extolled by Kemalism and provides them with an urban ethic with which to lead their lives. Indeed the Alevi are almost invariably supporters of parties sympathetic toward Atatürk and 'social democracy' such as the SHP or the DSP.[22] In addition, for those who have left the village, the rival system of authority between the state and the *dede* is far less of a dilemma; the state is their only feasible temporal authority in an urban setting. Individuals may show respect to the *dedes*, but they need pay no heed to what they say.

The research conducted here is based only on one sub-province, yet it appears from the work of other researchers such as Naess (1988) and Gökalp (1989) to be reflected across Turkey. If this is the case, its significance is great. The Alevi have hitherto been a rural population and the cities and towns predominantly Sunni. As the Alevi move into the towns it will be there, in urban Turkey, that a mix of sects will be found. Rural Turkey will become almost entirely Sunni. Thus for the first time in its history, rural Anatolia will be occupied by people of one single religious persuasion.

Secondly, we have no overall, unified way in which social change in Anatolia can be envisaged. Keyder (1983), for example, has suggested that villages can be classified according to the economic direction which they take, Hann has replied (1988) by suggesting that regional differences must be taken into account in evaluating the ways in which this occurs. This research suggests that though economics is vital to the process of social change, traditional social organisation and belief *independently* of the traditional means of livelihood must be considered when building models to account for it.

Notes

1. The government does not distinguish between Alevi and Sunni in official statistics. (Lewis, 1957, pp. 88-9).
2. Precise figures are given in my doctoral thesis, University of Cambridge, 1993.
3. I would like to thank also my many friends in the Middle East Technical University, who did much to make my stay in Turkey enjoyable and rewarding.
4. Stirling (1965, pp. 135, 271) notes that village boundaries became fixed by the state with the introduction of the Village Law in 1924.
5. For a standard work on local administration in Turkey see Keleş and Yavuz, 1989.
6. Stirling (1965, p.26) finds a similar pattern. Referring to Kayseri he writes, 'All the villages in the area...are self-contained clusters of

buildings separated from one another by stretches of unfenced land'. See also Sirman (1988, page 36) 'Rural Turkey is a mixture of nucleated villages and small towns which act as administrative and economic centres'. I would regard this as a characteristic of central Anatolian Sunni villages - but not necessarily of other areas of the country. See Hann (1990).

7. There have been periodic attempts at land redistribution by the state. These only reinforced the village ideal that all households should own some fields because the redistribution was aimed at creating smallholdings out of land taken from large landowners. Sirman notes; 'This law (the land reform bill of 1945) was supposed to provide "land to the tiller" by distributing land to the peasants...this land was supposed to provide for the subsistence of a family ... it was on the basis of the *households* (orig. emphasis) that the distribution took place (Sirman 1988, pp. 248-9). Contrast this approach with that of the Soviet government in Tajikistan; Gillian Tett, in her forthcoming Ph.D. thesis at the University of Cambridge, describes how similar Muslim peasant villages were integrated forcibly into a pattern of collective land use which was quite at odds with their indigenous organisation. See also Keyder in this volume.
8. Sirman (1988, p.87). 'Thus the village constitutes a unit within which a number of goods and services are produced and exchanged outside the sphere of commodity production. Village boundaries mark the outer limits within which these activities take place.' See also Stirling (1988, p.29) 'People belong to their village in a way they belong to no other community. On any definition of community, the village is a community - a social group with many functions, not all of them explicit, and to which many people are committed by birth or marriage and bound by many ties. '
9. This is explored in more detail in Stirling (1951) and in Delaney (1991).
10. Stirling (1951, p.58) describes similarly 'As I have said, several times, in discussing women or questioning men about their home life, I was told that women are *hayvan gibi* - like animals. Men do not altogether act on the proposition, but that they should affirm it so often and, on occasion in front of the women and girls, is significant of the relative prestige of the sexes.'
11. *Şeker Bayramı*, 'sugar festival', celebrating the last day of Ramazan, and the feast of sacrifice, *Kurban Bayramı.*
12. Sirman (1990b) notes that women play a separate role, though equally important, supporting ties between the household of the community through frequent visits to each other, out of sight, and independently of the men.

13. On this last see Sirman (1988, p. 384). 'Contrary to the experience of other similar communities in Turkey where change has produced massive upheavals...transition to commodity production in the *Söke* region has been rather smooth and has not destroyed the fabric of social relations within the community.'
14. For Alevi village ethnography see Bumke (1989), Gökalp (1980, 1989), Melikoff (1975), Naess (1988) and Yalman (1969).
15. This division into social life ruled by the state, and social life independent of the state is known elsewhere in the Muslim world, for example in North Africa, where the mountain tribesmen lived in a state of rebellion, *siba*, and the plainsmen and townsmen accepted the rule of the state, *makhzen*. (Gellner, 1969).
16. Gökalp (1980, p.205) found a similar ritual, though called by a different name; *sorgu ayını* (interrogation rite). See also Birge (1965, pp. 170-1).
17. I take this to mean, 'when *Tarikat* no longer has temporal authority over the events in the village...then *Alevilik* is finished.'
18. *Rakı* has sacred connotations for the Alevi and Bektaşi, some of whom use it in *tarikat* ceremonies.
19. i.e. the Alevi play songs previously regarded as religious in secular settings, and do so not to propitiate God but to celebrate their own society; they are going through the same shift that leads us in Britain to listen to Mozart's requiem in a concert hall rather than in a chapel and call it 'culture' The Alevi themselves call a neighbouring *mahalle* 'very cultural', *çok kültürlü*, citing their ability at music, dance and poetry.
20. *Şusesi* is not the actual name for the village in which I stayed, but the name I shall use when discussing it in print.
21. *Muhabbet*, shared drinking sessions, are not sufficient in themselves to provide a collective identity for a whole village community, *Tarikat* religious ceremonies gain much of their *frisson* by being closed, collective celebrations of a persecuted minority and it is difficult for the Alevi to use them as focal points for a village community (the diverse *mahalles* can only regard themselves as being a village in the first place by accepting the state's designation), and the villagers are not sufficiently attracted to the Sunni, mosque-based Islam led by the Directorate of Religious Affairs for it to be a sustainable alternative. See also Ragnar (1988).
22. The Social Democratic Populist Party, and the Democratic Left Party, respectively (ed.). Writers as early as Birge have noticed the possibility of a political alliance between the Alevi and the Kemalists. (1924, Reprint, 1965). See also Yalman (1969).

| 5 |

Peasants Without Pride

Migration, Domestic Cycle and Perception of Time

Werner Schiffauer

This article discusses the consequences of mass migration since the 1950s for the domestic cycle and the concept of time in Subay[1] (Araç, Kastamonu), a remote Black Sea mountain village.[2] I use an actor centred approach, that is, an analysis in terms of problems and problem-solving strategies. Migration, I argue, allows for new anwers to old problems but leads in turn to a new set of problems requiring new answers. It is in this active process that basic conceptions about society and self are formed.

I use material I collected during research in Subay from 1977 to 1986.

The Economy

The economic units in Subay are the households, which contain two or three generations. The crucial problem in any domestic economy is the constant need to reconcile economic and social imperatives. The solution must lie in the structure of production.

The economy is based on food production for self-consumption; wheat, potatoes, small scale husbandry. Additional income had been secured by seasonal migration (which ended in the late fifties) and is nowadays earned by cutting wood for the forestry department. A few farmers run a tractor, which they also hire out; four villagers have larger herds than the others, two run small shops; some get additional income from carpentry. A certain hierarchy in these activities can be observed. The food production and work for the forestry department constitute something like a 'core domain'; only after the basic needs are covered by these activities are more rewarding but also more risky 'entrepreneurial' activities taken up. The logic of production thus resembles a building kit. To a basic domain additional activities can be added, which can be given up again if the situation requires it. All this reflects the compromise between the socially necessary (security), and the economically desirable (profitability).

In this type of economy, production units are as large as possible. The core domain (food/forestry) requires four persons in the summer and three in winter. Risky but efficient enterprises can therefore only be undertaken by households with five or more working members. It is with regard to recruitment and organisation of the work force that the social and economic imperatives are often difficult to reconcile. This general problem appears in different forms according to the phases of the domestic cycle.

The Customary Cycle

Let us first reconstruct the 'customary ideal' of the domestic cycle, as it was before mass migration set in.

Four phases can be distinguished (1) The phase of the 'nuclear family' - usually a young couple lives together with their children in one household. (2) The phase of the 'composite nuclear family' - by marriage new members of the household are recruited and others (the daughters) are lost. (3) The phase of the 'extended family' - two or more married sons live together with their families in their father's house. (4) With the death of the patriarch the extended family breaks apart into the families of the sons. If the mother still lives she usually remains with the son who inherits the house. A new cycle starts.

There always had been some deviations from this ideal for demographic reasons. Bigamy was practised in case of childlessness, *iç güveylik* (in-marriage) in the absence of male heirs . Our interest here however concerns more the problems which result from conflicts of social and economic imperatives.

In phase one, the problem which had to be solved was the generational problem. I recorded several life histories of the older men in which the relation to their fathers was described as particularly difficult because of the 'coldness' and 'hardness' of their fathers. These conflicts generally led to friction on the household unit when they were aggravated by *güveylik*, a step relation resulting from remarriage. In these cases, young boys separated from their households in order to migrate to the city, often as young as twelve.

In phase two, it is the need to marry the children, and the corresponding need to restructure the work force which poses problems; in particular, the need to balance the loss of a daughter through marriage, by the marriage of a son, and the gain of a son's wife, a *gelin*.

Often the age differences between sons and daughters do not allow for a smooth arrangement. Two strategies are possible. Sometimes pressure is put on one of the sons to marry earlier than usual. This is considered to be undesirable, and the young men forced to marry in their teens are generally pitied. Because of the risk that such a marriage might result in marital strife, and a worse situation, the parents no longer insist on this type of marriage, though some may try. The other strategy is to attempt to postpone the marriage of daughters. This is only possible for a limited period. A social corrective is given with the institution of the *kız kaçırma*, the elopement. This however is a very risky undertaking. I recorded the case in which a girl whose father had postponed the marriage again and again for economic reasons finally agreed to an elopement. But she was left in the lurch, when it became evident that she was pregnant.

A careful balancing thus was required. Any attempt to ignore one or the other aspect may lead to serious secondary problems. It is the flexible attitude of the *bricoleur* (who works with prefabricated material and is as much determined by it as he determines it) which was required here rather than that of the engineer (who subordinates means to ends).

Difficulties were also posed by the in-marriage of a daughter-in-law. The household gained a female worker who had to be integrated socially and economically. This was considered to be very difficult and conflicts between mother-in-law and daughter-in-law were generally expected.

This situation was aggravated by a structural problem. With the in-marriage the nucleus of a new family was established - of a new social body which would break away sooner or later. The daughter-in-law was the 'daughter of the stranger' (*el kızı*). Her solidarity with the new household was questioned and there was the fear that she would alienate her husband from his parents. The obligation of a son to side with his parents, in particular with his mother, in these conflicts was stressed. These kinds of problems were usually, it seems solved; but at the expense of the *gelin* .

A different situation however arose when the second son married - phase three of the cycle. Oral history shows that most extended families broke apart at this phase despite the explicitly formulated ideal.[3] The decisive point seems to be that with the marriage of the second there were now two 'nuclear families' on the *same generation level* in the household, - which would be independent households sooner or later and which would then deal with each other on the basis of symbolic exchange. The ideal of reciprocity and equality which would characterise the relationship later was forshadowed. Despite the fact that the brothers still worked for their father, increasing conflicts about the distribution of work and resources seem to have been the rule.

A tendency to blame 'the women' for separation may have resulted from a desire to deny the conflicts between brothers. There seems to be some truth in the accusation, however. The wives of brothers probably had a tendency to pay much attention to equality with regard to distribution of work for structural reasons. The authority relation between them was less clear than between siblings - and structural equality encourages comparison. The strain between sisters-in-law is frequently expressed.

To sum up. The social conflicts - in particular those between brothers but also those between sons and fathers - gained momentum at the very moment when, from an economic point of view, the size of the production unit was optimal. Usually the production unit breaks apart at this moment. The inner dynamic of the social domain proves to be stronger than economic rationality.

Migration and the Domestic Cycle

The permanent migration which started in the 1950s to Karabük (a steel centre), to Istanbul and to Ankara was considerable. The village, which had 250 inhabitants living in 48 households in 1977, would have had about 750 inhabitants if no migration had taken place.

The possiblity of rapid permanent emigration led to a change in the ideal household cycle. Instead of trying to make the sons stay in the village, it now appeared sensible to let all except one (usually the youngest one) move into the city. This was not considered to be a 'separation' (*ayrılma*) but rather the establishing of a sort of urban branch of the farm. A separation would only take place after the death of the patriarch. The economic and social advantages (though not the political) of an integrated rural-urban household seemed to be convincing. It allowed for a solution of the problem of the scarcity of land and a flexible answer to the shifting demand for labour during the course of the year. The migrants could take their leave during the summer-time, in order to help with the harvest. The daughters-in-law could come for longer if necessary. Some were expected to stay up to three or four months during the summer-time in order to help out. Lastly an urban branch meant a regular cash income. This was less important for covering running costs - these were covered by forest work - than as a kind of insurance in the case of catastrophes, like fire or illness. Finally, the urban household would make it possible to give village children a secondary education. They would stay with their uncles in the city. The village household, on the other hand, was regarded as a guarantee of security in case of joblessness. And it was a place where the old parents could best be provided for. The integrated rural urban household also seemed to allow for a solution of the conflicts just described. Constant comparing lost relevance now that the brothers were working in very different domains. The migration thus at first seemed to allow for the realisation of the customary ideal better than in any earlier period. However, it soon became apparent that new problems would arise.

There was first the impact of spatial separation. While in the village the conflicts between parents-in-law and daughter-in-law were generally solved in favour of the former the spatial separation implied the growing structural importance of daughters-in-law. One of the peasants remarked with a rather grim voice: 'When my son is married, he will send no more money. He will care for his wife and she will interfere. That is always the case here'. This is particularly felt to be a problem when the son finds himself a wife on his own in the city.[4] In this case the *gelin* cannot be expected to come to the village in order to help out. It is not expected that the difficulties of the mother-in-law/daughter-in-law relationship can be solved if the *gelin* is a complete stranger. It is very questionable whether a stranger would accept the restrictions and sacrifices which, for example, are expected in the allocation of domestic space between family members. The whole concept of an integrated rural household is thus threatened by an urban marriage. The reaction of the parents therefore is usually very strong. I recorded a case where the father exerted so much pressure on the couple that the marriage finally broke apart.

Some of the young men in fact expressed their opposition to the concept of an integrated urban rural household by marrying a woman from Istanbul. 'I knew it exactly. If I had married Salığangoz's daughter (as his father had proposed) my father would have kept her in the village (in order to help out). But why should I marry if I cannot live together with my wife?'.[5]

A different set of problems usually appears in phase three, when the other sons have married as well. They are related to the appearance of a new type of economic rationality.

The migration of the sons was regarded by the patriarchs in the beginning like any other market-oriented undertaking, i.e. as within the context of an additional structure of production. It was seen as an undertaking which (similar to goat keeping or seasonal migration) could be added to the core domain of production but which would be given up again when the farm required it, for example in case of old age, illness or serious conflicts. It proved, however, to be much more.

New types of occupations became accessible. There was a growing resistance against giving up an urban employment in favour of the farm when the former was conceptualised as a chance which would not come again so easily. Someone lucky enough to find an insured (*sigorta*) job, would be very unwilling to give it up. Haci Sakır, then 45 years old, who had twice given up insured work in order to come back to the farm, was a clear exception. He told me that he regretted it. This led to a shift of emphasis. The work in the city now was considered to be basic, and farming secondary. There was a growing tendency give up farming for a job in the city.

Moreover for the families in the city, the city rapidly became the central focus in the life of the migrants. This led to a re-evaluation of the importance of the different types of income. For the seasonal migrants, the work in the cities had only been meaningful in the context of the activities of the other members of the household. It provided an additional and supplementary income. For the permanent migrants however the monetary income became central, and the products which were brought from the village became a mere supplement, given in kind, but evaluated at market prices. Work paid in cash became logically distinct from farm work. In principle one could live on it alone. The young men in the city came to regard their wages as their own . They certainly continued to send money to the villages, but they now sent something that basically belonged to them, which they also could have used otherwise, perhaps better.

This is reflected in a new type of conflict. The migrants in the city sometimes felt offended when the money they had sent to their fathers was handed on to their brothers. What fathers considered an act of pooling and redistribution, the migrant sons considered an improper use of a personal gift, given to benefit their fathers.

The whole structure of thinking about the relation of the individual to the others changed. The fathers tended to see the farm as a given unit, and the duties of the individuals were derived from that. In their reasoning, they started from the whole group - the continuity of which had to be secured at any price - and finally arrived at the individual. Their sons started with the particular, the needs and interests of the individuals, and finally arrived at the group. The urban-rural household was no longer perceived as a unit, the existence of which was given and not questionable - but rather as one possible kind of co-operation among others. If one kept it up at all, it had to serve the interests of all those involved. When looking at the enterprise from that angle the migrants felt that they were giving more than they received: 'I could have bought an apartment in the meantime. But we sent, sent, sent. And we received nothing.' To put it shortly; in the sixties and seventies the idea of the integrated rural-urban household did not 'pay off'. The necessity of finding compromises between the social and the economic requirements lost its plausibility. The attitude of the engineer replaced the attitude of the *bricoleur*.

During the sixties and seventies this way of seeing things spread to the villages. The men who had remained in the village had the feeling of working more and earning less than their brothers in the city. The peasants who had been dominant in the village in 1977 (i.e. the generation of the then 40-55 year olds) had the feeling of having drawn the worse lot.

They were too old to move into the city and tended grudgingly, to accept their fate. But their sons still had the opportunity to go. In 1977 none of the men under 30 said that they wanted to stay - 'rather leave today than tomorrow'.

The fathers were ambivalent about their sons' intentions to migrate. Some of them felt alienated from the village and wanted to spare their sons a life in Subay. A second group of fathers wanted their sons to stay in the village, but thought it unwise to apply any pressure. Then there was a considerable group which exerted some pressures on the sons for less pragmatic (economic or political) reasons. And finally there were those who insisted on the right to spend their old age within the village rather than in the city.

The sons of the latter two groups were in a difficult situation. If they left the village against the will of their parents they would violate the rules of respect for parents. If on the other hand they stayed till the parents were dead they would be too old for migration. There was yet another problem. Several of the young peasants said that they could conceive of staying in the village, as long as they had some kind of support from the urban households; for example, for the education of children. But since they could count on this support only as long as their parents were alive, they would rather leave the village today. They feared not only being trapped in the village - but also being left alone in the trap.

In this situation the young men took different positions. Very often they gave up. When I returned to the village in 1982, I was surprised how many of the young men who had declared their firm intention to migrate had stayed. Very often they mentioned the fear of the parents' curse as a reason. The frequency with which this metaphysical sanction is referred to may be due to the decreased importance of innerworldly sanctions.

There are, however, others who are not impressed by the threat of the curse. They move away and apply pressure on their parents to follow them and to spend the rest of their life in the city. As one said, 'In my opinion, a father should say: "For the sake of the future of my son, it is necessary that I move to his household"'.

Since parents sometimes refuse to move to the city, there is a growing number of households of elderly people from which all sons had migrated: eight in 1977, fourteen in 1983. Sometimes a member of the city household was delegated to take care of a single woman in the village. This high figure shows that the idea of the integrated rural urban household failed whenever no son agreed to stay in the village. See the bottom right-hand figure in the Diagram overleaf.

Diagram Family Cycle

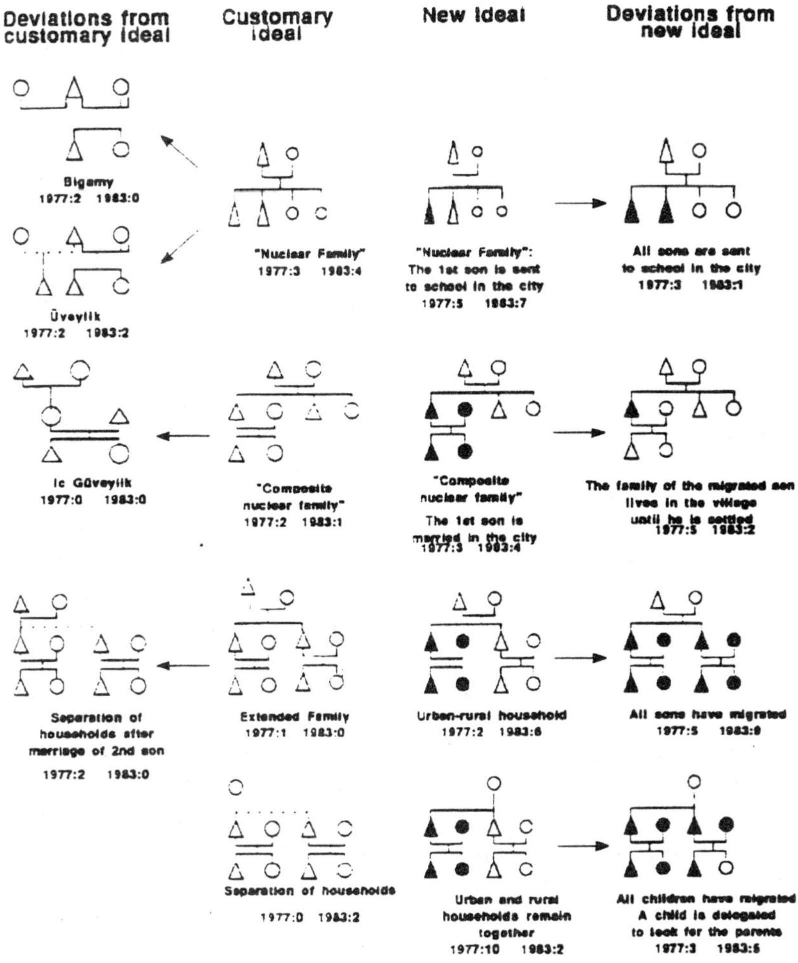

Composition of families in Subay in 1977 and 1983. The symbols filled black indicate migrants

A consequence was that for the first time the lonely death of the old folk became a social problem in Subay. During the winter of 1982/83 a woman whose relatives had all moved to the city had been found dead in her house. The villagers were upset. It is an almost sacred duty of the sons to keep watch with their dying parents in order to give them a drop of water in the moment of dying and to have the Quran recited. The purpose of both rites is to prevent the parents from dying *imansız* - without faith.

The great variety of family forms which I registered in Subay in 1977 and 1983 can be interpreted as resulting from the change of the ideal and practice of the domestic cycle. The two central columns show the customary and the new ideal of the domestic cycle; both cycles have their own characteristic deviations deriving from conflicts

Concepts of Time

The changes discussed have important implications for perception. They are reflected in a change in the experience and concept–ualisation of time.

Neither history nor traditionalism plays an important role for the peasants of Subay. The social memory is of a remarkably shallow historical depth. No incidents are remembered beyond the generation of the grandfathers of those now living. This seems to be related to the rules of inheritance. Equal inheritance implies that the ownership of land is regrouped from generation to generation. This does not allow for a strong identification with 'family land' or with a 'family farm' - and a general lack of dynastical thinking and memory seems to be the result.[6]

This does not mean, however, that time is considered freely disposable. The peasants do refer to *örf ve adet* (customs and morals) when they legitimise actions. But when they do so this seems to imply less a positive valuation of the past but rather a cautious attitude towards the future. Every change of *örf ve adet* seems to threaten the balance of obligations and counter-obligations - and thus implies a certain risk. This is related to the egalitarian and competitive structure of the society. Constant comparing implies that one cannot accept less without having to fear for one's status. Because of pressure to take account of what the other does, every new practice has a tendency, as the farmers put it, 'to become customary' (*örf haline gelmek*). An example is the development of marriage payments. The mechanism was described very clearly by

Hüsnü : 'One demanded one thing for his daughter; another one something else. One saw that and said to oneself: "Why shouldn't my daughter get the same thing?" - And so it became a custom'. Because status is involved, imperatives are set, which cannot easily be changed even if they seem to be irrational.

So it seems to be less respect for the past than anxieties about the future which leads to conservatism. It reflects a careful attitude toward time (and change). There is a sense of the weight of time.

That seems to be related to some kind of scepticism. The future does not hold promises. It cannot be planned. A basic experience of village life seems to be that whenever something seems to run smoothly a new problem is likely to appear. This is of course related to the intricacies of the production process which we analysed above. It is aggravated by the insecurities of village life. Almost everybody in the village had experienced plans or intentions being thwarted by catastrophes or illness. Things have a tendency to get worse instead of better.

The attitude towards the future, then, is less specific planning than wise precaution and provision. This is aptly summed up by the saying: 'We tied up the ass; if the wolf wants to eat it, it should eat it here'.

The basic attitude of precaution and provision implies in particular careful attention to one's obligations, *görev*. In general there is the feeling that one will get back in time of need what one gives in time of abundance. This was aptly expressed by Kuruçavuş:

> What do I need money for? I need men (*adamlar*). I need men who come when I call them. I need someone who does not care about distance and effort when I need him. Yes - earn money. But invest it in your relationships, give to those whose help you will need.

The central importance attached to the serving of the *görev* implies a concept of the future as *gelecek* - literally that which will come. This type of future is not opposed to the present but it is rather implied in the here and now. It is implied in the act of prestation which will lead to a counter prestation - which will be roughly equivalent. The time concept is determined by an idea of give and take and the balance and rough continuity which is implied.

The experience of migration and the change of the household cycle had a tremendous impact on this concept of time. Two experiences were connected with it. First, the setting up of an urban branch of the village household implied the experience of co-temporality. There is not only the here and now, with its own time rhythms and its particular future (*gelecek*) but there is also the there and now in the city, with a different time rhythm and a different *gelecek*. Of course there always had been the *knowledge* that there were other worlds than one's own; but what was different now was that one's own brother was living in a different world. And that meant that *in principle* one could be in his place. The abstract knowledge about other worlds thus became concrete and relevant knowledge. There was not only one future, but the individual had the choice between several 'futures'. In principle a different type of future was accessible. There was an option, even if one did not make use of it. The experience of time became two-dimensional; it demanded a 'perspective'.

But it was not only the experience of co-temporality, but also the experience of a new city structure of time. This second experience is related to the growing importance of the monetary income. The use of money has an impact on the concept of a future. Whereas symbolic - gift - exchange implies a concrete future centred in the present, rational monetary exchange implies an abstract future. The use of money requires different attitudes. It does not merely enable individuals to build up capital, it *requires* them to do so; and not only economic capital but also capital in knowledge. It requires a spirit of planning and wise investment. One has to learn how to 'deal with money'. A person who fails to develop this new kind of attitude is likely to find that money will run through his fingers like water. The future is thus transformed from the concrete *gelecek* into the abstract future, the *istikbal*. The different attitude which this new kind of future demands is expressed in the phrase of *istikbal sağlamak* ('to secure one's future'). To secure one's future demands planning. The future can be secured by schooling, by migration and so on. Future is thus conceptualised in terms of long-term and short-term aims. It is seen as something which in its nature is opposed to the present.

The 'discovery of the future' made time as it was experienced in the village appear in a new light. The *gelecek*, 'that which will come', is increasingly felt to be a 'lack of future'. There is a consensus among young men that there is 'no future in this village' (*bu köyde istikbal yok*).

The sequence of the *görevler*, the obligations the individual has to fulfil during the course of the annual cycle, or the life cycle, appears in that perspective to be an empty and meaningless rotation.

'We take something', Mevlüt said and illustrated it by taking his torch , 'and return it. But no money remains in the hand. In the city we do the same and we get money for it'. Whereas life in the city is associated with progress - by reaching intermediary aims you get closer to a final aim - the fulfilment of obligations does not seem to lead anywhere. The feeling connected with that is that 'this is a land without end, without remedy' (*çaresiz*).

Compared to the notion implied in the concept of *istikbal* that time should be something which should be rationally structured according to plans, the temporal experience in the village seems to be quite the contrary. It is not that the individual disposes of his time according to his needs; rather time disposes of the individual. The individual has to obey the sequel of imperatives set by *görev*. He or she does not dominate time, but is dominated by time.

This is felt very painfully in situations when serving the *görevler* seems to preclude the 'securing of the future' as it was the case among the young men who risked missing the right time for migration.

The most important consequence of the discovery of the future however seems to be a change in the perception of the self. For the traditional concept of self the idea of 'proving oneself' was decisive. From the fulfilment of the *görev*, which was an absolute imperative, one was able to derive a basic feeling of one's worth. As anybody of comparable status was confronted with the same tasks the idea of individuality was secondary. A person had to fulfil his or her obligations *just like* anybody else. Sameness was valued above difference. Individuality showed itself only with regard to better or worse performance.[7] With the idea of the future, individuality gets a different meaning. It relates now to the specific way through society - and it is claimed as a right by the young peasants. *Kendi hayatım yaşamak istiyorum* - I want to live my own life - was a phrase almost as frequently used as the other phrase: 'I want to secure my own future.'

This idea led to a significant devaluation of the idea of 'proving oneself'. There was a melancholic touch when Ahmet Akdemir, who had lovingly cared for his mother till her death said: 'Well, basically I always wanted to migrate. But, well - everything happened differently. But at least I have done my duty' (*hiç olmazsa görevimi yaptım*).

The implications of the new experience of time were also expressed by Koca Mustafa. I talked to him after conflicts had set an end to the co-operation of several households for collective shepherding. I asked him whether he would take a new initiative in this respect:

> Why should I call my men together? None of my sons is going to stay here. We will sell the sheep anyhow. It is *ayıp* (shameful) to send one's daughter-in-law to the pastures. Anyhow - the only ones who remain here are those who cannot secure their future and who are somewhat feeble *(zayıf)*.

The inner distancing of himself from the village, which is expressed here by one of the most influential villagers, is striking. Those who fulfil their traditional obligations now appear as the losers, as persons who are unable to develop a perspective of their own. The discovery of the future implied in the village the realisation of being without a future; the discovery of the individual implied the self-perception as loser. The migration thus led to a new type of peasantry: Peasants without Pride.

Notes

1. The name has been changed.
2. This refers to the classification Karpat developed with particular reference to the Black Sea region (1976, 175ff). He showed how migration had a very different impact on mountain villages, semi-mountainous villages and valley villages. The discussion here limits itself to the mountain villages.
3. This appears to be different from the situation in Kayseri. While the ideal of the household cycle is the same, there apparently always had been more deviation in Kastamonu. Stirling mentions brothers who stayed together even after the death of the father (1965, p.131). But see also Stirling, 1974, on changes in the separation of married sons.
4. A *şehir kızı* (city girl) is not necessarily a girl from an urban background. More commonly, she has migrated to the city from some other rural area.
5. The biography of Süleyman Doğan is extensively discussed in Schiffauer, 1991: 50-83).
6. This type of identification seems to be a characteristic of inegalitarian inheritance systems. If the inheritance is passed only to one heir, there seems to be strong likelihood of building up an identification of land and family. In such cases the farm tends to become a corporation (a unity of the living and the dead) - with a high tendency to loyalty to past and future generations. In this context the idea that 'corporations

never die' can develop. The Turkish peasant family definitely is a 'social body' but not a 'corporation' in the sense of a community of the living and the dead. The difference of social body and corporation as well as the relevance of the idea of the corporation for the conceptualisation of time is discussed by Kantorowicz (1990). Cf. also Meyer-Fortes (1969, pp.276-310). For the implications of inheritance rules for historical thinking see Todd (1985).

7. In most cases to worse performances. The individual traits played a crucial role in the discourse of gossip. It is the deviations from role expectations that are emphasised.

| 6 |

Gender and Household Resource Management in Agriculture

Cash Crops in Kars

Behrooz Morvaridi

Introduction

Neglect of gender issues is common to most development policies. The impact of development policies on farming households and women in production will be examined in the context of the commoditisation of agriculture in north-east Turkey and structural adjustment policy. Such macro-economic policies ignore the question of gender, yet they affect both men and women within the household.

The apparent gender neutrality of development policies hides a gender bias which stems from the omission of the process of the production and maintenance of human resources in policy planning. This conceptual bias, means that the 'economic' sphere has been defined in terms of marketed goods and services, thereby ignoring the unpaid reproductive labour of women, and their unpaid family farm labour within the household.

There is usually little mention in development policies and programmes of how women's work and welfare may be affected. The commoditisation process is engineered by macro-economic policies which intervene in agriculture, encouraging high capital-labour ratios and accelerating agricultural mechanisation. This does not necessarily mean lightening the burdens borne by women, many of whom work as family labourers. Integration into the commercial market can in some cases result in the intensification of women's work. Poverty can push poor farmers to exploit their resources and this often runs hand in hand with extra burdens for female family unpaid labour.

Macro policies, such as structural adjustment, which are aimed at achieving economic efficiency, tend to shift the burden away from the public sector to the private and unpaid economy. The effect can be to engineer changes in the gender division of labour, and in patterns of household resource management. In small family farming households the burden of economic efficiency in the spheres of household production and reproduction often falls on women. When small farming households encounter financial problems or economic crises, it is often female household members who are constrained to work under conditions of extreme pressure in the production process. Some farmers cultivate more cash crops than their resources permit or crops which compete for resources such as soil nutrients, fertilisers and female labour, with a negative marginal rate of substitution. Such production decisions pay little consideration to the increased burden on the women, who are often forced to work longer hours and under worsening conditions.

The key to understanding the relationship between macro-economic policies and the gender dynamism of the household is the study of intra-household relations - that is to say, how decisions on the economic and social aspects of household life are made, and how resources are distributed between, and controlled by, household members.

The question of whether market principles are applicable to the household or whether the household should be treated as a family unit is often raised. It can be argued that women who work in the field should be recognised as a key labour force and as such rewarded. In reality women in many Third World countries tend to work as unpaid family labour with limited access to resources. Men tend to control resources and exercise their power in making economic decisions. External agencies, such as government marketing boards, usually reinforce this by dealing only with men as household heads.

This Turkish case study looks at the introduction of new technology, the adaption of small family farms, the impact of structural adjustment on the household and how women's labour is affected. Gender-related differences in the distribution of resources within rural households are common, and resource abuse by male household heads which results in resource depletion is found to affect women directly.

State Policies in Agriculture

Policies which encourage farmers to integrate into the commercial market include price support controls, subsidies on inputs and credit facilities. The increasing use of new technology in agriculture among small farming households since 1960 is a direct result of the state-supported intensification of farming. For example, the number of tractors in use increased at the rate of 12 per cent a year during the 1960s and 1970s. Farmers tend to become dependent on state assistance in the form of subsidies and price controls in the period of transition from subsistence to commercial farming and many are dependent on state marketing boards.

In the 1980s government policy shifted away from import substitution to a policy of structural adjustment and liberalisation. Through the establishment of higher producer price margins under structural adjustment, many farmers were encouraged to increase cultivation of cash crops as the most profitable farming activity. However, many of the same farmers have suffered serious set-backs with reductions in subsidies on inputs that have come under structural adjustment.

Government agencies have been affected by tighter monetary controls and they often encounter cash-flow problems. The result can be inefficiency in payment to farmers for their crops. For example, the Sugar Corporation delays payment for the sugar-beet crop by six months most years. This along with rises in the price of agricultural inputs, such as fertiliser, has resulted in higher costs of production for cash crops reducing income per hectare. The increased cost of production together with the late payment for crops can place small farmers in a permanent state of debt.

Farming Households in Iğdır

The district of Iğdır is situated in north east Turkey, in Kars province.[1] The north-eastern region is listed among the least developed regions of Turkey. Iğdır is situated in a valley, one of the most prosperous districts of the entire region with first class arable land and a fertile soil structure. Cereal crops (wheat and barley) and cash crops (sugar-beet and cotton) are cultivated in 54 villages. Farm fields are irrigated from the Aras river, which borders on the Soviet Union, by a modern irrigation system.

Of the 40 villages visited, I chose to study Ak village in depth since I considered it to be more or less representative of the general pattern of field cultivation and land ownership prevailing in the region. The patriarchal household is the economic unit of the village. The eldest male family member heads the household and strategic resources, such as land and other means of production are owned, controlled and organised by him. He is the decision-maker of the household and commands respect from all other members, who are accountable to him. Investment in productive consumption and expenditure on personal consumption depend to a great extent on the household head's evaluation. On his death the second senior member, usually the eldest son, takes his place as household head. Other sons decide at this point to split and form their own households, since by custom inherited land is divided among male members. Women have legal rights to inherit land equally, but this rarely happens.

Within farming households, women are subordinate to men. The ideology of patriarchy, the domination of women's sexuality and labour both in the home and working environment, sustain the pattern of labour distribution between men and women in the production process (Barrett, 1980). The household is the forum of the most direct manifestation of patriarchal gender relations, with men designated as household heads and nominally controlling access to capital, land, and the instruments of production. Their authority is reinforced by the Civil Code, state agencies and credit institutions, which for official purposes normally deal with the household head alone. A woman participates in at least two households. She is always subjugated to the authority of men: in childhood to her father's will, in marriage to her husband's. Her work and duty is defined by the household head. Men within farming households exclude women from control of household economic resources, but confer on them responsibility for child-rearing and the household's general welfare. In some cases these responsibilities allow women to influence the household economy.

New Technology and Rural Women

The focus here is on only one component of women's work - farm work. The interrelationship between farm work and women's domestic work is, of course, often crucial for the process of household reproduction as a whole.

Prior to the mechanisation of agriculture, villages in the area tended to cultivate a limited amount of arable land, using wooden ploughs which tilled four decares of land a day. Chemical fertilisers were unavailable and the irrigation of the land was labour intensive. The introduction of new technology and capital inputs such as fertilisers, seeds, tractors and a modern irrigation system into the fields of Ak village in the 1960s increased the intensity of the cropping pattern. In the 1950s one third of arable land was cultivated, whereas in 1983 only about 7 per cent of the cultivated area remained fallow while 40 per cent - a fairly high proportion - was devoted to the cash crops, sugar-beet, cotton, vegetables and fruit, and the remainder to wheat and barley.

The process of commercialisation in Iğdır has been influenced by sugar-beet, the first commodity produced in the areas to be controlled by a state agency, the Turkish Sugar Corporation. Sugar-beet was first introduced in Iğdır in 1960. It substantially altered the agriculture of the region, which until that time had been based on crops such as wheat and barley, cultivated primarily for subsistence.

Unlike other crops, sugar-beet can only be planted through a legally binding contract signed by a household head and the Corporation. The Turkish Sugar Factories Corporation controls the cultivation, production, marketing and the processing of sugar-beet. Sugar-beet is a popular crop among cultivators because of guarantees and subsidies provided by the Corporation, such as the assurance of crop sale, pre-harvest payments of subsidies, and supplies of fertilisers to ensure the secure growth of the crop. Subsidies are paid directly to household heads.

Sugar-beet produces high cash revenues and farmers are eager to dedicate as much land as possible to its cultivation. However, the pattern of land ownership or the size of holdings in Ak influences the crops chosen by any one farmer and therefore the labour he requires.

Mixed crops are cultivated in 730 fragmented parcels of land spread around the village in nine different locations. The normal rotation in wet farming is: sugar-beet/wheat/cotton/fallow or sugar-beet/wheat/fallow/wheat. Sugar-beet is cultivated therefore on each parcel once in every four years. This means that if a farmer has only one parcel of land in one location in the village, he can only have a contract with the Sugar Corporation every four years and only then receive sugar-beet seeds from the Corporation. If a farmer has many parcels in different locations, he ensures that his rotation pattern allows him to be in the advantageous position of gaining sugar-beet seeds every year. This means that the latter has the potential to earn more cash, because sugar-beet is a high revenue crop. But he also has to ensure that there are enough wage labourers or family workers to weed and harvest the crop. Large holdings (above say 220 decares) need to employ wage labourers to do so.

A more detailed look at the degree of mechanisation of the specific periods of the agricultural cycle will illustrate what proportion and kind of labour is utilised in each, and to what extent women are affected by technological change. Agricultural tasks are gender specific, the main division of labour by gender for each crop being as follows:

Table 1: *Division of Labour for Each Crop by Gender*

Task	Wheat	Barley	Sugar-beet	Cotton
Ploughing	M	M	M	M
Seeding	M	M	M	M
Hoeing	-	-	F	F
Harvesting	M+F		F	F

M = male
F = female

Ploughing and seeding are traditionally done by men. Before the widespread use of tractors, men were forced to work hard during the ploughing season; only a team of oxen and wooden ploughs were available for ploughing. However, with the introduction of sugar-beet in the area, the number of tractors increased and all arable lands are now tilled and seeded by tractor. The ploughing and seeding periods for all crops therefore are fully mechanised. A tractor can plough approximately 4 decares an hour. In theory, 15 tractors could plough the total cultivated area of the village in 14 days by operating 8 hours a day. Together with the second ploughing, 28 days would be needed to till the total cultivated area. In 1988 80 per cent of households in the village had to hire a tractor for TL 5500 per decare (1 US$= 1400 TL). Sixteen households owned tractors and the male members drove them. The distribution of technical instruments of production, such as tractors and threshers, indicates significant differences among the households. The larger holdings have more access to the use of agricultural machinery. They rent out tractors to small farmers, giving them an extra source of income.

During the mechanised ploughing period, there is a surplus in the rural labour market. Except for the tractor drivers, no men work during this period. The tractor has taken over the most labour-intensive period of production for men.

The longest, most labour-intensive period in the cycle of agricultural production is hoeing. Hoeing begins at the end of April and continues until the end of July or early August. The hoeing and harvesting of cotton and sugar-beet are carried out by women only. These tasks are not mechanised. Women weed, using a short handled hoe with a wooden shaft and a sharp end. They hold the wooden part with the hand and root out the weeds with the sharp end, by bending or kneeling. This is the main method used in the region. Two alternative forms of weed control, herbicide and hoeing machines, have been introduced by the Sugar Corporation for sugar-beet crops, but not widely adopted. The cost of controlling weeds by applying herbicide was TL 15000 per decare, which was much higher than a female wage labourer at TL 4000-5000 per decare (1 US$=1400 TL). The majority of those growing sugar-beet are owner cultivators and use the female labour of their own households. Since women are subordinate to the will of household heads, they are expected to participate on demand in the production process, while continuing to bear responsibility for domestic labour and the well-being of the household. However, during hoeing, women are relieved of some of their domestic work. For example, bread may not be made in the home, but bought from the village shop.

In 1983 the population of active women in Ak was 185; 1,295 decares could have been weeded and harvested by the total female labour force in the village. Additional female labour was required to finish the sugar-beet and cotton crop fields and had to be brought in from Iğdır town, and from nearby villages which have a high population density. These were employed by the richer and larger households (those owning 100-200 decares, the largest being above 200 decares). Women from all households work, but the degree of participation and intensity of their labour differs. Women from the richer households only tend to work in the fields when female paid labourers are in short supply. In contrast women from poor households (middle 50-100 decares, poor 1-50 decares) have to work from early morning to evening, averaging 12 hours. One woman could weed and harvest 6-8 decares in one complete production cycle, by working 10-12 hours a day.

Since weed control is essential for adequate yields the demand for female labour is always high, although it varies with the area allocated to sugar-beet. The demand for female labour is also affected by the extent of weed growth, which can vary. The cultivation of sugar-beet and cotton is most successful if grown in rotation with other crops. The rationale of crop rotation is based on a complementary relationship between crops. By enabling the land to be cleaned, the soil rested and its fertility improved, introducing a rest crop into rotation can lead to increased yields in the crops subsequently grown and therefore to increases in profitability in the long-run. However, if crop rotation is not practised properly, weeds can outgrow the cash crop itself and soil exhaustion can result.

Some farmers cultivate cash crops, for example, cotton or sugar-beet, in two successive years on one parcel of land; or two different cash crops at the same time. Such decisions are forced by short-term financial need, but create long-term environmental costs. The cultivation of two cash crops simultaneously makes for difficult land management, since the crops compete for resources such as labour and fertilisers, with a negative marginal rate of substitution. A delicate balance of resources between cash crops is not always achieved and the incorrect application of inputs and misuse of fertilisers often result. Some farmers apply excessive amounts of fertiliser to sugar-beet fields to increase yield per hectare. However, this results in the quantitative growth of the sugar-beet root at the expense of sugar content to the annoyance of the Sugar Corporation, and also encourages unnecessary weed growth. Poor farmers, suffering financial stress, are sometimes constrained to sell the fertiliser allocated to them from the Corporation to wealthier farmers.

Inadequate fertiliser on their own land reduces yield per hectare, and means that the income women earn working as wage labourers for other landowners becomes even more crucial for the survival of the household.

Incorrect input application is not intentional but appears to be determined by lack of sufficient technical knowledge. The correct application of inputs to achieve qualitative and quantitative yield per hectare can reduce work loads for female labourers. Misuse of inputs can result in a faster growth of weeds, and contribute to soil degradation. In the long run inefficient resource use weakens the potential sustainability of the land.

Insufficient technical knowledge of irrigation may also lead to damaging environmental consequences and extra burdens for women. Over-irrigation reduces yield per hectare and contributes to waterlogging and salinisation, which arise from farmers' incomplete understanding of what is required to prevent or correct a rise in the water table. They can be prevented, either by reducing the application of water in excess of crop needs or by supplementing the natural drainage capacity by constructing subsurface drains. However, traditional methods of farm irrigation in the village have meant that over-irrigation is common. The results are waterlogging, soil degradation, and harder work and longer hours for women.

Technical change that resulted in an increased area of cultivation has worked unfavourably for women, creating a heavier work load for them even though they remain unpaid and their labour remains unrecognised. Technical knowledge of crop cultivation tends to be controlled and stored by men. Even though some women may know how to operate new instruments of production, men appear to exclude women from access to them. They have chosen to keep to traditional methods of weeding even though modern technology has provided an alternative which would reduce women's work intensity.

By tradition men in the village do not hoe. Even when times are tough, it is rare for a man to participate in hoeing unless he is from the very poorest of households. Men appear to prefer to see women working under difficult conditions rather than hoe alongside them. This indicates that the cultural definition of the gender division of labour creates a major problem for village women. Furthermore, the gender division of labour is reinforced by the women themselves, the majority of whom are conditioned to share the ideology of patriarchy. The commoditisation process in this case study depends on the intensification of female work in the agricultural cycle. The application of technical change to those parts of the cycle specified as male, has meant that female labour has become an even more crucial and, therefore, more exploited resource.

Mechanisation tends to be uneven when cheap labour or unpaid family labour is available for tasks which are costly to mechanise. In Ak village the cost of using herbicides during the hoeing period is three times higher than female wage labour. The differential in cost encourages farmers to push female household members to work longer hours, as they also do in South Asia and other parts of the world. The cost-effectiveness of using female labour means that households with both more technical resources and a high proportion of female members are in the best economic position.

Structural adjustment measures have threatened the income of farming households, and in some cases have reduced farmers' access to inputs. The Sugar Corporation encounters cash-flow problems and inefficiency in payment to farmers for their crops. The Sugar Corporation delays payment for the sugar-beet crop by six months most years. The delay in payment places many small farmers under severe financial pressure. Farmers are cash starved and those who can, borrow at high interest rates. Rises in the price of agricultural inputs, such as fertiliser, have resulted in higher costs of production for cash crops, reducing income per hectare. The increased cost of production together with the late payment for crops can place small farmers in a permanent state of debt.

I give an example of the farm labour process and gender division of labour of one middle-sized household.

The Labour Process of Production in a Middle-sized Household

The head of the household, Ferzali, owns 73 decares of land in 8 fragmented parcels in 4 different locations in the village of Ak. The household consists of three sons (aged 23, 19 and 9) and three daughters (aged 20, 16, and 13). A grand ceremony and celebration was held for the eldest son Murat on his return from two years' compulsory military service when, as previously arranged, he married the daughter of his father's brother. It is tradition that the bridegroom's family pays for the wedding and gives presents and money to the bride's family. In this case the total cost, TL 750,000, and the following items were given: one gold bracelet, five pieces of gold (4 bracelets and 1 ring), one sack of rice, one sack of sugar, one tin of fat, one pair of shoes, one overcoat, 12 pairs of socks and a roll of cloth.

After the marriage the bride's father died and Murat asked his father's permission to settle in his father-in-law's house to help them, since they had no men in the house. This was a great loss for the household.

The high expenditure of the son's marriage and Ferzali's inability to cultivate a high proportion of cash crops (see below) had forced him to mortgage 20 decares of his land to a rich landowner. In return the landowner lent him TL 600,000, which had to be repaid in a year. The landowner had the right to cultivate any crops he wished during this period. If the money was not paid on time the landowner had the right to cultivate the following year. This could continue for a number of years until the money was paid back.

Twenty-three decares of his 6 parcels of land in two locations were to be allocated to sugar-beet by the Corporation, so Ferzali felt able to plan ahead. Additionally he cultivated 15 decares of cotton, 5 decares of barley, 8 decares of wheat and 2 decares of vegetables.

Ferzali had already spent on the wedding the money which the Sugar Corporation had paid in advance for hoeing. He was under financial pressure and could only afford to hire a tractor once. He was therefore unable to undertake a second tilling in the spring, just before seeding, which is good both for the soil and controlling weeds. By tilling the land weeds are eliminated and yield per decare increases. Ferzali's wife knew that she had to work very hard in the field that year, because her two daughters could not manage to weed 38 decares by themselves, and her husband could not afford to employ female wage labour.

In April they started to hoe the sugar-beet, from 7 a.m. to 6 p.m. and sometimes during the first hoeing of sugar beet, they worked until 7 p.m. She said:

> The first hoeing of sugar beet is very hard, because the roots of the beet at this early stage of growth are weak and any damage to the roots would suppress the growth of the plant. Thus more time and energy is required for careful hoeing.

After they finished the first hoeing of the two sugar-beet parcels, they immediately moved into the next field on the other side of the village about two kilometres away from their house to weed cotton.

When hoeing the cotton the mother of the family became ill and had to retire to bed for a while.[2] The head of the household had to find an additional female labourer and enough cash to take his wife to the doctor and pay for medicine. He had already spent the wage money given by the Sugar Corporation and could not meet the expenses of an additional female labourer, so he tried to find an alternative.

At this time of the year, except for the rich, nobody in the village has money; they have all spent their crop money from the previous agricultural cycle. Cotton merchants visit the villages at this time of the year to buy any crops farmers are willing to sell before the harvest period at the cheapest possible price. Eventually Ferzali was forced to sell his cotton for TL 220 per kg. After the harvest, the market price for this commodity crop fluctuated around TL 300-350. The money was used mainly to pay for his wife's drugs and the doctor's expenses.

Now he had to find another female labourer, because the weeds were growing fast and could reduce the yield per decare. In the end he had to ask his son to send his wife, who was working on her husband's field, to work for a few hours more in Ferzali's field. She only came for a short time. He had no choice but to force the girls to work longer hours and faster. The girls now had to work from six in the morning to seven at night, with only ten minutes rest every two hours and half an hour for lunch. Lunch was cooked by the mother, who was still ill, and taken to the field by the youngest daughter of the family.

When the women finished the hoeing of cotton, they moved back to the sugar-beet field for a second hoeing which is usually lighter than the first hoeing, but not in this region due to the heat. In mid June during the second hoeing of the sugar beet, the girls slowed down due to the burning sun (35-40 C). According to their father many weeds escaped while they were hoeing. By the end of July hoeing was finished.

However, Ferzali did not have the yield he expected. He had a total of 55 tons from sugar-beet (yield per decare 2.5 tons) and 1.2 tons of cotton. The Sugar-Corporation did not pay for the crop on time. As a result he could not repossess his land from the large landowner; he was not able to repay the money.

This meant that for another year the eldest daughter, Tahire, had to remain in her father's house. The responsibility of finding a 'suitable' wife for a son is the task of the mother and for four years

Tahire's cousin had been sending his mother as a mediator to her father to get permission for their marriage. But year after year the father asked them to wait until the next year when he promised that after the harvest period he would organise the marriage ceremony, but once again Ferzali delayed the wedding. All of them knew the reason very well. Ferzali knew that for another four years he would have sugar-beet on only one parcel of land. He had already planned for the following agricultural cycle and he realised that if he gave her away, although he would gain a bride-price (*başlık*) of TL 750,000 in return, the cost of employing another female wage labourer would be far higher; above all he would not have the same control over a wage labourer as over his daughter. When his youngest daughter, who was 13, was of an age to work (14/15) then he could give his daughter away. But his plans did not materialise. The cousin threatened that he would kidnap the girl if the father did not give permission for their marriage. Finally, by previous arrangement with his close friends, the cousin kidnapped Ferzali's daughter. For a while there was bitterness between the two families, but a few months later on New Year's Eve by means of mediation and payment of TL 900,000 *başlık* instead of TL 750,000, the relationship between the two families was healed.

The loss of one female labourer forced the household head not only to cultivate a smaller area of cash crops but also to rely on the local system, which involves the exchange of labour and crops with another household, until his youngest daughter was older.

Ferzali would have liked to regain his land from the rich household, but that seemed a remote possibility. That year his younger son was going to do his military service in the army. During this period Ferzali had to provide his pocket money; and the likelihood of another marriage on his return increased his financial worries. Ferzali expressed disappointment in the Corporation's strategy:

> This year I received beet money in the fourth month whereas I am supposed to be paid in the tenth month of every year. That is why I face financial problems. This government is unable to govern. My father used to say that the luckiest people are those who have lots of sons, but I say that the more girls you have the luckier and wealthier you are. Of course one son is essential for each household, but more than that is not good. It was different in the old days, when my father was alive, everything was free, but nowadays everything costs money, even water. Farming is rough going; it is a very difficult job. This year I could not cultivate more than 14 decares of

cash crops and I do not even have enough labour for that. My plan was to cultivate 12 decares of cotton as well, but things went wrong. To cultivate more cash crops one needs women and cash. I do not have either. My wife can't work because she has become ill again; after all, one woman can only weed eight decares of sugar beet and eight decares of cotton; more than that is harmful for a woman.

You ask me why I don't weed. Well, every person in our household has a task. During the harvest of wheat and barley women obviously can't do the reaping, that is why it is a man's task. Hoeing is a woman's task and while hoeing is going on we take a rest. I would not weed even if you threatened to kill me. A few years ago when my children were very young, my wife who used to do the hoeing on my land, became ill as usual. That is the problem with women; they get ill for the slightest thing. Because I couldn't afford to hire a female wage labourer, I worked one day hoeing sugar beet and afterwards I stayed in bed for four days. A man can't do hoeing, it's women's work. There is nothing wrong with this. Worst of all when after four days I managed to walk to the coffee-house, the men made insulting remarks (*laf attırdılar*), 'Are you a woman doing woman's work?'. For a whole month, I was the topic of discussion.

Some men from poorer households who do have to hoe alongside the women, suffer humiliation and are often reluctant to go to coffee shops.

Conclusion

Existing development policies have failed to integrate women. Indeed, they have intensified the split between the genders in access both to resources and to knowledge. The State encouraged small farms to adapt to a more intensive cropping system. Under culturally shaped patriarchal control unpaid female labour within the household is exploited. Such exploitation is perpetuated under structural adjustment policy. This case study implies that inefficient resource management is common. Men within farming households exclude women from control of household farming resources, but confer on them vital labour tasks within the production cycle. Women are excluded from decision making on resource use. In times of economic crisis, or to prevent household disintegration, household heads often cultivate more cash crops than their resources permit. This puts increased pressure not only on land but also on female members, who are often forced to work longer hours and under worsening conditions.

Government agencies like the Sugar Corporation deal exclusively with men, thereby marginalising women's contribution to production and their access to economic resources. Agricultural and technological change affects women, therefore, primarily through internal household relations. The lack of a gender aware approach in macro-economic policies contributes to the gender dynamism of the household but the division of labour and the relationship between women and resources is first and foremost imbedded in local culture and the system of power relations at play. Only if policies explicitly directed towards women are formulated will their position be improved.

Notes

1. Two cultural groups - Azeri and Kurds - live in the villages and towns of the Iğdır plain. The religion of the Azeri is Shii Islam, as distinct from Kurdish Sunni Islam, the official and most commonly practised religion of Turkey. The Shii are often confused with the Alevi, which is considered an insult to the village people. Although like the Shii, the Alevi believe in the twelve Imams (direct descendents from Muhammad), they are fundamentally different in their religious practice. (See Shankland in this volume) Essential to the doctrine of Shiism are the Merjia Taqlid, clergy who, through their ability to interpret the Koran and Islamic law, have reached high status and respect. The people of Iğdır follow two very conservative clerics, who claim to be direct descendants of the principle Imams.
2. Health problems and medical expenses are perhaps the single most important cause of disaster to village households, as well as a major cause of direct suffering. Virtually all middle-aged women in the village had some form of chronic illness: and acute illness is common.

| 7 |

Labour Migration among Bursa Muhacirs

Some Wider Implications

Gabriele Paleczek

Since 1923 Turkey has faced a dramatic process of transformation, leading to urbanisation and migration.[1] This is especially true for the rural communities of Anatolia. As a result of increased integration into the world economy, highly differentiated types of agricultural production have developed, that range from market oriented farms to more or less self sufficient household economies (Leopold, 1978, pp.87-99; Hinderink and Kiray, 1970; Even et al., 1984, pp.116-193; Keyder, 1984, pp.89-131). Although numerous reform and modernisation programmes have been undertaken during the last decades, (Paleczek, 1987b, pp.13-45, 1988, 1989a, pp.59-77) some of the major problems of the rural population such as lack of agricultural land and employment, fragmentation of plots, and low incomes, have not been adequately resolved.[2] Thus many villagers are forced to earn their living either through employment outside the village or through permanent migration.[3]

In my essay, I aim to discuss some of the causes of migration and its effects on the social and economic setting of the village community, using my own field material on Fevziye Köyü which I collected between 1976 and 1980, and in later visits.[4]

The Village of Fevziye and its Inhabitants

The village of Fevziye, in the western Anatolian province of Bursa lies at the end of a valley at an altitude of about 900 m above sea level. It is a typical *orman köyü*.[5] Two mountain ranges covered with extensive forests separate the community from Lake İznik and the Bursa plain. The village is about 30 km away from the city of Bursa and 20 km from Gemlik.

Fevziye was founded around 1880 by a group of Laz Sunni refugees *(muhacir)*, who came from the south Caucasian province of Batum and had left their homeland during the Russian-Ottoman war of 1877/78.[6] Two other *muhacir* villages were established around the same time in the immediate neighbourhood; Şükriye which is Laz, and Hamidiye which is Georgian .

In 1980, 314 persons lived permanently in the village, and 55 people part time, forming 72 permanent and 14 semi-permanent households. The part-time residents consist, first, of people who work part of the year in the cities, but still undertake diverse agricultural activities in the village, and second, of old people who spend the winter months in the cities with their sons, but come back to the village in spring. Besides these, there are people who come irregularly to Fevziye on vacation, or to cultivate some of their village land, or to undertake specific activities like silk cocoon production and wood cutting. These people stay for some weeks in Fevziye but, unlike the semi-permanent residents, they only come for short periods to meet agricultural necessities, like preparing, tilling, irrigating and harvesting. This group fluctuates according to individual needs from year to year. In the course of field work I observed an increase of this type of semi-permanent re-migration to Fevziye. A large number of low income migrants (e.g. teachers, civil servants, unskilled workers) sent their women and children back to the village to produce food or to undertake silk cocoon production, animal husbandry or wood cutting, in order to gain extra income and to balance the effects of the economic crisis of the 1970s, when many families, due to an inflation of close to 100 per cent and slow wage increases, were confronted with a declining standard of living.[7]

The kinship system is built on two types of social unit; households - *hane* - some containing nuclear families, some various types of extended family (Table 6, p.107) - and patrilineal descent groups, *sülale*. Membership in a *hane* is necessary to get access to the means of production; land, tools and water. The patrilineal descent group, whose members generally reside in the same village quarters, *mahalle*, co-operates on a large scale. For example members are obliged to lend money, foodstuff, tools or animals and to support one another in disputes. Furthermore, the participants in the different reciprocal collective activities (laz:*nodi*, turk:*meciye*), e.g. grain harvest, are usually recruited from the patrilineage of the household head.[8] In contrast, affinal relations are less important. Extensive co-operation and mutual assistance exists only between the immediate households of the groom and his wife's natal household. Even here it is mainly restricted to female labour. Thus marriage does not break up the intensive co-operation existing between mother and daughter. They interact in a variety of tasks: child care, housework and agriculture, even if the daughter now resides in Bursa or Gemlik. Daughters will come to the village to help their mothers with the grain harvest, the production of silk cocoons and other activities. In the case of migrants, the co-operation between a woman and her migrant daughter might even be more intensive than between a woman and her migrant daughter-in-law. Contrary to the traditional pattern, in which a *gelin* (son's wife) was expected to wait on her mother-in-law and support her in her daily duties, *gelins* who visit Fevziye nowadays stay in their natal homes and help their own mothers rather than residing with their mothers-in- law (Kiray, 1976, pp.261-273).

My data shows no clear pattern of preference for marriage partners. People tend to marry outside their close kin, but within their own ethnic group.[9] From the 477 marriages for which data are available, 383 or 80 per cent were between members of the village: 340 or 71 per cent of these marriages were with non-kin; 26 cases or 5 per cent with a consanguine, and 17 cases or 4 per cent with an affine. Marriages to non-villagers were most often with other Lazis, either from the neighbouring Laz village of Şükriye, or from other Laz communities in the area. If no Laz marriage partner was available, the bride or groom was preferably from other *muhacir* groups like Georgians or Bulgarian Turks. This marriage pattern is not only followed by the villagers themselves but also by the majority of the urban migrants, who prefer a wife from Fevziye. Although most sons of migrants would take their wives from Fevziye, some changes are taking place, i.e. by marrying non-Laz.

The impact of migration can also be observed in the post nuptial resident patterns. According to custom, the newly-weds should reside in the paternal home of the groom, which still accounts for 72 per cent But neolocality has gained some importance as 18 per cent set up their own households upon marriage. Nevertheless as people still maintain the ideal that the son and the daughter-in-law should live with the groom's family, the newly-weds spend at least the wedding night and some subsequent days in the house of the groom's father. After some days they will settle down in the city, taking the bride's dowry (*çeyiz*) with them.

The Production Unit and its Economic Activities

The household, *hane*, is both a production and consumption unit. Access to the means of production is primarily established through inheritance. This applies to land, animals and tools, as well as to water rights. Whereas all sons inherit on equal terms, daughters are usually excluded from inheritance. Sometimes they are granted part of the movable property like a cow or some sheep.[10] Thus the villagers neither follow the provisions of the Civil Code, which, borrowed in 1926 from Switzerland, grants equal shares to males and females, nor the Şeriat, which endows a specific portion of the patrimony to the female heirs. In the take-over of the father's household, no preference for the first or last born son was recorded.

The village territory consists of about 10,000 *dönüms* (approx.1,000 ha).[11] Of this total 4,000 *dönüms* (approx.400 ha) are the private property of the villagers. This land is used as agricultural land - irrigated fields, *sulu tarla* and dry farming land, *kuru tarla*. Half of the latter lies uncultivated each year. Part of it is fallow land - *nadas* - and part of it, owing to lack of labour force to cultivate it, remains completely out of production. 4,000 *dönüms* are pasture land and 2,000 *dönüms* (approx.200 ha) forest. Both belong to the Turkish state, which grants the usage of this area to the villagers. Land ownership is not polarised. According to the villagers the mean farm size is 30 to 40 *dönüms* (3 to 4 ha). There are no landless households, because they have all left the community.

Erosion is a special problem of agricultural production, provoked by the unrestricted deforestation of the mountain slopes surrounding Fevziye which, as the villagers stated, resulted in the sharp decline of the grain harvest.

The economic activities of the villagers are primarily directed towards the self-sufficiency of the village households. In general agricultural production is divided into two sectors. First, subsistence production includes production of cereals, cultivation of vegetables and fruits, animal husbandry, and wood cutting. Second, the cash crop production of silk cocoons and tobacco yields a yearly income of around TL 20,000 (approx. $256 in 1980) per production unit.[12] This income is used for the purchase of goods which they themselves do not produce, like clothes, household tools, foodstuff, for the the repair or replacement of tools, for the payment of different taxes, e.g. the *salma*, fines (*ceza*), and religious dues such as *fitr* or *zakat*. Whereas silk cocoon production is stable, tobacco production declined in the late 1970s and was finally given up in the 1980s, owing to falling prices and the high labour input. Sometimes, especially in good harvest years, some fruit and vegetable surpluses are sold at the weekly market in Gemlik.[13] The quantity of commodities marketed depends not only on the harvest, but also on the sales possibilities at local markets. At Gemlik the villagers of Fevziye are in competition with farmers from the Bursa plain, who have the advantage of easier transport on better roads, a more favourable climate for production and a more efficient market organisation.[14]

Agriculture in Fevziye is characterised by a very clear cut distinction in the distribution of female and male tasks. Gardening, silk cocoon production, most of the tobacco cultivation and a great part of animal husbandry is considered female work. Male activities include the preparation of fields, help with the grain harvest, transport of grain and other products, cutting of wood and taking the flocks to distant pastures. The land is too mountainous for the use of tractors or other machines in Fevziye. Thus the villagers have to rely on simple tools like animal-drawn ploughs (*karasaban*), spades (*bel*), and hoes (*çapa*). The only mechanised process is threshing; threshing machines are hired from one of the villages in the Bursa plain.

Besides agriculture the villagers undertake a variety of crafts. Men are responsible for the renewal of agricultural tools and the maintenance of buildings and water canals. Women in all households spin, knit and produce pottery for home use. Three other craft specialists, a blacksmith and two basket makers, ply their trade as a supplementary source of income.

Because the profits deriving from agriculture are very low, most households try to make some extra income through additional work. Inside the community the possibilities are limited to a watchman (*korucu*), the busdriver, and the tea-house (*çaycı*). Outside the village, a considerable number of males go to Gemlik or Bursa during the winter season to work as temporary unskilled labourers in factories or in the construction business, securing a job by using a network of relatives and acquaintances who have migrated to the cities.[15]

Women also try to make some extra money. Their job possibilities are limited still further by their lack of education and the rules of female chastity and honour. Therefore only agricultural work seems suitable for women. Most of them work as harvest hands in the olive groves around Gemlik, Soluz and other olive growing communities of the region, where former villagers from Fevyize have settled and acquired olive groves.

Migration and its Effects

Migration has had a great effect on the economic and social structure of Fevziye. Emigration - though only in small numbers - started soon after the foundation of Fevziye.[16] In the 1950s it became a mass movement. Around that time several severe landslides occurred which, in the eyes of the villagers proved that a further transformation of the mountain slopes into arable land to cope with the rapid population growth would turn out disastrous. These push factors were complemented by various pull-factors - primarily by the increasing demand for labour in cities like Bursa and Gemlik. Thus since 1955, the village of Fevziye has been confronted with the continuous emigration of its inhabitants, mainly young people, leading to a drastic reduction of its population (see Table 3, p.104).

The Reasons for Migration

It was primarily lack of land that forced the excess population to leave the village at the beginning of the migration process. The inheritance practice had led to the establishment of small and fragmented plots from which it was impossible to earn a living. During recent decades -when shortage of land ceased to be a major problem, as some of the plots lie uncultivated owing to a shortage of labour - people left Fevziye mainly because of the low income from agriculture and the hard work that appeared increasingly unattractive to the village youth. In 1980 the average annual income of a five person household in Fevziye was around TL 25,000 to TL 40,000 (approx. $320 to $513) whereas a factory worker in Bursa earned some TL 120,000 ($1.538) per annum plus several additional payments. Rising consumer expectations that cannot be fullfilled within the framework of the traditional economy have been a further reason for migration in recent years. The low standard of living and lack of services play an additional role. Fevziye has only been connected with Bursa and Gemlik by a proper road since the beginning of the 1970s, and even this is impassable in winter and after heavy rainfall. Electricity came in 1978, and telephones only in 1988. Educational and medical facilities are still inadequate. Thus many villagers, especially the younger generation, view the village as a backward place and intend to migrate eventually. The decision to leave the village and to settle in an urbanised region of the province is quite often stimulated by seasonal migration and attendance at schools outside Fevziye. In general, only young males are permanent labour migrants. Women leave the village on the occasion of their marriage.

The Destination of the Migrants

The changes that have occurred within Turkish society during the last decades can clearly be detected from the migrants' chosen places of residence and the professions they have taken up.

The early migrants turned to the agricultural regions of the province of Bursa, e.g. Gürsü and Gürle, (75 per cent of 12 in the generation of the village founders and 55 per cent of 40 in the following generation). Later on, migrants went to urban centres, where the expansion of industry and trade had created new jobs (82 per cent in the third and 84 per cent in the fourth generation).[17] The city of Bursa became the main destination of emigrants from Fevziye (47%). See Table 1, p.102.

Similarly at the beginning people retained their agricultural professions by either acquiring their own farms in the new settlement areas or by becoming farm labourers. (75 per cent of the first migrants and 45 per cent of the next migrant generation). Later on a wider variety of jobs were taken up which ranged from professions requiring higher education, e.g. university graduation or teachers' training colleges, to qualifications that were acquired from scratch. Among the various occupations, work in business, offices, and the army, attracted an increasing number of people. Today, the majority of migrants work as skilled labourers in industry and crafts (47 per cent) or attend schools outside Fevziye (32%). See Table 2, p.103.

Table 1: *Places of Residence of Permanent and Semi-Permanent Migrants from Fevziye by Generation*

Place of Migration	Founding Generation		1st Generation		2nd Generation		3rd Generation		4th Generation		Total	
Gemlik	no.	%	no.	%	no.	%	no.	%	no.	%	no.	%
Gemlik	-	-	3	8	21	12	22	16	1	5	47	12
Other places	-	-	2	5	3	2	3	2	-	-	8	2
Province of Bursa												
Bursa	-	-	7	18	83	49	73	53	15	79	178	47
Other places	9	75	20	50	43	25	16	12	2	11	90	24
Other places Turkey	3	25	6	15	15	9	18	13	-	-	42	11
Outside Turkey	-	-	-	-	4	2	6	4	1	5	11	3
No data	-	-	2	5	-	-	-	-	-	-	2	1
Total	12	100	40	101	169	99	138	100	19	100	378	100

Table 2: *Occupations of Permanent and Semi-Permanent Migrants from Vevziye by generation*

Occupation	Founding Generation		1st Generation		2nd Generation		3rd Generation		4th Generation		Total	
	no.	%	no.	%	no.	%	no.	%	no.	%	no.	%
Farmer, farm labourer	9	75	18	45	40	24	17	12	2	11	86	23
Medical doctor	-	-	-	-	2	1	-	-	-	-	2	1
Judge	-	-	-	-	2	1	1	1	1	5	4	1
Teacher	-	-	2	5	12	7	8	6	-	-	22	6
Entrepreneur	-	-	2	5	13	8	9	7	-	-	24	6
Craftsman	-	-	-	-	14	8	8	6	-	-	22	6
Shopkeeper	-	-	5	13	21	12	14	10	-	-	40	11
Skilled worker	-	-	-	-	19	11	33	24	9	47	61	16
Unskilled worker	-	-	-	-	11	7	7	5	-	-	18	5
Education outside Fevziye	-	-	-	-	-	-	9	7	6	32	15	4
Imam	1	8	-	-	3	2	-	-	-	-	4	1
Civil servant, army officer	-	-	9	23	31	18	32	23	1	5	73	19
Pensioner	-	-	-	-	1	1	-	-	-	-	1	0
Unknown	2	17	4	10	-	-	-	-	-	-	6	2
Total	12	100	40	101	169	100	138	101	19	100	378	101

Demographic Changes: the Effects of Migration

The main effect of migration can be seen in the demographic structure of Fevziye. Today the village has fewer inhabitants than at the time of its foundation when, according to different documents, 346 to 378 people lived in the community (see Table 4). In 1955, the number of inhabitants reached its peak of 814. Since then the population, both male and female, has declined. By 1990, only 160 people were permanent residents.

Table 3: *The Population in Fevziye: (Permanent Residents only)*[18]

Year	Male	Female	Total
1880	-	-	346
1940	366	373	739
1955	383	431	814
1970	250	263	513
1980	148	166	314
1990	-	-	160

As Table 3 shows, there were 53.8 per cent females to 47 per cent males in 1980. This is due to male emigration.

Furthermore Fevziye is faced with a severe senescence problem (see Table 4): 40 per cent of the village population is over 50 years old. The number of 25 to 49 year olds, those in the most productive age group, is small, accounting for only 24 per cent. Likewise, the age group of 0 to 24 is 37 per cent; much smaller than the Turkish average figure of 59 per cent. With this age group distribution, Fevziye finds itself out of line with the demographic structure of Turkey which is characterised by a very large number of young people.

Table 4: *Distribution of Population According to Sex and Age Groups in Fevziye in Comparision to Turkey (in 1980)*[19]
(in percentages)

	total		male		female	
age group	Fevziye	Turkey	Fevziye	Turkey	Fevziye	Turkey
0-24	37	59	36	60	37	58
25-49	24	28	21	27	27	28
50 +	39	13	43	12	36	14
	100	100	100	99	100	100

Table 5: *Households of Permanent and Semi-Permanent Residents in Fevziye According to Number of Persons in 1980* [20]

Number of Persons in Households	Permanent Households		Semi-permanent Households	
	no.	%	no.	%
1	3	4	3	21
2	23	32	-	-
3	7	10	3	21
4	10	14	3	21
5	9	13	1	7
6	7	10	3	21
7	4	6	-	-
8	5	7	1	7
9	1	1	-	-
11	2	3	-	-
21	1	1	-	-
Total	72	101	14	98

Today (1990), 32 per cent of permanent residents live in two person households (see Table 5). These households are primarily old couples whose children have migrated to the cities.

At present, the average number of children per family is 2.8 children for the group of permanent residents and 2.2 children for the semi-permanent residents. Most families have two children.

Transformation of Production Unit and Changes in Agricultural Production

Migration has not only led to changes in the demographic structure of the village but has also provoked changes in agricultural production. In 1980, only 72 of the 113 farmsteads were permanently inhabited, 12 were used part time by migrants. Twenty-seven buildings were vacant and two had already become uninhabitable.[21]

The enormous loss of population primarily affects the production units and their size and methods of agricultural production

Recently the majority of households in Fevziye were 'simple households' (approximately 67%) which either consisted of one married couple (31%) nuclear families (29%t), or couples and other unmarried relatives (7%). People still had a residential commitment to the three generation household and perceived the patrilineal extended family as the ideal pattern of household composition. This was underlined during the wedding ritual when the groom and bride, in spite of establishing their independent home, were expected to stay for a certain period in the household of the groom's father. In practice, however, patrilineal extended families made up only 15 per cent.[22] The proportion of fraternal joint households was 7 per cent The effects of migration can be seen very clearly from the large number of fragmented households consisting mainly of single individuals or widowed persons and other relatives (11%, see Table 6). This kind of household composition, favouring 'simple' and 'fragmented' households, is still more evident in the case of semi-permanent households.

Table 6: *Household Composition of Permanent and Semi-Permanent Residents in Fevziye (in 1980):* [22]

Type of Household	No. of Households				No. of			
			semi-perm.		perm.		semi-perm.	
	no.	%	no.	%	no.	%	No.	%
1. **Simple Households**								
Married couple, married couple and unmarried relatives	22	31	-	-	45	14	-	-
Married couple and children	21	29	8	57	100	32	33	60
Married couple, children and unmarried relatives	5	7	1	7	31	10	6	11
2. **Joint Households**								
Extended family	11	15	2	14	71	23	13	24
Paternal joint family	5	7	-	-	47	15	-	-
3. **Fragmented Households**								
Widows and other	5	7	3	21	14	4	3	5
Bachelors and other relatives	3	4	-	-	6	2	-	-
Total	72	100	14	99	314	100	55	100

Migration, primarily of young males, has caused a severe lack of labour in the most productive age group in recent years, which in turn has made reciprocal collective labour a necessity in order to maintain certain work processes in agriculture such as the grain harvest, where 20 to 30 women participate, or cocoon cleaning. The labour shortage has also led to increasing amounts of dry farmland remaining vacant; and a reduction in animal husbandry. In the past, large flocks of sheep and goats were driven to the village *yayla* and there tended by communal shepherds. Nowadays the villagers keep small flocks which are tended individually on a household basis on pastures nearby, whereas the unused *yayla* is rented out to Yürük families from a neighbouring community. Some village families now specialise in fattening lambs, which are sold in autumn as they have no capacity to produce winter fodder for them. Due to male migration the division of labour among the sexes has also changed. Today, women and girls are forced to take over formerly male activities such as ploughing and wood cutting, whereas males may, if necessary, engage in gardening.[23]

Many crafts, such as shoe making, carpentry, and weaving have been given up during the last decades. Today people buy ready-made products. This is even visible in basket making, with the exception of a special back basket (laz: *kalati*) which is used only by Lazis. All other baskets are nowadays bought from travellers (gypsies or '*Roma*' as they call themselves) who come to the village to sell their products.

It is not only the number of people per production unit but also the unit's composition by age group that is of vital importance to agricultural production. A majority of the two person households, 32 per cent of production units, are old couples who have given up part of their agricultural production, such as grain production. They meet their cereal needs by sharecropping arrangements. In these cases the land is given to production units - mainly close relatives like a father's brother's son - with too little dry farm land for their grain requirements but sufficient young labour to cultivate the land. In return for the lease, the landowning household gets half the harvested grain and half the straw. Therefore, agricultural production in Fevziye today not only depends on the amount of land owned, but also on the size of the labour force and its age. I could detect a clear connection between the labour force potential, the amount of land owned and the number and kind of work animals, mainly oxen and donkeys. For example most of the old couples did not own draught animals, ploughs or transportation.

Other Changes

In general, Fevziye's inhabitants are increasingly adapting to urban values. This is especially true of clothing. Within the village, people keep to traditional clothes like *şalvar* and the large red-and-blue scarves (*peştimal*) of the women. But they consider this type of dress as inadaquate for the town. When going to Bursa or Gemlik, village women dress themselves in urban style clothes; raincoats, trousers and small scarves. At the increasingly popular salon weddings, *salon düğünü,* it is perfectly acceptable for the girls to appear in European short-sleeved low-cut dresses without scarves, using make-up, lipstick and nail varnish.[24] Today the younger generation has considerable influence on the choice of their spouses. The age of marriage is much higher, especially for girls. It is not unusual to find 24 year-old girls unmarried. Parents hesitate to marry off their daughters as these are quite often their sole helpers. Sons generally emigrate after finishing their military service. This has led to an increase of elopement (*kız kaçırma*) cases. As parents are reluctant to allow their daughters to marry - sometimes engaged girls are supposed to wait several years until they get married - girls decide to elope with their fiancés. For example out of the five marriages that took place in Fevziye in 1985, three were the result of *kız kaçırma.*

A dramatic change can also be observed in the keeping up of Laz customs. Because of emigration, the Laz are increasingly assimilated to the mainly Turkish speaking environment (Magnarella, 1976, pp.35-43). A large number of migrants' children do not speak Laz, although they might understand simple conversations. The assimilation process is likewise visible in the choice of spouses. Although a large number of migrants and their children choose wives from Fevziye, there is a trend to take a wife from outside one's own ethnic group. Contrary to former migrant generations when 73 per cent took their wives from Fevziye, this figure has dropped to 58 per cent in recent years. But still 53 per cent of all migrant sons marry a girl from the village. On the other hand village girls prefer to marry a former villager who has established himself outside Fevziye. As already mentioned Laz - either from the village or from other neigh–bourng Laz communities - are preferred as marriage partners. If no suitable Laz groom or bride can be found the marriage partner is sought among other *muhacir* groups such as Georgians or Balkan Turks. Only recently the number of marriages with *yerli* Turks is rising. Although the Laz are increasingly integrated into a larger social network they - migrants and villagers alike - try to re-intensify their relations, by establishing a club for the development of Fevziye (*Fevziye Güzelleştirme ve Kalkınma Derneği*). Once a year, a village festival (Köy Günü) is organized by the association in order to keep up contacts between the village and the migrants and to raise funds for development projects in the village, such as improvement of drinking water and irrigation schemes.

Developments in Fevziye show the formation of structural heterogenities (Leopold, 1978, p.20; Senghaas, 1977, pp.22 ff.), typical of nearly all the so-called developing countries. The establishment of a modern, dynamic, capitalistic and market-oriented agriculture, in the Bursa plain, contrasts with an increasingly marginalised subsistence economy in Fevziye, where people can hardly make a living from their agricultural activities, and have to look for alternatives to safeguard their livelihood. The subsistence orientation of villages, primarily those located in mountainous areas with a lack of transportation and communication facilities to the trade centres, and disadvantageous climatic and physiographic conditions, is at the same time a result of the transformation process in agriculture during the last decades. Whereas Fevziye had been an important marketing centre for agricultural products and products of village craftsmen in former decades, it has increasingly lost this function.

Until the early twenties a weekly market was held in Fevziye which was not only attended by neighbouring villagers to exchange agricultural products. Merchants, including Armenians and Greeks, from the local cities also came to purchase grain, vegetables, fruits, animals and dairy products, or items manufactured by the shoemakers, blacksmiths and basket weavers of Fevziye.

Increasingly since the 1950s, due to the intensification of agricultural production and industrial manufacturing in the more favourable regions of Western Anatolia, production for local markets has diminished. Thus cash crop production is now restricted to silk cocoons. Tobacco production was finally abandoned after the end of the 1980s. This progressive reduction to subsistence activities is one of the main reasons for further marginalisation of the village population, which in turn gives rise to further emigration.

These changes in the village economy are not restricted to Fevziye, which since 1955 has witnessed a steady reduction of its population and in consequence a decline of agricultural production. The same trends and developments can be seen in other villages with similar physiographic conditions in the Bursa area.[25] We may therefore conclude that, as the example of Fevziye illustrates, rural development took place unevenly. Whereas one part of Turkey's agriculture profited from modernisation, other parts, e.g. *orman köyleri* suffered impoverishment. 'Development therefore does not lead towards an integration of both sectors, but rather provokes further economic and social disparities' (Blaschke, 1981, p.8). One solution to this process of marginalisation within the peasant subsistence economy, to secure new sources of income, is emigration, which paradoxically contributes to a further disruption of the peasant household economy and may finally lead to its complete destruction (Meillassoux, 1976, p.149).

Notes

1. According to the census of 1990 only 41% of Turkey's population live in rural areas. In 1927 it was 75.8%. *1990 Census of Population*, p.2, Table 3. Nevertheless, with 9.3 million employed (=57.5% of active population) agriculture is the most important field of activity. TÜSIAD *(1987)* p.45.
2. Paleczek, (1988), pp.187-294; Mülayim (1985); Talım, (1985); Üner, (1980), pp. 1-10, 31-41; Köker, (1980), pp.136, 148-150. According to Üner p.10, the percentage of small landownership - one to five hectares - is steadily increasing, accounting for 73% of all rural households in 1973. The number of landless households is also increasing, accounting for more than one quarter of all rural households (Mülayim 1985 p.41). According to Werle, (1983), p.21, who is referring to data from the 1970s - as far as I know no more recent information on incomes has been published - around 76% of the rural families were living at or under the subsistence minimum.
3. Doh, (1985); Leopold, (1978). Mülayim, (1985) pp. 26 ff. presents the results on income sources among seasonal labourers in Adana in the late 70s, who on average own 2.3 ha of land. 40% of their income is derived from their own farms, 51% results from seasonal employment in agriculture and 9% comes from non-agricultural activities. In a study on *gecekondu*-inhabitants in Istanbul, 65% quoted economic reasons for leaving the village, Schirmer, (1977), p. 27
4. For details see Paleczek, (1987a). Since 1980 I have visited the village several times for short periods. Last stay was in spring 1990.
5. Approximately 17.000 rural communities are categorised as '*orman köy*'. Their roughly 9 million inhabitants belong to the most under-developed segment of Turkey's society, Talım, (1985), p.6. They are the main emigration areas of Turkey.
6. Some of the documents from the time of the foundation of Fevziye are dated 1881. Paleczek, (1984), Appendix 1, pp.7, 20 and 36.
7. According to TÜSİAD, (1980), pp.2 and 87, inflation was 94% in 1980.
8. A large variety of tasks are undertaken through reciprocal collective labour. Working teams consist of men and women or only of women;

grain and hay harvests, ploughing of garden plots, picking and stringing of tobacco leaves, cleaning of wool, and of silk cocoons, preparation of special breads for Ramazan and other festivities. For details, see Paleczek, (1987a), pp.149-152. This collective is vital for households that lack sufficient labour as some tasks require several people. For example, two persons are necessary to clean silk cocoons. Unfortunately, I have no information whether the reciprocal collective activities were traditionally undertaken by the Laz or whether they are a new development to cope with the current labour shortage.

9. Contrary to the often stated preference for the father's brother's daughter in Middle Eastern society my Laz informants said that bride and groom have to be distant kin seven steps apart. In the 26 marriages arranged among consanguines only five cases are with FBD and seven cases with a MBD. For details see Paleczek (1987a), pp. 84-90. Charachidzé (1968), p.64 and Luzbetak (1951), p.54 mention that the western Caucasian peoples, to which the Laz belong, consider marriages with close relatives as incestuous.
10. Increasingly women are fighting for their inheritance rights; e.g. demanding part of the irrigable plots or asking for possession of part of the village house. The latter applies especially to migrant women where the husband' s natal home is in poor condition, or where he is in dispute with his own family. This ensures the family a place to stay when residing in the village.
11. According to the villagers one *dönüm* accounts for roughly 1000 m2; and thus corresponds to the official '*hükumet dönüm*'.
12. In 1980 the exchange rate of the $1 against the Turkish Lira was between 78,00 TL and 89,25 TL. At that time for example a bus ticket from the village to Gemlik cost 100 TL (= $1.3) and the large scarves used by the women had to be bought for 500 TL (= $6.4). 1 kg. of silk cocoons sold for 100 to 150 TL (= $1.3 to $1.8).
13. Today (1991) grain is never marketed, as the amount produced does not exceed the consumption needs of the various households. With the exception of two households that do not own enough land and have therefore specialised in animal husbandry, no dairy products or animals are sold. In recent years some families have specialised in fattening lambs. Surpluses of the village households are given away to migrant relatives, mainly sons or daughters.
14. As the road ends in Fevziye, the only regular means of transport are two minibuses owned by the village community which leave Fevziye in the morning and return in the evening; and one privately owned truck. The buses were bought with funds raised by the Village Development Association, 'Fevziye Güzelleştirme ve Kalkınma Derneği' founded by villagers and migrants from Fevziye. Two villagers who are paid from

village funds, 'köy sandığı', are engaged as drivers.

15. These short term seasonal migrants are not included in Table 1, which only gives the figures for permanent and semi-permanent migrants.
16. The first emigrants were mainly late-comers to the village who could not find suitable land, as the plots close to Fevziye had already been divided. There might also be a connection with the population exchange between Turkey and Greece in the early 1920s, which emptied large areas of land in the Bursa plain and the Gemlik area.
17. Erder, (1976); Stewig, (1970). According to Erder (p.153), 2,500 new jobs were available in Bursa's textile industry between 1950 and 1960, and another 15,00 jobs in textile and metal industries between 1960 and 1975.
18. Sources for Table 3: Paleczek, (1984), Appendix 1, p.17, Fevziye population register, and Bursa 1973, İl Yıllığı (s.a.:57). In 1990 my stay in Fevziye was too short to collect exact data on male and female numbers.
19. The table includes only the permanent residents in Fevziye. Figures on Fevziye are derived from my field data (see Table 3); for the total population of Turkey in 1980 44,736,957, males: 22,695,362, females: 22,041,595) see Devlet İstatistik Enstitüsü, (1985), pp.44 ff.
20. Semi-permanent residents are persons who live at least half of the year in Fevziye.
21. In 1990 only 60 farms were permanently occupied.
22. The main reasons for splitting households are economic ones, primarily low incomes in the village. In addition, intra-family conflicts and tensions, e.g. between mother-in law and her *gelin*, were mentioned by the villagers, as well as the attractiveness of the cities. Another reason for the relatively few extended families is related to the villager's life cycle; households over the time of their existence change their composition, e.g. starting as an extended family, then upon the death of the household head splitting into various nuclear families which, in turn, develop into extended families when the sons of the household heads marry and beget their own children. Finally, separation of family members, to establish individual households, does not mean that these households are acting completely autonomously. Although living in separate households, a large part of the function of the extended family may be maintained. See Paleczek, (1988).
23. See Paul Stirling's scheme, (1965, pp.38 ff).
24. Gardening may be accepted as male labour, as generally the men are responsible for the improvement of fruit and mulberry trees in the gardens. Thus gardening may be understood as an extension of this traditional obligation of males to care for the stock of trees.
25. Salon weddings are especially popular among the groom families, who

are responsible for the organisation and the costs of the wedding ceremony, to which the entire village population has to be invited. Salon weddings are celebrated in Bursa and Gemlik. The groom's family rents one of the public rooms. At these weddings only soft drinks and some sweets and nuts are served, whereas in the village a complete meal is offered. As the villagers have to go to the city and are required to wear European style clothes, and as only modern music is played by a hired band, villagers, especially the older generation, are not very keen to participate in these weddings.

26. Most of the mountain villages in the province of Bursa show a decline in population, whereas villages located in the vicinity of cities like Bursa or Gemlik have an increase in population. Bursa, (1973), İl Yıllığı (s.a.:57).

| 8 |

Marriage, Gender Relations and Rural Transformation in Central Anatolia

Emine Onaran İncirlioğlu

My intention here is to ask a question, rather than to present a complete argument. I am hoping that it is a good question; and that a good question is better than a bad answer. How do we integrate the analysis of gender relations into the analysis of rural transformation?[1]

The argument I am working from is a very simple one - although the content is complicated, and, in this presentation, incomplete: integrating the analysis of gender relations is essential if we want better to understand and explain the variations in rural transformation. Here I have no intention of proposing a model to explain how rural transformation and gender relations are related (I wish I could). I simply focus on a single issue, marriage, an institution which is intrinsically cultural and intrinsically economic and ask the questions: 'What can we say about the changes in marriage patterns, while we are studying the processes of rural transformation? How do changes in marriage relate to the changes we call "rural transformation" and specifically to the "exit option"?'

I am relying on part of the data we have produced with Paul Stirling in 1986 and, for a short period in 1989, in two Kayseri villages, S and E. Although I am not directly using his 1949-51 research in the same two villages and his brief follow-up in 1971, I am certainly taking those studies as some kind of baseline.[2]

Both S and E have four main sources of income; agriculture, carpet weaving, construction work through pendular labour migration, and international labour constitute the four major economic activities that provide income for the villages. These activities are used by different households in different combinations depending on the landholdings and demographic compositions of the household.[3] S, a medium size village in 1949-50 with about 100 households and a little over 600 people, contained 153 households in 1986, and about 900 people. E, which was already well above the average in 1950-51, in terms of both population and the availability of land per capita, increased from about 200 to 238 households and from about 1200 to 1645 people. The natural population increase in the villages was actually much higher, but due to rural-urban and international migration, the village sizes did not grow to the same extent. In fact, there were more migrant households from S (at least 182), in 1986, located in various Turkish towns and in western Europe, than in the village itself. Household migration from E between 1950 and 1986 was less than that from S; nevertheless, in our E sample, which consisted of one-sixth of the 1950 households and their patrilineal descendents, there were 56 village households and 52 migrant households. Since 1950, many S and E households and villagers have clearly chosen the exit option.

As I conceptualise it in this paper, marriage is a means of reproduction. This includes both biological or primary reproduction and social reproduction (or social transformation, depending on the case).[4] By focusing on marriages, more specifically on how marriage decisions are made in households and how husbands are selected for village girls, I intend to learn (and show) the villagers' own identification of some viable paths of transformation or reproduction. Thus, I take marriage decisions and the changing criteria for 'good husbands' as a reflection or manifestation of the 'paths of rural transformation'.

Quite obviously, changes in various aspects of marriage between 1950 and 1986 are closely related not only to the changes in the village and household economies, but also to the changes in the national and international economy. And in turn, these changes in marriages play an important role in the reproduction or transformation of social life.

Marriage is a necessity in the villages, a rite of passage, an event everyone has to experience at some stage in life; remaining unmarried is not an option. Everyone gets married at least once, unless they have a serious handicap, like blindness or mental retardation. When the time approaches for a boy to be married, his family and neighbours begin to look for an appropriate *gelin*.[5] When the time comes for a girl[6] to be married, *dünürs*[7] begin visiting her household, formally asking for her, and her family tries to choose the best candidate.

Who is the Best Candidate?

When the villagers talk about good spouses for their children or for themselves, they indicate the 'unit of evaluation', in the language they use. When the boy's family evaluate girls as *gelin* candidates, they focus mainly on the individual. But when the girl's family evaluate boys as son-in-law candidates, they focus on both the individual and his household. The evaluation of girls as good *gelins*, the evaluation of boys as good husbands for daughters, and the evaluation of boys' families and households as good places for their daughters to live, are all, actually, the evaluation of the means of production, *and* of reproduction. In deciding whom their children will marry, the families decide about the way in which they will be reproduced, the way their households will be reproduced, the way their social life will be reproduced, and the way the two - or rather three - generations will continue, or transform, general living conditions and relations.

Girls' personal characteristics, especially hard work and temperament, are the most frequently used criteria. On several occasions, women told me that their husband's sides wanted them because they were hard workers, they were strong, and they were good farmers. Of course, villagers are worried about a girl's 'origin', because if a person has a 'good origin' (*aslı iyiyse*) she is considered to be more likely to have a good temperament. And a good temperament means, primarily, obedience.

With boys, however, there are two 'units of evaluation.' One unit is the boy himself, his personal characteristics, and the other is the household he belongs to. The relative importance of these units depends on the size, type and wealth of the household he belongs to. When the girl's family evaluates the prospective son-in-law, they say '*yeri iyi,* his place is good,' if he comes from a relatively large landholding, wealthy, multiple family household. If the boy has a non-agricultural occupation, if he is hard working and if he has proved able to bring money to his household, they say, '*oğlanı iyi,* 'the boy is good', when they evaluate him. In S, this non-agricultural occupation is almost always construction work, whereas in E a variety of other occupations also apply.

In 1986 and in the summer of 1989, both Stirling and I observed that there was a notable shift from an emphasis on the boy's household to an emphasis on the boy's personal 'achievement.' I have not heard of any girl in 1986, who actually wanted to marry a farmer. All girls of my acquaintance looked for an 'occupation' or 'profession' (*iş, meslek*) in boys. Many girls and their parents explicitly said that they *did not* want to be married into a household which owned a large herd of sheep or a large landholding or both.

Ayşe's case in E is a good example.[8] Ayşe is the eldest of the six children in a comfortable, middle-range household. Her father had worked in Western Europe as a migrant labourer for several years and brought back some money; they had enough land in E, for subsistence and even for some accumulation,[9] in addition to some benefits they get from her mother's home village. They owned a large herd of sheep, and the girls wove silk carpets for a merchant based in Kayseri. In 1989 when I last talked to them, Ayşe was 22; several *dünürs* had come for her, and they were all refused. (Changes in age at marriage are discussed below.) We had a long conversation with her parents and they explained to me why they turned down all the *dünürs*. Their reasoning was typical in the villages, in the sense that many villagers shared them.[10]

Her father said, '*Hoşuma gitmedi onlar, sevmiyom onları...* (they did not please me . . . I do not like them).'
Her mother explained in detail, '*İşimize gelmedi. İrençberlikleri ağır. Tarlaya giderler. Bir kere, görgü yok, giyim yok, yiyim de yok. . . . Tarlaya git, tarladan gel, otur halı doku!* (They did not suit our interests. Their

farmwork is heavy. They go to the fields. First of all, they do not have manners, no proper clothing, no decent food. . . Go to the fields, come from the fields, sit down to weave carpets!).'
The father added, '*Yani köle gibi* . . . (You see, just like slaves. . .)'
And her mother, '*Rahat etsin diye. . . Oğlan iyi olsun, çalışkan olsun, sanatı olsun. Sanatı ne? İrençber. E, irençberin arkası olur mu? Ömür boyuna kadar güreş toprağınan! Hani aylıklı olsun, memur gibi, şoÿle ögretmen ğibi . . . diyok. Onun için vermiyok Emine. Burdan gidecek oraya varıp halıya oturacak. Köy yeri diyok. ... Şehir yerlerine gitsin diyok.* (So that she can be comfortable. . . We want the boy to be good and hardworking, and have an occupation. What is his occupation? Farmer. Does a farmer have security? Wrestle with the soil all your life! You see, we want someone with a salary. Such as a civil servant, such as a teacher. That's why we do not give her, Emine. She will leave this household, for what? To go and weave carpets when she gets *there*? We don't want villages. . . We want towns).'

Here I can formulate two significant changes in marriage patterns from the 1950s through the 1980s. First is the change in the preference of village endogamy; and the second is the change in the age at marriage.

The Changes in Village Endogamy

Virilocal post-marital residence is the norm in S and E, as it is throughout rural Turkey[11]. Brides still come to their husbands' parents' household at least for a few months, often for years, before the young couple establishes a new household.

Clearly, virilocal post-marital residence has very different consequences for men and for women. For men, marriage is not a breach in residence nor in immediate social relations. For women, however, the change is normally total and traumatic. It is possible for men to be born, grow, marry, have children and grandchildren, and die in the same household, even the same house. With rare exceptions, all women, on the other hand, experience, at least, two households: the one they are born into, and the one they are married into. This difference between women's and men's experiences in continuity greatly affects gender relations.

The experiences of brides who marry and move to other villages and those of brides who marry within their own village are quite different until they pass their 'novice' stage '*acemiliği çıkanaca*', as they say in the villages.[12] Women married within their natal village have a degree of continuity in their lives which makes it easier to adapt to a different household. Brides who change villages go through a stage of adaptation not only to a new household but also to a different village, which may include learning and undertaking unfamiliar tasks. There are variations in the gender division of labour, even between neighbouring villages. For example, in K village, women are specialised in full-time carpet weaving and are not usually expected to do farm work, while in S, women fully participate in farm work and carpet weaving is only a seasonal occupation. A girl who is raised in K and married to a boy in S has to learn a set of agricultural tasks during her first few years. The few wives in the villages who come from different cultural backgrounds - from eastern Anatolia (some of whom are Kurds), from *Avşar* villages of the Kayseri province, and *muhacirs* (immigrants from Eastern Europe) - may never fully pass their 'novice' stage, and remain outsiders all their lives - that is, of course, if they can stand the isolation and stay in the village.

Women who marry within the village do not have to go through a stage of adaptation, and, being close to their natal households, their support network is already in place. But the ones who come from other villages are called *gürbetlik*.[13] From the perspective of women's ties and protection, then, there is a preference for village endogamy;[14] and the provisional results of our data support this preference. About two-thirds of all married women in both S and E are local. When given the choice between their own village versus another village, the majority of girls prefer to marry within their own village. However, if they have the option of marrying to a town, most of them prefer the town. This preference of village exogamy dovetails nicely with the 'exit option' in rural transformation.

Although avoiding *gürbet* has so far been an important factor in the selection of husbands for daughters, now *gürbet* is preferred provided that it is a town. Most women are fed up with village life, and they look forward to go to *gürbet,* with towns in mind, in the hope of a decreased work-load. In reference to Ayşe's marriage I asked her parents, 'if she goes, say, to Kayseri, won't you miss her?' Her mother's answer was ready: 'She will come. I can go, she can come.' Her father added, 'there is no such thing as close or distant. Buses run, taxis run.'[15]

Changes in Marital Age

In 1949-51, according to Stirling, a boy was 'normally married between the ages sixteen and twenty-two or so,' and a girl, 'at about fourteen to eighteen years of age' (1965, p.179). In 1986, although there were a few young women in the villages who were married at a young age, right after *menarche*, age at marriage for most girls was much higher than in 1950. There were numerous girls in both S and in the E sample who were in their twenties, not married, and *not* considered to be *evde kalmış*, 'spinsters'. Stirling recorded only one in 1950-52, and she was in the wealthiest family.

Both the girls and their families regard marriage as an opportunity to better the girls' conditions. They make a careful decision in choosing the best candidate by comparing the conditions, particularly the labour requirements, of their own household with that of the boy's. Girls are married at an older age because the families want to wait an 'optimum' length of time, hoping to find a suitor better than the existing ones. Both Stirling and I ran into many cases where girls' families refused *dünürs* by saying that there was too much work to do, and boys' families were deeply concerned because they could not find girls who were willing to work in the farms and tend the animals.

Women's, Work, the Exit Option, Production, Reproduction and 'Emancipation'

Now, clearly, household migration to town after marriage is preferred, because in the village a *gelin* has too many responsibilities: farmwork and weaving carpets, in addition to the usual reproductive activities. In 1949-51, Paul Stirling wrote, 'the main resources of a household are threefold: land, animals, and able-bodied ploughmen' (1965, p.83). If we leave aside the male bias - women are not even mentioned - and take the description as a baseline, in 1986, there was a major change in the main resources of a household. Women *were* recognised as significant resources in the household economy, partly because of the shift to weaving carpets as a main source of income, and because of the shift to labour-intensive crops such as onions, potatoes, beans and lentils.

Women are productive in the village. By opting for marriages through which they migrate to towns, they are, quite deliberately and decidedly, withdrawing from direct production. Nor, from this area, are they going into wage labour in towns, except in a very few cases. Actually, while they are involved in paid labour in the villages through weaving, in most cases they are turning to unpaid domestic work in towns - housekeeping and childcare.

A number of conclusions can be drawn concerning the ideological dimensions of rural transformation, but here I will focus solely on women's emancipation.

It is commonly argued that women's emancipation is directly related to their contribution to production. Women's contribution to production is usually defined as their entry into the waged labour force and is seen as a prerequisite for improving their social position.[16] If this is so, how come women are eager to leave their direct contribution to production, by marrying someone who is not a farmer?

To answer this question, I think it is essential to analyse women's production in different dimensions and to draw an 'access and control profile' By this, I mean, analysing women's access to resources and benefits, as well as their control of resources and benefits. Resources include land, equipment, labour, capital, and education and training; benefits include income, assets, in-kind goods, education, political power and prestige.[17]

If we look into women's access to and control of land, labour and income in these villages, the pattern shows that they *do* have access, but very little control. In this perspective, when we examine women's production in the villages, it is clear that their involvement with both farming and weaving carpets is in their *practical interests*.[18] They belong to households, they identify themselves with their households, and their own economic well-being is almost exclusively connected to the economic well-being of the households they belong to, but they certainly do not receive any strategic benefits, such as political equality.

I cannot here give a detailed account of the gender profile of resources and benefits, such as the land inheritance norms and the control of labour and income. But the critical point is that women have *access* to resources. What they do not have is *control* over these resources, or access to, or control of, *benefits*. They do not have control over the products of their own productive labour. In plain language - as we say *Türkçesi-* - they work hard from sunrise to sunset and they do not have any prestige; their labour is taken for granted and is not even acknowledged. They do have some degree of satisfaction, because their identity is derived from their households and families, but for *sub*-subsistence peasant women that is not enough. What women are doing by withdrawing from production, then, is not working against their liberation; actually, they are very willingly giving up, or more correctly, getting rid of, at least one major kind of control over their labour.

In summary, changes in marriage patterns and the selection of husbands are intimately related to the predominant gender relations at the household and village levels. Having to participate fully in rural production but not being in control of the production process nor in the distribution of the products, young women, like young men, prefer the 'exit option'. For women, the most significant, if not the only, way of realising this exit is through marriage. Rural-urban migration is, undoubtedly, related to external factors - the current state of the national and world economies, the availability of jobs and the rate of unemployment. However, given that the external conditions favour the exit, the access and benefit profile of gender relations encourages rural-urban migration. A comparison of the variations in gender relations and women's position in different regions may help us to understand and explain the variations in the employment of the 'exit option'.

Notes

1. By gender relations, I mean the relations between and among men and women who are related to one another in different ways, in different contexts. These relations take different forms: complementarity and co-operation, but also domination, subordination, exploitation and oppression, in the everyday interactions of women and men, as well as in their 'intimate' relationships. For the identification and description of different 'paths' of rural transformation in Turkey, see Keyder, 1983, pp.34-49. Also Akşit and Keyder, articles in this volume. Rural transformation, in my understanding, includes the transformation *from* agriculture to other sectors, as well as the transformation of social relations within the agricultural sector. In other words, the 'exit option', that is, permanent rural-urban migration, is an integral part of rural transformations.
2. Stirling, 1965 and 1974.
3. İncirlioğlu, 1991. For a discussion of the place of carpet weaving in Sakaltutan economy, see Ayata, 1987.
4. The concept of reproduction has been used uncritically, in different contexts, and for different purposes. For the different uses of the concept as well as their critiques, see Seccombe, 1974, pp.3-24; Edholm, et al.,1977, pp.101-130; Cousins, 1978, pp.62-70; Evers, 1984;

Barrett, 1980, pp.19-29; Collier and Yanagisako, 1987, pp.20-25. Here, the term is used in the sense of '*re*-producing' a social system and a set of social relations, as opposed to 'transforming' them, from generation to generation through marriage decisions. In structural-functionalist terminology, one would use the term 'maintenance', not, probably, with much difference in the specific meaning.

5. *Gelin* means both 'bride' and 'son's wife' a derivation of the word *gelen*, 'the one who comes'.
6. I use the word 'girl' for *kız*, when referring to an unmarried young woman, which also implies virginity in Turkish; and 'boy' for *oğlan*, when referring to unmarried young men. In both standard Turkish, and in the village dialect, *kız* is the female counterpart for *oğlan*, and its usage does not reflect a derogation of women, as it often does in English.
7. *Dünür* here means the party who visits the girl's family, to ask for the bride. It also means the parents of one's child's spouse.
8. Ayşe, and the other names I mention in this paper, are pseudonyms.
9. At household level, 'subistence' or 'below-subsistence' as opposed to 'accumulation' or 'surplus' production are difficult to define 'operationally' outside the context of cultural standards.
10. During the fieldwork, in both 1986 and 1989, I had the chance to record the life-histories of some villagers, with the permission of the informants. Through the text, the Turkish is given, verbatim, for the readers of Turkish, because it is so telling.
11. See Timur, 1972. Duben showed in 1990, that in contrast to rural Turkey, neolocal, rather than virilocal, post-marital residence was the norm in urban Istanbul, during the late 19th and early 20th centuries.
12. *Acemi* means 'new recruit', 'inexperienced learner' and *acemilik* is that 'clumsy' and 'awkward' state.
13. *Gürbet*, another Turkish word for which it is difficult to find an English counterpart, is glossed in the Redhouse Dictionary, in the colloquial use, as, 'place far from one's home' and 'living away from one's home.' In 'standard' Turkish, *gürbet* is 'foreign land.' The lyrics of numerous folk songs are devoted to the suffering and difficulties of *gürbetlik*, 'the state of being away from home.'
14. There is not necessarily a one-to-one correlation between marrying out to another village and suffering. Because of complex inter-village kinship networks, mainly matrilateral, many women who marry out have close relatives in the village, and sometimes in the very household into which they marry.
15. In the villages, *taksi* is used for 'automobile,' private or hired. *Araba* (the more inclusive term for 'car' in 'standard Turkish') denotes animal-drawn carriages and trailers.

16. Long before the revitalisation of feminism in the West in the 1970s, it was argued that women's subordination stemmed from their economic dependency on men. See for example Gilman, 1966. After Ester Boserup's classic study (1970, 1986) and the 1975 U.N. International Conference on women in Mexico City, serious attempts were made to study rural households, women's participation in the labour force and their unpaid work. The foci of many of these studies were gender inequality and the *conditions* of women's economic participation in different societies. It has been stressed that women's participation in the labour force was not adequate for improving their status in society: women should also participate in the control and distribution of the fruits of production. See for example Croll, 1986.
17. For a clarification of the 'access and control profile' see Overholt, et al., 1984. The framework was originally presented as a guideline for evaluating the 'gender sensitivity' of development projects.
18. Maxine Molyneux (1985, pp.227-54) differentiates between *practical* and *strategic gender interests*. 'Practical gender interests are given inductively and arise from the concrete conditions of women's positioning within the gender division of labour. In contrast to strategic gender interests, they are formulated by the women who are themselves within these positions rather than through external interventions. Practical interests are usually a response to an immediate perceived need, and they do not generally entail a strategic goal such as women's emancipation or gender equality.'

| 9 |

The Sexual Division of Labour in Lazistan

Chris Hann

The interaction between culture and economy is revealed as the weakest link in studies of women and development.

(Kandiyoti, 1985)

Introduction

This paper is a preliminary attempt to explore the sexual division of labour, and more especially some representations of women, in a region of north-eastern Turkey where fieldwork was conducted in the 1980s.[1] I hope that further fieldwork in the 1990s will enable me to test what are at present very speculative and tentative arguments, and to deal more adequately with a wealth of potential comparative materials, in Anatolia and elsewhere, as well as with recent theoretical work in anthropology pertaining to gender.

The term Lazistan is used here to denote the area of Laz speakers along the Black Sea coast between Pazar and the Soviet border. This Laz language has never been written, at least not by any local speakers. It is closely related to Mingrelian, more distantly to Georgian, and the group's self-designation is *Lazi* (Geiger *et al.*, (eds.) 1959, p.14). Almost all of the inhabitants of this region today have a fluent command of modern Turkish. Their non-Turkic tongue is not much used in public places and it may be disappearing altogether among the younger generation. The term Laz is, of course, used imprecisely and ambiguously in the rest of Turkey (Meeker, 1971, Benninghaus, 1989). It seemed to me in the 1980s that most Turks were unaware of the persistence of a Mingrelian language in this corner of Anatolia. When people in Ankara or Istanbul speak of the Laz they are usually referring to the entire East Black Sea region (say, everywhere east of Samsun), the inhabitants of which are distinguished from other Anatolian Turks by a variety of linguistic and other cultural criteria (see also Stokes, this volume). Alternatively 'Laz' is sometimes used to designate the inhabitants of a smaller zone centred on Rize and Trabzon. Rize is the most easterly of the major towns along the coast, but it is still some fifteen miles west of the main belt of Laz speakers. Nor is this belt congruent with the historic Lazistan of late Ottoman times, which included the zone around Rize. I use Lazistan to designate the territory, lacking any major urban centres, in which the Laz language (and perhaps other aspects of culture too) has survived, albeit unofficially and discreetly, with somewhere in the region of 100,000 speakers resident in the region at the present time.[2]

As every Turk knows, Rize is the centre of the country's dynamic tea industry. This industry was the main focus of my fieldwork, and there is no doubt that it has revolutionised the economy of the region over the last half century. In this context the Rize region denotes an area from the Soviet border to the environs of Trabzon - indeed, there are isolated pockets of tea production in much less suitable ecological conditions as far west as Ordu. Representations of the Laz have become caught up with new images related to this industry, and to the prosperity and new divisions of labour which it has brought. In this paper I am concerned with a certain stereotypical representation of women which is widely thought (i.e. throughout much of Turkey) to apply to all the people who live east of Trabzon. I refer specifically to Lazistan because this is the part of the Rize region which I know best, but it would not surprise me if further research revealed more variation *within* the Laz-speaking districts than I have been able so far to observe, as well as a more general contrast with the westerly parts of the tea zone.

A Popular Stereotype

According to what I shall call the general stereotype, the women of the Rize region are dominated by men in ways which would be considered unacceptable elsewhere in Anatolia. For example, women are said to perform the heaviest operations of farming, whilst men stand idly by or sit gambling in their coffee houses; and women are the normal means of transportation in the marketing of produce, such that they are often left to stagger under heavy burdens whilst their husbands walk unencumbered a short distance in front of them.

This image has been reinforced by any number of foreign commentaries, including some I consulted before even starting my research project.[3] It was generally endorsed by Turkish friends in Ankara. Consequently, though it was by no means a main theme of my enquiry, I decided to include some questions about gender equality in the household survey which I conducted in 1983. The salience of this stereotype was generally acknowledged by respondents. Indeed the most popular newspapers in the region gave the topic publicity from time to time. In one episode in 1978 a *kaymakam* (presumably originating outside the region) was so shocked by the spectacle of Laz women being used like pack animals that he initiated action to prevent such practices and, in the presence of the reporters, picked up heavy baskets himself to set the local men a good example.[4]

In spite of such apparently clear-cut evidence I now find this stereotype deeply problematic. Initially I assumed it had a substantial degree of validity as a commentary not only upon the actual sexual division of labour but also, in a more difuse way, upon the 'balance of power' between men and women within Lazistan. I groped for explanations in terms of local economic factors, and more specifically, the demographic pressures which had pushed many Laz males to seek wage labour opportunities outside the region in the generations before the arrival of tea. If women were left alone to look after the subsistence farms, I reasoned, this might explain why they had been drawn into field activities to which females were unaccustomed elsewhere in Anatolia. Some Laz offered similar explanations themselves. However it now seems to me possible that the sexual division of labour in this region was distinctive over a very long period, before migratory pressures intensified in the twentieth century.

I am also aware, in the light of recent anthropological work, of the need for great care and caution in analyses of the 'position of women' (Strathern, 1988; Tambiah, 1989). Apart from the problematic assumption involved in treating 'women' as a homogenous category, all such analyses reflect certain ideas about equality and individualism which belong to modern Western industrial societies - and to the social science traditions of those societies. Turkey is a most interesting case to examine from this point of view, given its dedication from the 1920s onwards to the emulation of those Western ideas. From this angle I wish to suggest that the dissemination of this aspect of the Laz stereotype may have something to do with an increasing awareness of Western ideals on the part of the modern Turkish elites. Given the new emphasis upon a national Turkish identity in the republican period, it was easy for such a stereotype to be foisted upon a small group who obviously deviated from so many Anatolian norms, irrespective of its objective validity. Laz villagers themselves have been made aware of the stereotype, but I have come to question whether they endorse it, and whether it is meaningful to them at all.

An Anthropological Model

I do not yet have adequate data to enable me to pursue these questions of local meaning in Lazistan, so let me turn instead briefly to the very rich arguments developed by Michael Meeker on the basis of his fieldwork in the district of Of, between Rize and Trabzon (1970; 1976). Meeker, like Paul Stirling before him (1965), approaches kin groups essentially in terms of their male members. Unlike Stirling, he gives priority to the domains of religion and politics in his analysis of pervasive cultural categories. He takes the concepts of honour and shame to be fundamental to social organisation in this region, arguing that the 'patronymic groups' (this designation is intended to avoid any confusion with African-style corporations) are more important entities for society in this region than nucleated communities such as hamlets or villages. These groups are, however, generally associated with a specific home territory, as a result of the way in which women are transferred between groups and denied any possibility of inheriting land. Meeker pays close attention to the place of women, reporting the emphasis laid upon ideas of female chastity, and the manner in which women are depersonalised through the use of a veil or shawl whenever they enter public spaces. He also provides a detailed account of weddings and the material payments associated with marriage. Various rituals are interpreted to show how rights over women are transferred at marriage between groups of males. Material payments are complex.

A bride invests time and her family invests money in her trousseau, but she does not receive property in the form of land. There is also an element of indirect dowry, i.e. gifts received from the groom's parents. However the sum paid by the groom's parents to the parents of the bride is substantially larger than all other transactions associated with marriage: this is known as the *başlık*.

In Meeker's account it is taken for granted that women are controlled by men, and yet the picture is by no means one of bleak subordination. Like many other anthropologists, he argues strongly against viewing these marital payments in terms of the purchase of women. On the contrary, within the patronymic groups men and women form a moral unity, sanctioned by religion, and rendered particularly explicit in the rituals associated with marriage and sexual intercourse. The question of gender equality cannot be posed in such a context; but arguably, neither can the question of domination, at least not in any conventional sense. Meeker's implication here is perhaps compatible with Marilyn Strathern's radical critique from a Melanesian perspective (1988). Both would find the stereotype outlined above seriously deficient as a satisfactory cultural description, and insist that the problematic of equality is ours, not theirs. Must we then conclude that no questions of power and control can be addressed here?

The Sexual Division of Labour in Sümer

Of course Michael Meeker's arguments, following fieldwork in the west of the Rize region in the 1960s may not apply in Lazistan twenty or thirty years later. Certainly my fieldwork materials are not comparable to those of Meeker, since I concentrated on productive activities associated with tea. Although tea was present and important in the Of districts in the 1960s, Meeker says very little about tea growing and processing, or indeed about the sexual division of labour. I think this is important, for by privileging the spheres of religion and politics and the more ideological aspects of patrilineal kinship organisation he may unwittingly be introducing androcentric bias (Olson, 1986).

In Sümer (Laz: *Sumle*), the valley which I studied in the *ilçe* of Fındıklı (Laz: *Vitze*), I have very little information about sex roles and the division of labour which prevailed before the arrival of tea as a cash crop to transform the local economy in the course of the 1950s. My hypothesis is that women were the mainstay of the local farming labour force even before the incidence of male out-migration reached higher levels in the context of demographic pressures in the twentieth century. I would like to argue that this greater prominence of women in agricultural production had long afforded them significant power resources which are overlooked in the anthropological model summarised above. In other words, leaving aside the 'informal power' (Friedl, 1986) available to women in the 'domestic' sphere of peasant societies, it seems to me at least possible that their position is stronger in a situation where scarcely any manual activity on the land is considered too hard for women, and where a number of income generating activities have been open to them. [5]

During thc 1980s many local practices in Lazistan were consistent with the picture sketched by Meeker. Men and women were segregated in many activities. The coffee houses of the village centre in Sümer (most houses here are scattered, so this consists merely of a cluster of new buildings) and of the small market towns along the coast were for men only. Women did not attend the mosque but they gathered separately for mourning and other rituals. Most marriages were still apparently arranged by the parents through the mediation of a go-between (*görücü*).

Turning to the economic transformation of recent decades, it might be expected that the massive expansion of tea gardens would have intensified the exploitation of female labour, as it has in other parts of Anatolia (Morvaridi, Chapter 6). In addition to housework and subsistence-oriented production it is women who have had to take prime responsibility for the harvesting of a very labour-intensive cash crop. Unlike the patterns of commercialisation in some other parts of Anatolia the introduction of tea around Rize was not at first accompanied by any significant mechanisation. Most of the labour expended in tea plucking as I observed it in the 1980s was indeed female labour, and it was comparatively unusual to see men old enough to have completed military service doing this work. Women carried the tea in baskets or sacks to the collection points, and they carried heavy (50 kilogram) sacks of fertiliser to the gardens every spring. They also carried firewood on their backs in large piles, as well as foodstufs for the animals of the household. Indeed most tasks associated with the gardens and the animals were primarily a female responsibility. At the same time female labour remained dominant in the home, in terms of cleaning, washing, cooking and child care (though some men did enjoy cooking for foreign visitors).

However, it would be wrong in my view to see the new crop as causing some sort of 'deterioration' in the position of Laz women. Rather I see their position in the new rural economy in terms of successful consolidation on an already secure basis, built up through many generations of being more actively engaged in production than other Anatolian females. The change in labour requirements has not at all been a change for the worse as far as women are concerned. Once a tea garden has been established the tasks of maintaining and harvesting it are less demanding physically than the earlier labour process associated with maize, the production of various vegetables, and hazelnuts. By the 1980s many families had converted virtually all their lands to tea, preferring to buy in most of their provisions from the regular weekly markets in the coastal towns. Many had also begun to invest in machines (*teleferik*) for transporting tea up and down the steepest slopes, which brought significant economies in female as well as male labour.

What did people say about such matters themselves? My questionnaire was inevitably crude, and the relevant questions came at the end of several pages designed to elicit 'hard' statistical data about farm size, output, credits used, other souces of income, and related matters.[6] People were generally amused to be asked their views as to whether women worked harder than men, and whether tea had made any difference. The majority response, among women as well as men, indicated that the introduction of tea had, in their estimation, required both men and women to work more than they had previously. More than two-thirds of respondents said that on balance women still worked harder. The usual reason given was that, whilst the productive activities outside the house might be more equally shared than in the past, in and around the house many tasks still fell solely to women.

In order to investigate these questions further it is essential to look more closely at the work of men. Some still sought and held jobs outside the region, returning home to their village only infrequently until final retirement. Some had permanent wage-labour jobs within the region, to which they commuted from their village homes (very few women have such jobs). Other men have opened shops or artisan workshops locally, enterprises made viable by the relative material affluence which tea has brought to this region.

Many had contracts which specified 120 days per year of manual labour in a local tea factory, working shifts that included night work, often in very noisy and over-heated factories. This work of course coincided with the period of greatest labour demand in the gardens, partly explaining the relative absence of the men from the tea gardens. Some men, particularly when not engaged in wage labour, or at times when their wives were busy caring for young children, were active tea pluckers. They also carried tea alongside women, and sometimes in place of women. Establishing a new tea garden was emphatically seen as a male job, along with other activities such as road maintenance and forest work. Among the many men who have some eight months of the year 'free', a small minority probably did spend a high proportion of their time gambling in the coffee houses. Others took every opportunity to seek further remunerative work, or they undertook major renovation tasks in their own households, or their 'leisure' activities were designed to bring in substantial material benefits (fishing and hunting). The idea that most able-bodied males spent much of their time loafing around could not be sustained.[7]

I now feel that my early questionnaire results conceal more than they reveal. The questions were naive and treated as such by the villagers. Other observations over several months in 1983, and again in 1988, call both model and stereotype into question. For example, contrary to the anthropologist's model, many women seemed to retain close links with their natal families, visiting them regularly. Inside some households the women seemed much more forceful personalities than their husbands. Some widows exercised management powers over large tea estates, even when grown sons might have taken over. The welfare of daughters was of continuing concern to parents, even when they married some distance away; nor did financial provision necessarily cease at marriage. In these respects the picture in Sümer in the 1980s seemed rather different from Of in the 1960s. Perhaps Lazistan is genuinely different from the rest of the Rize region. But it is also possible that paying more attention to economic factors and to what Jack Goody (1976; 1990) terms the domestic domain would have led Meeker to modify his picture of the position of women.

The question of women's property rights is of particular interest here. In Lazistan everyone will tell you that women do not and never have inherited land, though they may be generously provided for in other ways. The reality is that a daughter *can* inherit through entering into what Goody terms a filiacentric union when she has no brothers. This possibility is not explored by Meeker. Perhaps he would feel that to ask such proprietorial questions is at once to introduce ethnocentric Western assumptions. Strathern (1988) argues that mistaken proprietorial assumptions underlie some explorations of gender relations in Melanesia, for example, in the case of some diagnoses of economic exploitation of women. Her argument depends upon giving priority to complex indigenous understandings of the person in the context of a gift economy. Meeker could maintain similarly that persons in the Rize region are not constructed along the lines of the modern Western individual. A woman who inherits landed property because she has no brothers does so to maintain an estate and this does not alter the patrilineal foundations on which society is constructed. However, as Goody's work has demonstrated, this possibility is not always present in other patrilineal systems and more comparative analysis of what he terms the 'woman's property complex' throughout Turkey can help us to correct the bias implicit in the Meeker model.[8]

In summary, I am arguing that among the contemporary Laz the 'position of women' differs significantly from that implied by both popular stereotype and anthropological model, both before and after tea became the dominant cash crop of the region. Closer attention to females' property rights, to their roles in production in contexts of large-scale male migration and male domination of wage-labour opportunities, and to their interpersonal relations both inside and outside their families, with other women and with men, suggests to me that the position of women may actually be 'stronger' here than elsewhere in Anatolian peasant society.

Women and Development

The next step must be to acknowledge again how dangerous it is to generalise about women. The strong personalities and the forceful widows noted above were mostly located at the upper end of the local society in Sümer. At the other extreme, among the sharecroppers who had no gardens of their own in Sümer there was a very different division of authority. Here it was normal for a patriarch to enter into arrangements committing the labour of his wife and children, whilst reserving absolute control over the proceeds for himself. These families were commonly recruited from poorer districts adjacent to the tea zone, both westwards along the coast and southwards into the Anatolian interior, though some came from the districts around Rize itself. It was among these immigrant families that the sociological realities seemed to conform most faithfully to the general stereotype of the region. I have suggested elsewhere that such sharecroppers have come increasingly to form a new rural proletariat in prosperous valleys such as Sümer (Hann, 1985). Very few of these families have been able to purchase land and become permanent inhabitants: most will return eventually to a marginal economic existence in their poorer homes outside the Rize region, or end up as urban proletarians in Istanbul.

Having tried to show that gender relations among the indigenous inhabitants of this region were not as unfavourable to women as outsiders liked to suppose, I want briefly to turn to broader theoretical questions concerning development, and to suggest that Evans-Pritchard (1965) was right to emphasise that the key to improving the position of women may lie in general economic improvement. Contrary to the arguments of some later writers (e.g. Boserup, 1970) I would argue that the greater involvement of Laz women in a commercial economy has not been detrimental to their interests. On the contrary women have played a vital part in the transformation process which has brought great prosperity to both men and women of the region. In my view this process has been embedded in strong cultural continuities. As far as I am aware there never was any deliberate attempt to incorporate gender considerations into the planning which lay behind the massive expansion of this agro-industry in the Rize region after 1950. But if my arguments about the unreliability of prevalent stereotypes of gender relations in this region are sound, then it is perhaps just as well that no specific goals were set in this respect. Rather, if policymakers are concerned with avoiding the extremes of patriarchy they should be seeking ways of preventing the recent upsurge in sharecropping immigrants, for it is among these people that the harshest exploitation of women is continuing, rather than among the native Laz.

I realise that in the 1990s this may be an unfashionable, even a reactionary standpoint. In recent years development studies have been affected by a powerful feminist current and it is now almost received wisdom that greater attention should be paid to targeting females - everywhere. Such policies would seem highly desirable in many parts of Turkey, for example, in those regions which have been exporting sharecroppers and labourers to the Rize region. But, in the light of my argument about the position of women here, I am not sure that such policies would have been advantageous in Lazistan. I find it difficult to imagine that any special policies to target women in this region could have been more beneficial than those pursued to promote general economic development based on tea since the 1950s. There is even the danger, given the popular stereotypes about this region, that well-intentioned policymakers might have counselled against the introduction of tea, on the grounds that as a highly labour-intensive crop it would inevitably have increased the exploitation of women. I do not deny that the development of the tea industry has added to demands for female labour in a number of ways. We see here the reinforcement of an established division of labour, with women still providing most of the primary field workers and largely excluded from new wage labour opportunities in the region. The sexes are in many ways highly segregated and a long way from the familiar Western, conjugal, 'companionate' marriage pattern. But women's labour burden has been in other ways reduced, and again, it is hard to imagine how they could have been provided with any better alternative source of material provision than tea. I do not think that, say, reserving a quota of the new manual wage-labour jobs in the processing factories would have improved their position significantly (women *are* increasingly employed, in white-collar positions, in the associated bureaucracies). Women too have benefited from the general prosperity of the region. Better health and educational services are among the things they expect from would-be interventionist forces outside the region, and these needs have to a very considerable extent been met. Certainly it would be unwise to justify targeting Laz women today for special development initiatives on the basis solely of the stereotype and model discussed above.[9]

Conclusion

In conclusion I return to consider the origins of the stereotype. I do not wish to dismiss it as simply as a concoction of the Republican period. Positivist appeals to a new code of equality probably built upon older notions of a cultural boundary around the Rize region, whose otherness was so striking. The people who spoke with strange accents, and whose men did not grow wheat on the plain but ate the maize which their women grew on the hillsides, were a strange mixture in the context of Anatolian peasant society. I suggest that, far from the representation that has been widely disseminated in the twentieth century revealing the essential exploitation of women among the Laz, it has served instead to conceal the advantages which their economic roles earned for Laz women, and perhaps to conceal from women elsewhere the extent of their own subordination. In other words the stereotype may have developed as it did because it served the interests of patriarchal society in the rest of Anatolia. It has persisted in part due to the currency of Western gender ideals and a concept of equality which ignores more complex indigenous ideas. The latter involve not only segregation but also balance and complementarity, as Evans-Pritchard pointed out. At the same time it is a pity that sophisticated anthropological accounts which recognise the importance of indigenous ideas should tend to conceal very real differences in the position of women in different parts of Turkey as a result of the undue emphasis they place on male-dominated kin groups and their public statements and activities (in particular ritual and religious activities).

I therefore arrive at the following tentative conclusions. The stereotype of the dominated Laz woman may reveal more about how women have been kept subordinate in the rest of Anatolia than it does about the established pattern of gender relations in Lazistan. This stereotype does not correspond to 'insider' views of gender relations. Michael Meeker's exploration of local 'knowledge practices' in this regard is not entirely convincing because it pays insufficient attention to economic practices, and in particular, to the practices of the domestic domain and the quality of interpersonal relations. I suggest that new working patterns, associated mainly with the spread of tea as a cash-crop, have served overall to reinforce pre-existing ideas about complementarity and balance between the sexes. In further research I hope to be able to show how gender relations are entwined with traditional ethnic distinctions within the Rize region, and also with emerging class distinctions, and with generation differences and the life cycle.

Notes

1. This research was financed by grants from the Social Science Research Council (later Economic and Social Research Council) and the Turkish Ministry of Education. Full acknowledgements are provided in Hann

(1990). I should emphasise that I used Turkish in carrying out this fieldwork and have no competence whatsoever in Laz.

2. Other estimates are provided in Andrews (1989, p.176). I make allowances for many who no longer use the tongue, especially in the youngest generation, and for the presence of a significant number of non-Laz immigrants in Lazistan, many of them state officials or teachers. It is likely that a similar number of Laz speakers can be found in their diaspora, with large concentrations in the major cities of Western Turkey.
3. See Hann (1990, p.82, n.9).
4. An account of this episode, which was publicised on national television as well as in the local newspapers, is provided in a compendium of local history (Yazıcı, 1984, p.65).
5. This is a hotly debated subject. It is not my purpose here to argue that greater participation in productive activities always implies higher status for the women concerned. Arguments which have been put forward along these lines have come in for much criticism (Engels, 1972, Friedl, 1975; cf. Dubisch (ed.), 1986, Moore, 1988). It would certainly be safer to argue that nothing can be determined *a priori* about women's status in society from a knowledge of their role in production. But in the general Anatolian context I suggest that the exclusion of women from certain productive tasks may plausibly be related to prevalent ideas about male supremacy and the devaluation of women: hence the active participation in such tasks by women in Lazistan may be more likely to imply less rather than more in the way of oppression and exploitation. I do not have evidence to assess, for example, to what extent Laz women in the first half of the century actually controlled the products of their labour; but given that so many men were absent in these years it seems likely that the degree of female control was quite considerable.
6. My research in 1983 was carried out during the tea plucking season when labour demands were highest, and involved administering questionnaires to 150 local households. The questions were all designed for the head of the household (*hane reisi*), who was of course usually male. However, other females and males were frequently interested participants, and as I recall my questions concerning gender relations generated a good-humoured consensus.
7. To test the validity of the model and stereotype outlined above it is essential to make a closer inspection of domestic economic practices and interpersonal relations. As far as household finances are concerned, my impression (until more data are collected I cannot phrase it any more strongly) is that in many households, even those with resident male heads, control over the money earned by females through tea

plucking is indeed exercised by the senior female. Payments for leaves collected are normally made at the local tea factory to a male wage-worker from each household concerned, but even in cases where this person is the head of the household such moneys may be handed over to the senior female when the income derives from female effort.

8. Changes in marriage payments are also of great interest in this context. The *başlık* was unknown in many parts of Lazistan, including Sümer; but even where it was formerly present recent decades have seen a decisive shift away from *başlık* and a corresponding increase in the value of the *ceyiz* (trousseau). But as Sharma (1980) and others have shown, forms of dowry cannot be viewed simply as a means of pre-mortem inheritance, and they do not necessarily imply greater security or power for women; this topic too will be taken up in detail in further research in the Laz region.
9. On the other hand I do not think it is essential to follow through very carefully the differential consequences a new cash crop may have for men and women, and the state agents which promoted tea in the Rize region may indeed be faulted in this context. For example, at the Conference when this paper was presented Professor Dr Nermin Abadan-Unat argued that women's health was severely affected by the conditions in which they worked in the tea gardens, with rheumatic diseases a continuing problem. This may well indicate an area which merits concerted intervention, e.g. to promote new forms of protective clothing whilst working in the tea gardens, and it follows from the division of labour outlined above that this would imply a particular focus on women. I have no reliable information on health problems in the region, but it seems to me that both sexes have benefited greatly from the modern medical facilities now available throughout the region; that many health and nutritional problems have been largely eliminated since the 1950s; and that men too suffer in large numbers from rheumatism as a consequence of the climate of this region.

| 10 |

Traditional Modes of Authority and Co-operation

Carol Delaney

A common thread of the papers in this volume is an interest in Turkish villages; but is it reasonable to assume that the interest is the same? Is the interest merely intellectual or is it meant to have some practical effect? Is the interest to improve the lives of villagers, ourselves or the state? Change implies measurement, direction and evaluation. But by what or whose standard are changes measured? Meaningful changes also imply a teleological narrative - but whose script is it and for what end? Change is usually evaluated as better or worse, but again, whose judgement is decisive? Is it to help villagers preserve their values, knowledge and way of life or to use our knowledge to destabilise that way of life as means of changing it? Drawing villagers into the national economy simultaneously breaks down the integrity of their way of life. Despite a common concern about Turkish villages, there can be no disinterested perspective.

Having spent several years of my life living in a Turkish village, I have great respect for their way of life and the hospitality, tolerance, sense of humour and forgiveness I experienced there. At the same time, there are changes that could enhance that life and shore it up against the currents that are tending to destroy it. For such change to come about, villagers' dreams, hopes, knowledge and goals must be taken into account and taken seriously.

Part I

My paper is about two kinds of relations that affect the economy and are always implicated in the direction that change will take. These relations are relations of authority as well as relations of co-operation. I will discuss these relations not in the abstract but as they are enacted in the practices of everyday life and especially as they are embodied in and expressed by the concepts of *izin* and *imece*. The first part of the paper will deal with authority relations and the second with co-operative relations. I spend more time on authority relations because, in my opinion, these are an impediment to both co-operation and creativity and have deleterious effects on the economy.

As notions of authority and co-operation are made quite specific, so too is the context of my study. The village I refer to is the village in central Anatolia where I conducted anthropological fieldwork between August 1980 and July 1982[1] and to which I returned again in the summer of 1986. While my observations are drawn primarily from that village, I believe they apply to many, for in the process of choosing that village I visited more than fifty others and stayed in several for periods of up to a week. During my fieldwork I, along with the villagers, had continuing connections with several neighbouring villages. The village I lived in is composed of approximately 850 people, evenly divided by sex, who profess to be Sunni Muslims. The production of wheat and sheep for subsistence and for the market are the predominant forms of livelihood. Ever since the introduction of tractors in the 1950s there has been a steady migration of some of the people to town in search of work, but few have migrated directly to Europe. Despite out-migration and birth control devices made available after 1965, the population has been relatively stable for several decades indicating an overall growth. This is due not only to a reduction of infant mortality and greater life expectancy but is also an indication of the viability of the village way of life and a sense of dedication to fostering it.

Authority relations in the village are enacted against a background of authority that has characterised the nation as a whole for a long time. These authority relations are hierarchically ordered and patriarchal in character as has been discussed in numerous works on Turkish villages, e.g. Stirling's classic monograph, *Turkish Village* (1965). Twenty-five years later, my discussion both confirms and hopefully extends his. The model of authority can be imagined as a pyramid with God at the top. His authority extends to the edges of the world; in his shadow and under his mantle is the ruler of the nation. At the lower end of this pyramid is the eldest male whose authority encompasses the household, and finally the husband-father whose authority covers his wife and children. This diagram nicely captures the top-down (*tepeden inmecilik*) direction of authority as well the bottom-up direction that respect and obedience should take. It also shows that regardless of the enormous difference between God and man, a man, however lowly, nevertheless stands in the direct line of power. A Muslim theologian has confirmed this. He says:

> The Muslim family is the miniature of the whole Muslim society ... In it the man or father functions as the imam in accordance with the patriarchal nature of Islam. He is in a sense the priest...In the family the father upholds the tenets of the religion and his *authority symbolizes that of God in the world.* (Seyyed Hossein Nasr, 1966, pp.110-11, emphasis mine.)

Because God gave us life we owe him obeisance; analogously but at very different level, it is because men are presumed to be the ones through whom the life-giving power is conveyed in procreation that they stand in line with divine power and partake of it. Elsewhere (Delaney, 1986 and 1991) I have discussed the way patriarchal authority is intimately involved with notions of fatherhood or paternity and entails a specific theory of procreation. It is important to realise however, that the culturally perceived ability of men to engender children is part of the meaning of being male and bestows status on men regardless of whether the potential is actualised. While male power and authority intimately involves the perceived ability to procreate, a man's *honour* depends on his ability to ensure that the progeny is his own and this entails the control of women by men (Delaney, 1987). In the village, a man without a family is a rarity and a man's authority can only be exercised if he has a family. Then he is counted as fully adult, as head of a *hane* (household). Nevertheless, this does not give us a sense of what his authority consists of, and how it is expressed.

Villagers did not discourse abstractly about authority or its legitimacy; instead authority relations became obvious in their effects. A father's authority, besides representing the house and making decisions about its inhabitants and its management, manifests itself in the concept of *izin*. Usually this is translated as 'permission' or 'leave' and even by some as 'vacation'. Nothing could be more alien to a villager than the last. *İzin* is not freedom to do whatever you want; it is authorised permission to do something specific, or to go to another specified place. It is what conveys you from one place or duty to another. People who are legitimately 'out-of-place' are *izinli* - with permission. Such a category would include a soldier who has come home to visit, the imam, midwife or teachers who are permitted to leave the village for a time, or someone who works in town but who has returned to the village for a specific reason. Being *izinli* implies being embedded in a whole network of social relations and obligations; without *izin* one is cast adrift, one is defenceless and especially in the case of women, fair game. Indeed, the person who bestows *izin* is also held responsible for the 'protection' of the *izinli*. If one is to understand the context in which life in a village is lived, it is essential to understand the meaning of this concept.

My understanding of authority structures developed along with my understanding of the concept of *izin* and I first became aware of its importance because of the questions villagers put to me. They wanted to know if I had *izin* from my father to be there, then whether I had *izin* from my university and finally whether I had *izin* from my government. Who 'sent' me? Who authorised me to come? It is especially important for a woman to be under this kind of 'protection', which is symbolically if not actually male, for it conveys the idea that someone is responsible for her, someone cares about what happens to her. The notion of autonomy and the fact that I had chosen my work and the village myself was extremely difficult for them to understand, if ever. And it became critical for me in the village. My presence there was obviously an anomaly; not only was I a foreigner, but I was also a woman and living alone in one small quarter or *mahalle* of the village.

In order to learn about the village and become acquainted with other villagers it was necessary for me to walk around. '*Çok geziyorsun*' - you're wandering around too much. A woman's proper place is working at home or, at most, sitting just outside the house. Such behaviour conveys that she is properly 'protected' and is, in turn, protecting the honour of her husband, father or brother. Women do work in the fields, of course, but they must have *izin* to do so and often they are accompanied by a male relative. Since the streets are really the legitimate province of men, a woman strolling about too much is provocative. She is not where she ought to be, she is definitely 'out-of-place'.

My free movement was unsettling and disorienting for them especially since there was no man to give me *izin*. Since men control, or like to think they control, the movement of women, my free movement implicitly undermined their authority and set a bad example. Such ideas are not, of course, confined only to Turkish villages. In modern America women often complain of being 'chained' to their desks and cannot get up to leave without informing others. Generally, men have much more mobility on the job, and generally control that of women.

The fact that I had no man from whom to obtain *izin* became a very sensitive issue on the occasions when I decided to go to town. Villagers would ask me 'Who gave you permission (*izin*)'? They compared me to the teachers and midwife who, in order to leave the village (their place of duty) needed *izin* from their supervisors who lived outside the village. In order to allay their anxiety and to maintain the good will and support of the *muhtar*, I tried to let him know when I was leaving the village and when I planned to return. He was, after all, the person who had given me *izin* to stay in the village and who could terminate it at will. Since he had assumed the burden of 'protecting' me, the least I could do was to inform him of my whereabouts. This was also a matter of respect so that he would not be shamed by lack of knowledge of my movement in and out of the village. In this way I also made my own precarious position more secure.

İzin, in a sense, is a source of power and movement; on whose authority are you 'sent'? One does not control one's mobility in space and time, one is conveyed by *izin*. To a large extent this lack of control applies also to the choice of one's occupation, university major, and marriage partner. Ultimately all people need God's *izin* to leave life: 'No soul can ever die except by Allah's *izin* and at a term appointed.' (Sura 3, pp.145)

The idea of *izin* and its complement - who gives *izin* - has extremely wide application. Nevertheless, it is in the home where the idea and attitudes are instilled. Authority, except in the case of the elder male (and even that is relative) is always outside the self. Nevertheless, its range affects people differentially.

Young men are allowed more freedom to walk around the village and its environs. Their place is in the village but outside the home and therefore they need *izin* from their father to go to town. Girls and women need it to go anywhere. Women's place is in the home; except for brief visits to immediate neighbours, they need *izin* to leave it.

A young man can look forward to a progressively more embodied authority - as he grows older, marries, establishes a family, and takes over the management of the household. A woman can only look forward to a relative relaxation of it - when she is older, has a married son and a *gelin* (bride, son's wife) to whom she can delegate work.

Following are a few examples of the application of *izin*:

(1) A new bride needs *izin* from her in-laws before she can go back to visit her natal family. Indeed she needs *izin* either from them or from her husband to visit anyone.

(2) Another important area in which *izin* operates is school. While primary school is obligatory, middle and high school are not. Since most villages do not have a middle or high school, a village youth who wishes to continue his or her education has a formidable hurdle to surmount. A relative living in town with whom he or she could board must be found and be agreeable to the arrangement. At the same time, such an arrangement deprives the village family of the help and companionship of that child. The problem could, of course, be solved if a village *dolmuş* was used as a school bus to transport children to and from the school every day. In any case, both boys and girls need their father's *izin* to continue school beyond primary school. For girls, however, there are additional obstacles.[2] Headscarves are not permitted in state supported schools. Since girls customarily cover their heads at the end of primary school, which coincides with social, if not physical, puberty, girls would have to flaunt village custom to continue their schooling. More importantly, if girls wish to pursue their education so they might become teachers or midwives, it is government policy that they cannot be appointed to their own village. Since most fathers would not think of sending their daughters out into the world unprotected, this policy is a further impediment to the education of women. It must also be noted that materialistic reasons for sending a girl to school held very little

weight among villagers I knew. Some of them would have let married girls attend school but that, I believe, is also forbidden by the government.

(3) Another school-related example involved me. Our village was fortunate to have a middle school although few children and even fewer girls were 'sent'. English was the foreign language being taught in the middle school. I suggested to the teacher that I come once or twice a week to read the lesson or a story or just to help out. Although I offered in a spirit of co-operation, he experienced it as a threat to his authority (and masculinity - for the two are combined). He also said that if I wanted to do this, I would have to get *izin* from the Ministry of Education. I did not want to embark on a lengthy involvement with the bureaucracy and even had I been granted permission it would have meant a far more rigid commitment and schedule than would have been feasible. But thereby the students, the teacher and I lost out on an unusual opportunity.

(4) Our village also had a library - almost unheard of for a village. Perhaps this was because the village was relatively remote but it also attested to a former interest of villagers in education. Although the library was supported by the government which sent books and a staff person and should therefore have been accessible to everyone, women were not permitted to go to the library. Their husbands/fathers would not give them *izin*; the excuse was that unrelated men would always be present and their mere presence was considered defiling. This problem could easily have been resolved if one day a week, or even half a day, was reserved for women. This suggestion did not go over very well not only because of the presence of unrelated men but also because male relatives would be unable to control what women read. 'Women are meant to do handwork not headwork'; but by not being able to go to the library, women are ironically denied books on cooking and sewing.

(5) The library could also have served as a lively centre for the discussion of current events if we had been able to get a newspaper on a regular basis. A subscription would have required *izin* from the government, and since it could not afford to give subscriptions to all papers, it could not authorise it for any one paper since that would have indicated political preference.[3] In addition, books I donated to

the library could not be displayed because no *izin* from the government had been granted. Some of the villagers' caution may be related to the fact that the country was under military rule and they did not want anything to precipitate military intervention. Their attitude may have been exaggerated due to events of the time, but it was not new.

(6) Belma Akşit's paper illustrates that health-seeking behaviour is another important as well as insidious area where the concept of *izin* operates. Although our village had a resident midwife-nurse who was trained and supported by the government, women needed *izin* from their husbands or father in order to visit her. A number of women and children did not receive timely health care because they were not given *izin* in time. Even more difficult was getting permission to go to the doctor or dentist in town. That visit was a major undertaking and cost about $5.00 roundtrip by the village *dolmuş*, in addition to the expense of medicine, tests and perhaps an overnight stay. Since a woman would have to be accompanied the cost was multiplied.

(7) Health was also jeopardised by the fact that in village custom, although not in Qur'anic law, women needed *izin* from their husbands to eat and drink if they were pregnant or nursing during Ramazan. The month of Ramazan fell in August and July respectively during the period I was in the village. These are the most gruelling times for the fast. Although the fast is difficult even for the most heroic to accomplish, several pregnant and nursing women went without food or water for the daily eighteen-hour fast. Several of them complained that their milk supply dried up and their babies were sickly. Some very strict men forced 'their' women to work in the fields without food or drink (cf. Morvaridi, this volume); meanwhile quite a lot of men working in the fields did eat and drink and postponed their days of fasting until the winter, if at all.

The attitudes behind these various examples display a certain consistency. The concept of *izin* exhibits a structure of authority that is both hierarchical and patriarchal. Social relations are construed in terms of those who have the power to impose their wills and those who must obey. At the same time, it motivates resistance and creates a situation in which people will try to circumvent authority. For example, one head of the household was nicknamed 'Khomeini' because he was so strict, especially with 'his' women - his wife and daughters and his dead brother's widow. He would not give them *izin* to have their photographs taken (by me), nor would he let the widow, who lived just down the lane from me, visit neighbours. After the women assured me that he would never see the photographs I went there one day when he was absent. Similarly, the widow would come to visit me or send for me at times she knew he was away for several hours.

Whether this kind of circumvention is really an expression of resistance or is endemic in a Muslim upbringing is unclear, for the desire to get around the 'law' is consonant with the kind of reasoning involved in Islamic legal training. Because God's law is written it cannot be legally or humanly changed, but it can be re-interpreted. The structures of authority and the symbols of its imposition are retained, but the reality can be manipulated to a certain extent.

İzin is a concept that also exposes a lack of trust - trust that people can make intelligent decisions, and perhaps even more important, trust to let them make mistakes and thereby learn from them. This attitude undermines initiative and creativity; indeed, Islam discourages innovations.

Distrust of creativity can also be discerned in the authoritarian methods of teaching and learning regardless of the subject matter. What is stressed are facts and knowledge that can be transmitted from teacher to student. This model of education contrasts with one that attempts to draw out the talent and creativity of the student. One seems to foster independence while the other instils obedience to authority.

In relation to outside authority, villagers are infantilised. They become *memleket çocukları* - children of the 'country' (in the sense of nation); no wonder they wait for *Devlet Baba* (Father State) to solve their problems and to ease their lives. Everything conspires to show them that 'Father Knows Best'. Inside the village, however, villagers did take initiatives and were quite creative but this goes unacknowledged by the government experts or officials. Government authority often comes to the village in the form of various experts who, by their attitude and condescending manner (which I experienced myself on a number of occasions when I was perceived as a villager), exhibit its authoritarian and paternalistic style.

Villagers do not disdain the learning of the experts, but the relation is not reciprocal; the experts disdain the knowledge of the villagers and do not treat them as equal partners in either the preservation and production of knowledge or in developing its applications. In addition, it must be acknowledged that villagers and I shared a suspicion of progress; unlike most of the experts who visited, they were not positivists. Villagers are very well aware that each 'progressive' change entails the destruction of something else with which they were more familiar. Furthermore, they know that there is no guarantee the substitutions will bring about changes that will really be better. Some changes will undoubtedly destroy aspects of their life they value. John Berger writing about his experience of living in a French village for over seven years has captured this sentiment very well. A villager he said 'may admire knowledge and the fruits of knowledge but he never supposes that the advance of knowledge reduces the extent of the unknown' (1979, p.202). There are simply too many things that cannot be anticipated, that can go awry. Berger goes on to say that:

> this non-antagonistic relation between the unknown and knowing explains why some of his (a villager's) knowledge is acommodated in what, from the outside, is defined as superstition and magic. Nothing in his experience encourages him to believe in final causes, precisely because his experience is so wide. The unknown can only be eliminated within the limits of a laboratory experiment. Those limits seem to him to be naive.

Not only do villagers not want to be used as a laboratory, but they realise how erroneous are outsiders' views of village life. Contrary to the view that village life is timeless, unchanging and of course, boring, I suggest that it is just the reverse. Precisely because there is so much change, is village life so satisfying. A number of men who worked in town for a while told me they preferred the village not only because of the variety of tasks but also because each could be done at its own pace. The monotony of work is more an urban experience and creates in those who live in town a need for ever-changing pleasures.

Change in the village is rooted in the lives, the history, and the topography of the village. Villagers have excellent memories and remember significant events in minute detail. Places, too, store memories and as villagers walk about their land, these places release the memory of the events that took place there. In the management of their daily and seasonal tasks, villagers must take into account so many changes and make allowances for so many unforeseen events, that they must always be improvising and creative in small ways. The wealth of this enormous talent has rarely been acknowledged, let alone mined. Instead, it is undermined.

The intrusion of authorities into the village implicitly questions the ability of the village to manage itself. Men of the village are put in a humiliating and subordinate position; *vis à vis* the authorities, they are like women and children. They may feel that they have lost control over their own lives. In order to regain some measure of self-respect they are liable to turn to women to exert their authority and control.[4]

Social planners as well as villagers might benefit from a model of authority that is neither oppressive nor condescending but, rather, one that *empowers* villagers by including them as full co-operative partners in both the planning and implementation of any development projects. To date, development schemes are usually conceived in government planning offices by planners who have little experience of village life and tend to disdain it. Not only are their plans imposed on villagers whose co-operation they then seek for the implementation, but the plans generally either fail to include women or fail to anticipate the impact on women. In the process of so-called development, women have been left behind; their tasks and roles have changed very little (cf. Morvaridi). They have lost a considerable amount of power they had as partners in the management and productive activities for the survival of the household and are now much more dependent on their husbands who control the arenas wherein large revenue is made. This process is not unique to Turkey but has been documented in a number of developing nations (cf. Beneria, 1982; Hill, 1986; Moore, 1988; Rogers, 1980).

If progressive action is desired, all must be empowered, for too much individual assertion in getting ahead of his/her fellows is seen as a negative quality in a village that also prides itself on community spirit. It is to that I will now turn.

Part II

Given the above, it might seem difficult to imagine space for co-operative behaviour which, by its very nature, cross cuts and undermines hierarchical structures. There are, in fact, numerous kinds of co-operative actions; if they did not exist, the village could not exist. In this context I can only outline a few.

Much of the co-operative action is done by women - both within and between households. The provisioning and upkeep of a household and of persons - housework, cleaning, washing, food preservation and preparation, spinning of yarn, making of clothes and bedding - in addition to and along with agricultural work and childcare - must be a co-operative enterprise. No one woman can do all of it. Within the household, the women must co-operate in trying to keep up with these never-ending tasks.

Between households it is only women who can dart in and out of neighbours' houses - men's relations to other houses is more formal and they need *izin* from a resident male to enter; women do not. Women co-operate by sharing food if it runs out and by sharing labour and providing companionship in the daily, weekly and seasonal preparation of food. This includes making bread, cheese, butter, sausage and *pastırma*, noodles and *salça*, drying vegetables and fruits, and making *komposto* and jam. Women share their labour in preparing food for large gatherings - at weddings, *bayram* and funerals for example. They help each other spin yarn, knit sweaters and socks, trim headscarves, make *şalvar*, embroider sheets and pillowcases, and stuff and stitch quilts.

Women are also the ones who primarily care for the sick and elderly; in a very important sense the village is the nation's welfare agency. Relatives from city and town come to the village when they run out of money or work, or when they are sick. Children of villagers living in the city were sent back to the village for the summer. Widows were taken care of and not always by relatives. I remember one family who cared for an elderly widow who was unrelated to them. She used to spend her days with them and return to her own house only to sleep, and not always did she do even that.

Women's co-operative behaviour sustains the village in small ways; it is informal and often invisible. In contrast, men's co-operative behaviour is often formalised in an arrangement called an *ortak* (partnership). When I asked if women ever form an *ortak* a female neighbor of mine joked about our *kedi ortağı*. We had an arrangment whereby we shared the care and responsibility of a kitten between us. We agreed that I could have the kitten with me as long as I was in the village; but she had to care for it when I left the village - when I went to town for a few days as well as when I eventually left to return to the United States.

Men's *ortak* usually involve a sharing arrangement for buying and using heavy equipment such as tractors, combines, or a *dolmuş*. Theoretically, agnates are expected to co-operate, but in practice this was not always or even often the case. Such arrangments were quite often made between non-kin. Because of this it is conceivable that a village as a whole could form an *ortak* for buying such equipment.

One extraordinary co-operative act took place while I was in the village. Villagers built a house for a poor and elderly couple. Since it was directly across from my house I was able to watch the entire process. Because of their poverty this old couple had been living for seven years in the *yayla*, located half way down the mountain and used as a corral for sheep. Occasionally people would drop off bags of food for them, but their situation was a blight on the village conscience. Money was collected from everyone including villagers who were then living in town. Materials were bought and an *usta* (skilled craftsman) was hired. Others volunteered labour, machinery and provisions for the workers. (I occasionally made tea for them.) The house was built fairly quickly and the old people were brought back and installed once again in the life of village. A few years previously villagers had built a house for a widow and her children after her house collapsed. I used to frequent their house often and noted that it was finely built.

In the near past a number of village projects had been undertaken by the whole village at their own initiative. Such co-operative endeavours included: building bridge over a ravine where several villagers had been killed in a tractor accident; building the midwife's house, building a grand new mosque; laying down the pipes for both a sewage project and for water to be piped to each household. An irrigation project had begun but it was never completed and when I returned in 1986 it lay in ruins. In addition, several co-operatives were formed for bringing commodities such as sugar to the village. Other projects had a more social than economic purpose, for example, village-city social exchanges, co-operatives to help send poor children to school, inter-village sports meets, and so on.

All of these projects were referred to as *imece* which means 'community project' and to which, if necessary, each household contributed labour and money. In some places, I have heard that *imece* can have negative connotations; in that case it means something like an enforced work party. It seems that the connotation has much to do with the way in which projects are decided upon. In our village, this was by a consensus arrived at in fairly democratic manner, albeit one that included only men and then only household heads. Each head of household would be consulted and have a say in the decision-making process. He, of course, could consult with members of his family but only he had the power to delegate someone from his household to work on the project. Projects that would or could involve the whole village but that were proposed from outside, were received more negatively. For example, the state proposed building a new road from the village; villagers would have been hired and paid for their labour, but no one wanted to work on the project and they refused to become involved.

In our village *imece* projects were discussed in a positive way, so much so that I assumed the word meant 'community spirit'. In fact, there is a sense in which the kind of co-operative activity they exhibited does display a community spirit. Villagers' photographs and recollections seemed to indicate a time when there were periods, at least, of collective effervescence without which a sense of community withers. During the time I was in the village, the only occasions for something like that were either weddings or the communal meal given by those leaving to go on the *hac* (hajj).

Most of the co-operative ventures had died sometime before I got to the village in August, 1980; in other words they had collapsed before the military coup (September 12, 1980) when all such associations were officially closed. At first I was told that part of the failure of these activities had to do with the lack of trust between participants; a generalised fear that some clever person would divert the funds to his own use. But this suspicion is a fairly endemic aspect of Turkish village life and, in any case, had clearly been transcended for certain periods of time. Others explained that during the preceding years of political upheavel co-operative behaviour had come to be labelled 'communist' and thus tainted. (My attempts to explain that most American capitalist companies also demanded co-operation met with disbelief).

The villagers' assessment of the reasons that *imece* projects and community spirit broke down emphasised the political polarisation of the village which, they said, came about through the importation and establishment of two political *derneks* which were supported by two opposing political parties. Not only did these polarise the village, but by linking each side with groups outside the village, broke down ties within the village and weakened the community as a whole.

Previously, there had been differences of opinion between villagers but these were kept within the village and the spirit of the village was united against the outside. With the politicisation of the village, loyalties were divided and channelled into two factions and people were forced to take sides. I might add that this phenomenon not only divided the village but also divided families. Brothers living next door to each other ended up on different sides; so did fathers and sons. When a project was suggested by those on one side, the others refused to go along and vice versa. Such a state of affairs brought the village to a standstill, a state in which the village as a whole can only lose. It also creates an atmosphere of suspicion and a desire for retaliation. Villagers' views of the breakdown of *imece* spirit supports the hypothesis of C. H. Dodd (1983) and Tachau (1984) concerning the breakdown of the government at the national level.[5] Clearly, politics affects economics and economics affects politics; but both are shaped by and embedded in specific cultural concepts, structures and practices.

Conclusion

Although Turkey considers itself a democracy, the term too often seems to mean only whether or not there are free elections. This is surely much too narrow a definition. Democracy is not just about voting but has to do also with the feeling that people have about the power to affect their own lives. When voting is presented as the primary means to achieve that, the struggle for dominance ensues and the structure of authority relations reasserts itself.

The structure and content of authority relations have deeply destructive effects on feelings of agency and consequently on taking initiative. This kind of authority thwarts the creative spirit which tends to be subversive of received opinions and ways of doing things. The lack of trust implied by authority structures and attitudes also thwarts the development of bottom-up or 'grassroots' projects and organisations, projects that depend upon trust and co-operation. It is these kinds of projects that would give back to villagers a sense of their own power to make positive changes in their lives.

As I was writing this paper I heard of several instances in the United States where the state has turned over the management of some housing projects to the poor tenants who live in them. In a very short time, it was reported, these tenants have been able to turn these areas of high crime, violence, drug use, and vandalism into attractive, clean and safe apartment buildings. The tenants themselves now have control and are making improvements because they have a direct stake in their building and their lives. No doubt there will be setbacks and they admit to mistakes, but they are learning valuable lessons in the process. These lessons might have something to teach the experts in the field of economics. One such expert, Albert Hirschman, has written an inspiring report (1984) of co-operative projects in Latin America. Admittedly, rural projects are not the same as urban housing projects, but the assumptions and the implications are similar.

Rather than thinking of villages as instrumental for the goals of the state, it may be more productive to encourage and support villagers' view of villages as separate, semi-autonomous units. This would enable a village to negotiate its relation to various state agencies as a partner in mutually conceived and mutually beneficial enterprises. When villagers are empowered to make changes they feel are created by themselves and for themselves, their energy and commitment is insured. Paradoxically, it may just be that the more grassroots projects are allowed to grow, the more the nation as a whole will reap the benefits.

Notes

1. I wish to express my thanks to Professor Paul Stirling for the kind invitation to participate in the conference, 'Culture and the Economy: Changes in Turkish Villages', in London, May 1988 and for his numerous editorial comments. Thanks also to G.Paleczek and B. Morvaridi whose questions and comments were especially helpful.
   The results of that fieldwork have been published in Delaney (1991).
2. See Delaney (1987 and 1989) where I discuss these issues in greater detail.
3. The lack of a government subscription does not preclude an *ad hoc* arrangement whereby whoever went to town would bring one back for the library. That suggestion, however, was not picked up.
4. My experience among Turkish workers in Belgium confirms this hypothesis. Men who were out of work and therefore deprived of the authority and autonomy which work implied, became more authoritarian in the home and became more concerned about controlling 'their' women - wife and daughters.
5. See also the articles in Part Two of Schick and Tonak (1987).

11

Rural Health Seeking

Under Fives in Sivas, Van and Ankara

Belma T. Akşit

Introduction

Ill health is the greatest source of misery and anxiety for the poor, indeed, for all humans. Improvement in health is plainly one major effect of increased real wealth per capita; and a contribution to it.

High infant mortality and its persistent urban/rural and regional variations in Turkey have already been demonstrated (Shorter and Macura, 1982; Tunçbilek, et al., 1988; Akşit and Akşit, 1989; Bertan and Guriş, 1989). There has also been some explanatory work using local and national survey samples. Yet the relation between child mortality, morbidity and survival, and the health-seeking behaviour of rural households have scarcely been studied. Anthropological research on the sociocultural and medical determinants of child mortality in Turkey is urgently needed. Although many epidemiological surveys have been conducted, there are few studies on the 'production' of health at household level.

The success of health development depends on a combination of appropriate technology, sound health care delivery, and social and economic changes affecting households and the community (Berman et al., 1989). It is not sufficient to develop effective clinical health technology. It is not even sufficient to make it available on a wide scale. The technology must be utilised consistently and correctly at the household level, in order to realise its potential significantly to improve health (Leslie, 1987).

'Health seeking behaviour' is sociocultural; it is not simply an individual activity but also a social one, which concerns and involves other members of the individual' s social environment (Frankenberg, 1968).

Most of the studies on the production of health are limited to the health-seeking behaviour of ill people (Igun, 1978; Kroeger, 1983; Cleland, 1989). Instead of focusing on the behaviour of patients, we must take into account the behaviour of parents, grandparents and the community; even more so in the case of children. Only in this way can we develop more appropriate health production models, and ensure better survival for children; and indeed everyone.

Of course, health care services cannot be ignored. Distance, and the attitude and behaviour of health personnel are important. But so also are the type of family and household (Kroeger, 1983), the relations among family members, decision-making power (in terms of money, wisdom, education, experience), the status of the women in the family and the community, the external or internal locus of control (Simons, 1989), and the value of children (Kağıtcıbaşı, 1981). In sum, the sociocultural and economic behaviour of individuals, households and communities greatly affect the child's morbidity and mortality.

Objectives and Methods

It is important to understand the reasons for the lack of information in rural families, for their 'child neglect', for their 'misconceptions'; and for delays in seeking medical care (Akşit and Akşit, 1989; Spradley, 1979). A high proportion of deaths are from preventable causes such as infectious diseases and environmental factors. Since production (including health), consumption, and social reproduction all take place in households, I shall in this paper examine the stages of health seeking behaviour for children under five in Turkish rural households.

This study has two phases. In the first phase, 'focus group' interviews (Folch-Lyon and Trost, 1981) were conducted in Sivas and Van Provinces for three weeks in February-March, 1989. In each area, sessions were held with diverse groups, covering variations in settlement location, local economic activities, health services, religious and ethnic affiliations, educational and marital status, age and gender. We conducted forty-one sessions, sometimes with the help of a medical research assistant from the Department of Public Health of Hacettepe University. Moreover, we used information from observations, unstructured conversations, and sometimes depth interviews in various households which welcomed us as guests; and with many other informants.

Depth interviewing is vastly better than normal pre-coded surveying, but less effective than more prolonged 'immersion' research, specifically directed to health.

The second phase was carried out a year later in March-April, 1990, with the assistance of fourth-year students of the School of Social Work of Hacettepe University, in Etimesgut and Çubuk, both districts of Ankara. In accordance with the same criteria as in Sivas and Van, the villages were selected with the help of the Heads of the Training and Research Areas. In each village, two teams (composed of a female and a male student) visited families chosen by the *muhtar* (headman), with at least one child under five, including both nuclear and extended households.

During this second phase, we visited twenty families, with each of which we spent a day conducting informal observation and depth interviews. A total of 52 depth interviews were carried out with fathers (19), mothers (20), grandfathers (6), and grandmothers (7).

The Interview Sites and the Families

The focus group interviews were conducted during the winter months, when acute respiratory infections (ARI) are most frequently encountered (Akşit, B.T., 1989). Sivas in Central, and Van in Eastern Anatolia, two of the 'cold' provinces of Turkey, were chosen as the research sites because ARI are very common, particularly in children under five. Ankara was also added to the 'cold' provinces with quite a high rate of morbidity in the same age group.

Sivas also has a Socialised Medicine Programme as of 1975; and the Ulaş Training and Research Area, formed in 1981 through collaboration between Cumhuriyet University and the Ministry of Health.

Socialised Medical Services began in 1964 in the Province of Van. Van also participated in an ARI Programme, which aims to decrease child deaths due to pneumonia in Turkey by the year 1992.

The goals of this project included an increase in general information about ARI, and a change of attitude and practice among mothers, families, and certain social leaders (such as teachers), through active participation in health education and other programme components (UNICEF, 1988).

On the other hand, Çubuk and Etimesgut are rural districts near Ankara with semi-urban town centres, where health services have, since 1965 in Etimesgut, and since 1975 in Çubuk, been socialised and run by the Ministry of Health in co-operation with the Department of Public Health of Hacettepe University.

We visited seventeen villages in Sivas and nine in Van. These were selected on the basis of variations in the presence, distance, quality and usage of health services; the distance from town; ethnic group - very important in both provinces, especially in terms of women' s openness to outside and behaviour; jobs; and relationships with the local town.

With only twenty households for intensive study, each of only one day, the sample is clearly not representative, quantitatively or qualitatively. The families were chosen on the basis of having at least one child under five. The original intention to visit five extended families and five nuclear families in each district, could not be achieved, since some of the families which the *muhtar* had chosen for us as nuclear, were not so; they shared their compound, toilet and food with the husband's family, that is, the husband's father or mother, or his brother's family. And as expected, in these cases, the budget of the younger newly separated family was determined by the husband's father, with the assistance of his mother. In this study, this type of family is classified as semi-extended.

We visited five extended families in Etimesgut and seven in Çubuk with average economic conditions[1]; and four semi-extended families in Etimesgut and one in Çubuk, mostly with fairly good economic conditions. The two nuclear families which we visited in Çubuk lived in poor conditions, whereas the nuclear family interviewed in Etimesgut was well off.

As expected, all were farmers, and most also kept animals; most of the men and women were primary school graduates, and none of the women worked outside the home.

Findings and Conclusions

The following conclusions of the present study provide clues both about common diseases in childhood, and for future research.

These findings are divided into two parts. The first is concerned with the structure of the households, with the status of women and their values, and with health-seeking behaviour as a whole. The second part sets out a series of specific steps in health-seeking behaviour.

A. The Socio-cultural Structure of Households

(1) Household Types and Internal Authority.

On the basis of our observations we question the soundness of accepted distinctions among family types. Although it has been established that the proportion of nuclear families is high in rural, as well as in urban, Turkey (Timur, 1972; DPT, 1989); young rural couples with children under five are more likely to live with the husband' s family, or at least very near to them. This leads us to question the soundness of the formal definition of simple or nuclear family, in terms of decisions about the health of the children. It seems that the increase in the number of separate houses cannot explain the networks between closely related families in many social environments. Even if the young couple live in a separate house, if the house is in the same compound as the husband's parents' house, they may well live as extended families under the supervision of the husband's parents.

In the context of this study, it is important to know who decides; who buys clothes, food, and especially medicine. In extended and semi-extended families, it is normally the senior man, head of household, who buys almost all the goods, food and clothing. As they say, 'He earns the money, he spends the money'.

The crucial person for this study is the *gelin* (literally, the one who comes, the son's wife), the mother of the under fives. But she cannot herself decide on spending for her child's needs - clothes, books, equipment, medicines, medical care. Like other family members, she has first to approach the head's wife, her husband's mother, for anything she needs. Only if this senior woman herself approves will she in turn convey needs and requests to her husband, the household head. Even a young wife's personal friends are controlled by her affines. Indeed parents even have the last word on the friends of a married son; even if he is living in a separate household. 'They are experienced; they know who is good and who is bad for us.'

Even in independent households, a young mother is not free to decide what her child needs, nor with whom she can make personal contacts and friendships. Both her spending and her social life are controlled by her husband, who in turn - depending on circumstances - may be indirectly controlled by his mother and father.

Almost all the informants stress the strength of the link between parents and children. Fathers and mothers interviewed said that they love and feel intimacy for each other and their own children. Most men and women name their own parents as 'the most respected and most reliable persons in their lives'. Interestingly, this finding varies little between household types.

(2) World view

'World view' is not a precise concept. The comments of informants which I have chosen to report here are in part informal and spontaneous remarks in conversations. But we did use some standard questions, and we coded and counted responses. I give estimates of the results for some of our questions.

The world views of many of the people interviewed were traditional. They claimed to believe that whatever they did, they could not change the fate of the child. However, this reply could easily be a conventional cover for non-action; we do not know how literally they take this idea. As expected, this view of causation is more common among people living in extended and semi-extended families.

They claim that they start fasting from the age of ten or eleven; with few exceptions, the Sunni believe that a woman has a duty to fast in pregnancy or in the post-natal period. Alevi villages do not require fasting for men or women.

We asked informants to react to a number of general statements. In the Ankara villages, only half, most of them women, agreed 'It is possible to be a good person without strong religious beliefs' ('*Kuvvetli dini inançlar olmadan da, iyi insan olunabilir*'). Most agreed that 'Whatever you do for your child, you cannot entirely change morbidity, mortality or survival'.

To the proposition 'You can prepare your own future', ('*Kendi geleceğini kendin hazırlayabilirsin*') there were some paradoxical responses; most of the women and some of the men were undecided. But everyone agreed 'You cannot change what God has written.'

(*'Allahın yazdığı yazıyı değiştiremezsin'*).

(3) A Young Mother's Autonomy

The status of the child's mother in the family and in the community is very important for health-seeking behaviour for the child. She is not autonomous (Delaney, 1987 and 1990; and Chapter 10), but is always controlled and supervised directly by her mother-in-law and her husband, and by other members of the family and the community. For her to extend her relations outside the home is quite impossible. She cannot easily take her child to a doctor, particularly a male doctor, by herself. It is still true for some men, though this is an extreme formulation: 'If a man hears a woman's voice for more than one minute, it is fornication'. In spite, or because, of this high degree of control, most mothers said that the most reliable person, and the best adviser for them, was their mother-in-law.

Most women and men agreed strongly that 'a woman should tell her ideas only to her husband'; 'a woman cannot travel alone'; and also 'only a man can make the right decisions'. Again all these types of belief are very important for the mother's behaviour at the time of a child's illness. Some men said that 'rural women cannot travel alone, but educated women if married, and with an occupation, can'; some women expressed anxiety saying : 'What can I do, if something happens to me?'

A woman's age, and the number, age and particularly the sex of her living children influenced a woman's status in the family and the community, although this varied considerably with the locale, the community (particularly between ethnic groups), the household, and the individual. Women normally go through four stages in their life cycle:

(i) 'young *gelin*' , aged 15-30, - lowest status (son' s wife in an extended family).
(ii) 'middle-aged' , aged 30-45, - medium status (wife in a nuclear family).
(iii) 'mature', aged 45-65, - highest status (first lady) (grand-mother in an extended family).
(iv) 'old', aged 65 respected but not powerful (great grandmother in an extended family).

In short, the status of women, and the values and norms about, and behaviour towards health, and particularly children's health, change more slowly than other social aspects of Turkish rural communities, such as integration with modern urban centres, male education, and so on (Akşit, B., Chapter 13).

B. Steps in health-seeking behaviour

Researchers in various countries (Igun, 1978; Kroeger, 1983) have developed models of the stages of the health-seeking behaviour of mature ill persons. My model here is concerned with the behaviour of members of relevant households, and of the wider community, towards the health of children under five. In their models, the starting point is the illness and curative behaviour, whereas mine combines prevention with cure. Our research suggests the following steps of health-seeking behaviour for children under five.

(1) Physical, environmental, and sanitary conditions
Although there was general awareness of the correlation between 'dirtiness' and illness, it did not extend to an understanding of the causative role of germs and viruses. Concepts such as 'germs' and 'hygiene' are not well developed. The use of soap is not widespread.

Those families with an external locus of control and a strong belief in God's will, are less concerned with personal and environmental sanitation, thereby increasing the likelihood of childhood diseases.

(2) Caring for the child
According to the interviews, the main causes of these illnesses are cold and heat; lack of proper diet, and lack of clothing. For many respondents, the lack of proper care was due to having too many children. In Sivas and Van only one group of women in one of the villages mentioned cleanliness and germs, but in Ankara considerably more mentioned it promptly. The responses of groups to questions about germs varied greatly. They find the concept 'germs' abstract, and their concept of cleanliness was highly relative. Clearly, these populations are unaware of many crucial aspects of hygiene and germs. Moreover, hygiene cannot be provided by merely 'knowing the rules'. Some respondents said: 'It is necessary to keep things clean, but that is very difficult here.'

The common explanation of the cause of illness is an imbalance of hot and cold; this is widely reported from other countries (Helman, 1986). People get diarrhoea from being subject to too much cold or too much heat; and pneumonia from extreme cold. Most of the preventive measures put forward by the people were as follows:

The child should be dressed according to the weather, and should be protected from the cold.
Some families will not even wash their child' s face for fear that they will catch cold.

We used some probing questions. For example, when asked, 'When your child is sick, do you, as a family, continue eating out of the same dish or do you separate the sick child's plate, glass, and cutlery?', some replied: 'Oh, those poor kids! That is still our child. We cannot discriminate like that. We cannot be so mean to our children.'

In both Sivas and Van, but more often in Van, we were told that many families did not want to have their children vaccinated, saying: 'What can vaccination do against illnesses given by God?'

This might of course be a defence for people's fear of vaccination and the trouble it causes, such as high fever and uneasiness of the child following vaccination.

(3) Symptoms and signs of illness

Crucial symptoms of ARI (i.e., rapid or laboured breathing, wheezing, and stridor) were not well conceptualised and known by the people interviewed, although they were aware of differences in breathing.

Many respondents said that the symptoms were fever, chest congestion and coughing for respiratory infections; and fever, watery and frequent stools for diarrhoea.

When asked what they do when symptoms such as fever and coughing appear, most of them said: 'We take the child to a doctor'.

These responses to a great extent represented what people thought ought to be done, and probably is done by young adults with few children who live very close to a local health centre and have some level of education. However, for others, especially those living some distance from health care facilities, and who are poor and relatively uneducated, these responses are suspect. Therefore, to get more accurate information, we went deeper in more casual conversation. Our results are presented in the following steps.

(4) Home remedies

When symptoms appear, people respond according to their social position, their available resources, the proximity and cost of health services, and the degree to which they take the symptoms seriously. Home based remedies are used first.

In general, the people interviewed knew about treating a feverish child by uncovering him/her and applying cooling agents (e.g., rubbing with alcohol or a wet cloth). Warming the child's back and giving cough syrup are widespread practices to treat coughs. Cough syrups given to the child are generally purchased from a pharmacy or left over from previous illnesses. Coughing, like intestinal parasites, is not thought to be a serious symptom because it can occur in anyone at any time. Only if the child has a prolonged fever will the parents be concerned enough to seek help outside the home.

I cannot refrain from giving one description of a treatment related by a paternal grandmother while I was in Sivas:

> The child coughed all night long until the morning. Now what was I to do here on the top of the mountain? What was I to give the child? I couldn't find anything, so I gave the child some Linvarin (a deworming agent for veterinary use). I melted it down and gave the child two spoonfuls of it. Thank God, the child opened its eyes and 'shone'!

(5) Pharmacist as Consultant

As Hardon has pointed out (1987) among Filipino villagers, it is very common to consult the pharmacist before visiting the doctor and to begin treatment with 'pharmacy medicine'. Often an assistant with no formal education plays an important role.

The following statement by a pharmacist indicates his role clearly:

> People respect the pharmacist more than the doctor, here. They come to us before they go to the doctor anyway. If their problem is something beyond us, we refer them to the doctor. Otherwise, we help out with minor things. Actually, if we didn't refer them, the patients wouldn't go to the doctor.

(6) Waiting for recovery

We asked how long people waited before taking the child to a doctor. There was considerable delay between the appearance of symptoms and a visit. Some respondents said, 'We take him/her right away'; but as conversations continued, we got responses like the following:

'The child has to stop eating and drinking completely before I take him/her to the doctor. We don't have the means.'
The following words by one of the women were also significant: 'Don't you think we have any understanding? We don't have any means, so we can't take them to the doctor'.

We conclude that the period before children were taken to a doctor varied significantly with economic capability, ease of transportation, and perception of symptoms. People with the lowest socio-economic status, the greatest transportation difficulties, and who were least able to recognise key symptoms waited the longest. 'Educated' and 'western' parents with better resources responded quickly.

(7) Deciding to take the child to the doctor

Responses to the question about who makes the decision to take the child to the doctor varied between 'mother-in-law' and 'father-in-law', mostly the latter. In extended and semi-extended families, the fathers' fathers were very significant. Most of the men interviewed gave their father as the decision maker.

In a group, a grandmother had the following to say: 'While we are around, the child' s mother and father will have no say. They are just kind of auxiliary caretakers.'

We surmise from these comments that it is men rather than women who have the final say on visiting a doctor; and rarely a young child's own mother; in extended families, virtually never.

(8) Evaluating gender and birth order

Findings from international research on child survival indicate preferential treatment (Levine, 1987; Scrimshaw, 1978). Our research confirmed this finding, particularly in Sivas and Van. Older people generally said that they do not discriminate between children, whereas the younger women said that sons are more valuable.

From these interviews, it was possible to reach the general conclusion that a first or only child is the most valued. If there are three daughters and one son, the son is most valued; but if there are three sons and one daughter, then the daughter is highly-valued. Nurses, in general, said that there is a preference in favour of sons, whereas some of the doctors said that there is no significant difference.

However, some groups expressed quite different views. For

example:

> Sons are very important. When we get old, it is the son who will look after us.

It is my observation that the Ankara people seemed more equal in their treatment of sick children.

It is impossible to think that discrimination is unconnected with social security, and with having too many children.

(9) Which doctor?

Those respondents with a health centre in their region generally said that they made use of this service. Many people in the villages of Sivas said that they attended hospitals for health services. Several informants in Sivas also said that they went to private doctors in Sivas city centre. In contrast, several people in Van and Ankara said they first went to the local health centre, and then if necessary the doctors at the health centre referred them to larger health institutions. 'If the child is really sick, we take him/her to a private doctor, and if only a little sick, we take him/her to the hospital.'

People who were employees of establishments which had insurance could make use of hospitals run specifically for them. Other comments included complaints that, because hospitals are very crowded, children do not receive adequate care. Informants said that doctors generally have neither time nor patience to examine the patients sufficiently, nor to explain the illness and how to take medicines. In this context, even though it is very expensive for them, people concluded that private doctors are better:

> Hospital doctors will not thoroughly examine the child's illness and tell you about it. They will examine the child perfunctorily, and the medicines they prescribe might or might not have an effect.
> Actually, although the private doctor is good in his own office, he will get nasty in the hospital.

(10) Pharmacist as Dispenser

When we first asked, 'Do you purchase all medicines that the doctor prescribes and give them to the child in the way and at the times instructed?', virtually all groups claimed to do so: 'We take every medicine that the doctor finds necessary.'

But, when we pressed for more clarification, the responses were very different: 'We consult the pharmacist. We take whichever medicine is most effective and cheap.'

Generally, people with insurance purchase all the medication prescribed. Pharmacists or their assistants dispense medicines for parents who buy them with their own money according to the stage of illness of the patient, the dispenser's own judgement, and how much the parents can afford.

Both the pharmacists and their customers reported that fever and pain-reducing medicines, and cough syrups, are frequently purchased.

(11) The uses made of medicines
One major and crucial question is how people actually use the medicines which they have purchased. Even those who purchased all the medicines prescribed, did not necessarily use them appropriately. 'When the child's complaint or coughing stops, we interrupt the medicine. If your child begins to cough, we give the medicine to you, and if the other guy's child coughs, we give it to him.'

To understand better why such practices occur, we asked health centre doctors whether the use of medication was sufficiently explained to their patients. They replied: 'The use of medicines varies according to the severity of the illness.' 'People refrain from giving medicines, so that the child will not get used to them' .

Differences between men and women, and between the research sites were interesting; Sivas and Van men did not seem to know much about how medicines are given to their children whereas almost all women, and the men in Ankara, knew that they were not giving them correctly.

Of course these eleven stages do not necessarily occur in every illness, but generally the model fits well enough. Variations from the patterns described depend on the kind of illness; or the sociocultural, economic, and demographic characteristics of individuals, households and communities, and on the health service.

Some Problems and Suggestions

The present research was based on qualitative methods, based on 'rapid assessment procedures' used in anthropology (Pelto and Pelto, 1978; Folch-Lyon and Trost, 1981), medical sociology (Patrick and Scamber, 1984), and medical anthropology (Scrimshaw, 1989; Scrimshaw and Hurdato, 1989). The methods we adapted to this research ran into problems.

1. The organisation of 'focus groups' based on the criteria of age, socioeconomic status, and the number and age of young children was difficult. Some of these groups were too large.

2. Some were shy and reluctant to come to meetings. The poor, and the less articulate tended to be excluded as potential hosts and informants by the *muhtars*. These are often precisely those in greatest need of services . In planning similar research, more time and effort should be given to organising groups and selecting households with special needs.

Informants were also influenced in their responses and comments by informal controls in the immediate social situation; not only their perception of the researchers, but of the 'significant others' who were present at every point in the interviews and discussions.

3. Most young parents who had children under five lived in extended or semi-extended families. So it was difficult to find truly independent nuclear families, and hence the variation was limited. On the other hand, 'nuclear' families - particularly in urban areas - have also to be studied in the context of production of health for children under five. Moreover, the children of many of them are raised by the maternal parents if the mother works outside the home.

4. The methods to be used, and the place, time, and duration of the study therefore require careful attention. In order to gain understanding of peoples' attitudes and behaviour, researchers should reside in the community for as long as possible; and to maximise validity and reliability multiple methods of data collection should be used, from a single population.

5. Lastly, physicians and other health personnel should try to understand and use the results of this kind of study in order to reach the people. To ensure this, research on health issues should be carried out and analysed by teams of health personnel and social scientists, (Pflanz, 1975) and very firmly incorporated in the training of doctors and other professionals.

Note

1. The economic condition of families cannot be measured adequately, particularly in a one-day visit. So we evaluated the condition according to our impression of the presence of TV, refrigerator, sewing machine, radio, cassette-player, and their general conditions - food, clothes and so on.

| 12 |

The Genesis of Petty Commodity Production in Agriculture

The Case of Turkey

Çağlar Keyder

In this paper I discuss the formation of the present agrarian structure in Turkey, which is characterised by the predominance of small farmers or petty commodity producers. I argue that the rise of family farms, as against capitalist agriculture, was not inevitable, and that genetic determinism is not a sufficient argument in understanding their emergence. This paper sets out an agenda for discussing the point of transition when alternative outcomes were possible and the conjuncture in which small ownership gained the upper hand.

I

When we look at Turkish village studies of the 1940s, it is obvious that both the village community which was the social unit, and the households which were the economic units, operated very much in the 'traditional' mode.[1] The village was often the only life-world, and all national and world concerns were filtered through its structure; market transactions were few and infrequent; most of the output was for the household's own consumption or for local exchange; hardly any of the productive inputs required for a technology of wooden plough and a team of oxen were purchased from outside the domestic sphere. The procurement of credit, usually through some form of usury, was a local affair; a significant degree of reciprocity operated in the obtaining of commodities and labour from outside the household. Furthermore, there were only a few regions where a labour market operated to some extent via temporary migration. These were distinguished by geographical proximity to large cities and to historically established connections. The picture is one of arrested development - in the exaggerated words of an American observer, nothing much seems to have changed since Hittite times (Thornberg et al., 1949).

This is not to say that all regions in Anatolia were equally closed and isolated from the market. There were certainly regions which, since the early nineteenth century, had been open to commercialisation, where households bought and sold and made production decisions according to market prices.[2] These, however, were in a minority: in most of the interior, especially after the demographic catastrophe of the 1914-1922 period, closed village societies and subsistence-oriented peasant households were the rule.

By contrast the literature of the 1950s is full of descriptions of market adaptation, new inputs and changing technology, the importance of banks and other formal credit institutions, and, of course, the beginnings of urbanisation.[3] In the 1950s the Anatolian peasant seems to have resolutely started on a road towards commercialisation of output, of inputs, and of his own labour. The manifestations at the macroeconomic and sociological levels of this new momentum are well known. Agriculture began to receive the attention of post-war governments, in part due to the pressure of American development agencies. After 1946, the Republican People's Party was more willing than any time before to appease the peasantry; they accepted the recommendations of visiting experts to channel the new foreign funds into rural development. Tractors and other machinery began to arrive in Turkey after 1948, accompanied by various schemes were also initiated to increase agricultural productivity.

The full impact of this new orientation, however, was not felt until the early 1950s when the populist Democrat Party came to power, receiving most of the peasant vote. It was then that a credible commitment to rural development emerged and land reclamation received a new impetus. New land was opened up because of the promise of the market and because credit became available; tractors made the move technologically possible. As a result of the great expansion of land under cultivation, and with the help of good weather, output increased rapidly. Terms of trade had initially been favourable to agriculture due to the Korean War boom. Subsequently, the inflationary policies of the ruling party continued to reward the electoral loyalty of the peasants.

There are two additional factors which should be added to the picture. First, the labour market became much more extensive for individuals living in the rural sector. Opportunities for seasonal work increased, labour demand in the cities made migration practical and shanty towns began to develop. Even if the number of individuals who actually moved remained limited, permanent and temporary migration became an option that households could realistically include in their income-earning strategies. In other words, the labour of some of the household members could potentially be remunerated elsewhere, not only on the farm. Second, the physical possibility of movement increased, both for persons and goods. The road network received a good deal of public investment. In imitation of the American mode, with its emphasis on the motor car and derision of railways, and responding to the advice of the foreign aid establishment, which favoured such market-expanding infrastructure, after 1950 the ruling party made the rapid social integration of the Anatolian countryside one of its major aims. Parallel to the expanding road network, individuals purchased trucks, cars, vans, and buses to carry persons and goods to and from markets. Tractors and their trailers also served this purpose.

Physical movement, the existence of input and output markets, and the availability of work outside the village increased the ability of peasant families to specialise more effectively. Production, however, was still based on the predominance of unpaid household labour, and household income derived preponderantly from household production, using means of production owned by the family. The transition, therefore, took place in the degree of market integration which in turn provided the impetus for all other changes. Money income allowed the purchasing of simple manufactures which might earlier have been locally or even domestically produced. Specialisation could advance and with it the ability to calculate on the basis of comparative costs and prices. Hence, the market-integration process briefly described here provided the initial push which set commoditisation on its path.

II

This description of the threshold of the 1950s is very much in the conventional mould of commercialisation or commoditisation approaches.(Vandergeest, 1988). At this level of identification of the transitional mechanisms there is not much difference between the modernisation (commercialisation) and Marxist (commoditisation) frameworks. In both, a peasant economy is shown to prevail at some anterior period which is then gradually penetrated by the market. Eventually outputs, inputs, land and labour become commodities, and the accounting logic takes hold. Small producers find themselves in a competitive economy where they must make rational decisions and accumulate in order to survive. In the Marxist version peasants are said to become 'petty commodity producers', situated in and dominated by a capitalist social formation (Friedman, 1980; Bernstein, 1988). Through self-exploitation, community reliance, and sheer tenacity when it comes to property, petty commodity producers are able to survive, although they are unable to hold on to the value they create.

The modernisation approach treats the same transition as the liberation of the rational calculator. The peasant, breaking out of the shackles of tradition concretised in the village society and kinship relations, emerges as a farmer who responds to prices and potentially becomes an atomised citizen operating in modern society. It is true that this interpretation is much more optimistic in its appreciation of the transition from 'peasant' status, but aside from the nature of the analytic tools involved, there is not a radical difference between the commoditisation and the commercialisation perspectives on the process of transition. For this reason I will confine my critique to the Marxist approach of transition to 'petty commodity production'.

The often unelaborated model of the 'rural society' existing before the transition posits a village community which is necessary for the survival of a peasant household. The peasant household enters into a spectrum of non-economic relations with the rest of the community in order to sustain itself as an economic entity. In other words, the simple replacement of the material inputs into the production process, and the physical reproduction of the members of the household, often require the networks established through the rural society. In most arable agriculture, there are tasks that require co-operation, either in the form of communal participation (clearing of land, digging ditches, and so on) or in the form of labour pooling and reciprocity (in the harvesting season, for example). Furthermore, in open field regimes and rotational cropping and fallow, corporate decisions have to be made or community custom has to be respected in order to make the system work. A second type of consideration derives from the requirements of mutual assistance within the community. A bad harvest, the death of a cow, an illness, an extraordinary tax, may easily push a peasant household below the line of accepted subsistence, or make it deficient in terms of the inputs required for purposes of reproduction. Under such circumstances the community (or the real and fictive kinship unit constituting a segment of the community) is the first line of defence. There may occur a borrowing of inputs, of money, or a deficit in the exchange of labour, all designed to temporarily sustain the peasant household in distress.[4] It is not necessary that such exchanges are expected to be, or in fact are, strictly reciprocal. There are other currencies available and one well theorised model suggests that the obtaining of political power in exchange for the redistribution of surplus is perhaps the most common exchange encountered within peasant societies.[5]

These peasant relations end when the market replaces the community as both the source and the measure of economic reproduction. From the point of view of the household, the crucial differences derive from its participation in commodity circuits which require a notion of calculation, rationalisation, and maximisation, a nexus between the internal balances of the household and the market logic of an external economy. Products and credit are measured in prices - in money terms - more definite, variable and closely watched than before. Even when reciprocity continues, there will be implicit prices attached to various kinds of labour or goods that are exchanged.[6]

The foregoing story of the destruction of the 'natural economy' of the peasant through the penetration of the market is of nineteenth-century origin and found its full Marxian expression in Kautsky's

Agrarian Question. (Banaji, 1976). It later became the starting point of Lenin's analysis where the market provided the solvent of the rural society which would then undergo a transition toward differentiation and class polarisation (Lenin, 1964). The important dimension which constituted the proximate political reason for both Kautsky's and Lenin's interventions in the debate, was the relationship between the domination of the market and class formation. In other words, it was the impact of the destruction of the rural society on agrarian classes in which Kautsky and Lenin were interested. As Carol Smith has observed, the curious point about their (but particularly Lenin's) analytic approach was the dominance given to market relations as the determining instance of class formation (Smith, 1984). In other words, according to Kautsky and Lenin, the history of the German and the Russian countryside in late nineteenth century was not one of class struggle; it was rather one of progressive commoditisation.

A similar bias is apparent in the contemporary debate concerning commoditisation and the genesis of petty commodity production, in that the market mechanism is uncritically accepted as the determinant of the transition from peasant to petty commodity production.(Friedman, 1980; Kahn, 1982). In fact, however, it is not at all certain that this transition is either unproblematic or inevitable. Simply because petty commodity production was the historical outcome, we cannot argue that it followed inevitably from the destruction of the peasantry. Commoditisation may result in capitalist landownership rather than family farms; if petty commodity production does prevail this is due to the political struggle unfolding in favour of small ownership rather than a bias in market relations towards one type of property relations versus another. The factors which determine whether capitalist agriculture or petty commodity production emerge out of the peasant background are those mediated by and directly emanating from the state. Essentially, they result from the class struggle; although it must be remembered that the actions of the state do not directly reflect the balances obtaining in the class struggle. Especially in the case of what may loosely be called 'modernisation from above', the state has its own agenda that it pursues with a relatively high degree of autonomy.

My argument may become clearer by reference to a well known debate in the literature.[7] The transition from feudalism to capitalism has been a privileged field of study and a point of reference for various approaches in historical Marxism. In the celebrated *Science and Society* debate the principal sides were defined according to the weight they attached to the role played by the rise of trade and markets relative to that of class struggle. In the more recent 'Brenner debate' as well, the major discussion revolved around Brenner's attempt to bracket the role of the market (and of population dynamics) within a context of class struggle and state action.(Aston and Philpin, 1985). Both of these debates referred to the parallel antinomies of circulation vs. production (where class conflict was located) on the one hand, and state vs. the economy on the other. In the discussion of transition to petty commodity production, however, circulation (the market) and the economy are taken as unproblematic determinants. By presenting the economy, or even the market, as autonomously providing sufficient impetus to propel the transition, the political dimension has been ignored. It is my intention to point to ways in which class struggle and the state may be brought in as explicit variables in understanding this other transition.

III

Peasant societies move slowly. Property structures and class relations tend to be perpetuated over generations as long as the ultimate reference of non-economic power, the state, retains its relations with the powerful groups. A greatly increased level of integration into markets introduces a new logic, that of the economy, and opens the route towards a potential transformation of the social relations governing the peasant society. The old balances may be disrupted and new arrangements may emerge to accommodate the economic reality. But since all sides involved will attempt to benefit from the newly emerging opportunity, the moment of transition is characterised by 'undecidability'. The old order will have to change, but it is not clear in which direction. For this reason it is not possible to read off the post-transition structure from the contours of the pre-existing agrarian society. To put it differently, it is at the moment of transition that class struggle and the intervention of the state gain additional importance because they may now play determining roles in designing the new relations of power.

A good example of an explicit class struggle and state intervention was provided by the experience of south-eastern Anatolia during the 1960s, a case studied by Nur Yalman.[8] Unlike most of western and coastal regions of Turkey, the market integration of the south-eastern region occurred in this later decade, and it was at that conjuncture that some landlords attempted to enclose their possessions by driving out their tenants. These tenants were not contractual renters of land, rather they paid traditional dues to the landlord (of the order of 10-20%of the output), but otherwise enjoyed full rights of possession on their plots. As commoditisation spread and production for markets became attractive, some landlords purchased tractors and attempted to establish capitalist agriculture, an option which would not have been feasible before markets in commodities and labour became widespread. In most cases the attempt failed because the villagers resisted the landlord, who could only maintain his farm by recourse to armed retainers and government troops. Changes in the political climate as well as the difficulty in keeping the peasants out at gunpoint eventually led to settlements where some aspiring landlords left the village and former 'tenants' became full owners. In other words, in many villages of the Southeast, the successful struggle of the small peasants forced the would-be capitalist landlords to give up their project, and also persuaded the political authority implicitly to shift its support away from the landlords.

The transition experience of the rest of Turkey, while not so dramatic, still reflected the prevailing balance of social forces. In terms of historical background, landlordism did not have as much a chance in the rest of Turkey as it did in the Southeast. Social differentiation was either less prominent or was based to a much smaller degree on the hereditary control of land. It would therefore seem that the chances of success of a capitalist transformation from a peasant background would be limited even if the moment of transition opened up all options. Nonetheless, an important battle concerning property relations in the countryside occurred immediately after the end of World War II, at the beginning of what I would like to identify as the 'decade of transition' (1945-55). I am referring to the acrimonious debate around the land reform legislation of 1945 (literally the Law for Providing Land to the Farmer), which became the test case and occasion for the factionalisation of the ruling party and its eventual split.

It is possible to argue that the struggle around this legislation was a proxy for other fights, and that there was, in fact, no grounds for a land reform, since landlessness was not a widespread phenomenon.

This perspective would lead to the conclusion that the debate occurred in the ethereal realm of politics, and its bearing on the real property relations was accidental.[9] On the other hand, if we adopt the view outlined above, i.e. that conflict intensifies during the period of transition because the balance of forces is being redefined, then the political struggle emerges in a different light. It is the particular course of the transition to a commoditised countryside which is being disputed. The proponents argue about the direction of state intervention during a period of much accelerated commoditisation, and not about the preservation or destruction of patterns of ownership of the previous period. In other words, what we observe during this debate is the reflection of a class conflict directed at determining the outcome of the transition. The land reform bill was designed precisely to ensure the continuation in the countryside of property relations dominated by small property, while its rejection might have opened the way for a capitalist transformation. Hence the bureaucratic wing of the ruling party which defended the legislation did so with the intention of foreclosing the capitalist option. The reform would pre-empt the 'provincial notables' in their probable bid to seize the new market opportunities.

Although the legislation passed in a diluted form, it clearly recognised that new lands which were to be opened up would go primarily to peasants who held little or no land.[10] In fact, land distribution, or rather the ratification of the reclamation process in accordance with the new legislation, was already under way by 1946. The significant point about this reclamation was that the expansion of the land under cultivation served to increase the number of small owners. By 1963 the number of owner-occupied holdings had increased by one-third, from 2.3 millions in 1950 to 3.1 millions.[11] The true significance of such an outcome becomes more clear if we consider the counterfactual alternative, i.e. if we suppose that all the new land was appropriated by large landlords. In this case there would have been at least 800,000 families in the countryside (this is the number of new owner-occupied units set up in the period) who held no or little land, and the newly enriched landlord class would have found it possible to engage in large-scale agriculture employing wage labour. Instead, a widely dispersed pattern of landownership made the emergence of permanent wage labour in agriculture highly unlikely, and the period 1945-1955 witnessed the consolidation of petty commodity production.

A further element in the political reflection of the class struggle was the conversion of the new opposition party (Democrat Party, founded in 1946) to the cause of the petty commodity producers. Although the founders of this party had initially been in the 'provincial notable' camp and had opposed the 1945 legislation, the exigency of popular electoral contest quickly won them over to wooing the most discontented segment of the population: the rapidly commercialising peasantry. First in 1946, and then in 1950, the peasantry voted in reaction against the wartime policies of the single-party government which had imposed on them forced sales, confiscations, and arbitrary exactions carried out by the gendarmerie and the tax collector (Pamuk, 1988). When the Democrat Party came to power they had no choice but to deliver on their election promises, a task made immeasurably easier because of the American funds and their intended destination. Hence the new availability of credit, various purchasing schemes which developed to support the small producer, and the continuing policy of ratification of land reclamation, acted to reinforce the outcome of the transition against the option of capitalist enclosures. This decade of transition succeeding the War, under the rule first of the Republicans then the Democrats, effectively put to rest the old canard of a politically dominant landlord class.[12]

IV

A significant dimension of the involvement of the state in the constitution of either petty commodity production or capitalist agriculture concerns the definition and determination of property rights. As conservative theory recognises, the principal prerequisite of the capitalist model of possessive individualism and accumulation is absolute and enforceable private property rights. A brief look at the legal arrangements concerning land ownership in Turkish history shows that the advent of such property rights was rather late. Although legal reformism and adoption of western laws arrived during the Tanzimat period, Ottoman bureaucrats were uncomfortable about the institution of private property in land. The 1858 land legislation was ambiguous in its stipulations and full of restrictions which made the alienation and concentration of agricultural land difficult.[13] Hence, with some exceptions, the 1858 legislation tended to preserve the status quo as far as agrarian property relations were concerned. Besides, potentially cultivable empty land in Anatolia remained abundant and under state ownership. Following a time-honoured tradition individuals could open up, appropriate, and take possession of state land. Together with the rather high ratio of land availability to population in Anatolia, the *de facto* reclaimability of state land made the ambiguous 1858 legislation operate predominantly in favour of consolidating peasant rights.

The demographic catastrophe (McCarthy, 1983) of the First World War and its aftermath made the situation even less conducive to the establishment of private claims on landed property because the real conditions of possession were so fluid. In fact, the vast movement of populations resulted in the abandonment of up to one - fifth of the cropped land in Anatolia and its subsequent seizure by the remaining population in a rather haphazard fashion.(Keyder, 1981; Tekeli, 1990). As is well known, there is no enforceable law of property in the frontier and the situation that characterised Turkey in the 1914-1924 period could not have been very different. As Greeks and Armenians died, departed or were expelled in haste, most immovables were abandoned with no clear principle to govern the massive transfer. Without the availability of labour-saving technology, the decline of population from seventeen to twelve millions resulted in the shrinking of land under cultivation. Hence, the concrete application of the 1926 Civil Code, which made property rights much more absolute than previously, could not have been very extensive, simply because the resources to bring all the land under cultivation were lacking (Arıcanlı, 1991).

This situation continued into the 1930s, when market opportunities declined, terms of trade turned against agriculture, and most Anatolian households moved towards greater subsistence production. Various taxes were imposed on the peasantry which, together with the decline in money incomes, resulted in the indebtedness and insolvency of poorer peasants. Consequently, poorer peasants were forced to sell their animals which left them only the choice of accepting sharecropping status, working on the lands of wealthier peasants (Keyder, 1983). Hence, the second decade after the end of the First World War could not have been a propitious period for the enforcement of individual rights in land either. The commercial incentives were not present, and sharecropping introduced an element making possession a rather fluid category.

The importance of the decade of transition between 1945 and 1955 is that individual property in agricultural land finally became established. The expansion of the market made factors of production valuable, and land became a sought-after commodity because it produced marketable output. More land could not be cultivated, however, unless labour-saving technology was introduced. Tractors supplied precisely such technology, with the consequence that all the readily reclaimable land was in fact opened up during the 1950s. Land under cultivation had increased during the first two decades of the Republic, more or less in tandem with the growth in population. Between 1948 and 1956, however, land under cultivation, in total, increased by 57 per cent and per rural dweller by one-third.[14] As easily reclaimable land became more difficult to find, the state also became jealous of its ownership, especially of forest land, and took measures to deter clearing. Meanwhile, the common grazing land of the villages shrank, leading to a collective outcry against its private appropriation. In addition, favourable terms of trade and growing commoditisation increased the money income of the poorer peasants and vitiated the conditions that had led to sharecropping arrangements. The reclamation of land especially benefited such poor sharecropping peasantry, and the practice gradually declined. Hence, the material conditions for the establishment of a stable private property structure had obtained during the decade of transition.

On the legal front the crucial development was the Law for the Distribution of Land to the Farmer. As I have said, the implementation of this legislation consisted mostly of ratification of individual appropriation of previously public land. What the state did was to consolidate the already existing situation by sending to Anatolian villages commissions which were empowered to register the property situation *as related to them by the villagers*. Even where cadastral registration was not completed the countrywide situation was such that the much advertised news of these travelling commissions sufficed to lay out the conditions for the subjective awareness of property claims. In other words, during the early 1950s, the overwhelming majority of Turkish peasants actually became, or were expecting to become, legal owners; or had subjectively and inter-subjectively accepted a village structure in which property (in the modern capitalist sense of private and individual ownership) was a definite and demonstrable category. No longer were property rights relative, dependent on prevailing power balances, or negotiable: they now became absolute, and land turned into a commodity. From this point on, in most of Turkey, land could not be appropriated by a would-be capitalist landlord. The exceptional south-eastern case has already been discussed, and even in that region the period of transition and 'undecidability' had ended by the 1970s and property rights had been established, usually in favour of individual households.

The two fundamental features of petty commodity production are commoditisation, and land (or means of production) ownership by the household. For this reason, the legal recognition of private property and its inheritability is definitionally a necessary component of the establishment of petty commodity production. It is this ownership which allows petty commodity producers (or farmers) to control their own labour, to improve their means of production, and to engage in productive accumulation. Individuals or households do not invest unless they are certain to reap the benefits, i.e. unless they are certain that the fruits of their accumulation will accrue to them or their estate. In other words, the legal ratification of absolute individual property (through a change in the state's conception and enforcement of property rights) is a requirement for the establishment of petty commodity production.

We have already seen that commoditisation makes a transition out of 'peasant society' possible, but it does not determine whether the transition will be towards owner-occupied or labour-employing holdings. I have argued that there is a class struggle involved at this transitional juncture: for petty commodity production to be established the outcome of this struggle must favour small cultivators and preclude capitalist enclosure of the land. As in all political conflict the nature of the intervention of the state, either as relatively autonomous from the contesting parties or as a reflection of the balance of forces, will be crucial in determining the outcome. The argument concerning property rights further underlines the importance of the state in the emergence of petty commodity production. In the case of Turkey the state intervened at the moment of transition in order to preclude the capitalist trajectory. If the state had chosen at this moment to honour dubious claims (as it did in the Southeast in the later decades) or to delay the ratification of small ownership, the outcome might have been different. There are also historical cases when the state intervened *after* the transition in order to reverse a path already taken. This is the example of land reforms which created petty commodity producers in contexts as diverse as Mexico, Korea, or Egypt. In terms of its effective outcome, the role that the state played in Turkey was equivalent to a land reform. The difference was that it occurred before the capitalist option was given a chance.

V

There is a social dimension to the recognition of property rights which refers to the legitimacy of the private appropriation of land. As is well known, the Ottoman self-conception and practice militated against the notion of private appropriation of land.(İnan, 1991). The legitimacy of sultanic rule and the notion of justice propagated by the ruling class made land into a public trust. For this reason, it was one of the great turning points in belief when absolute property rights were accepted by law and by the citizenry as legitimate. The distance from patrimonial or communal types of property to the exercise of individual property rights cannot be traversed by simple decree; the change involves the subjective acceptance of private appropriation. It may be argued that the conditions most conducive to the subjective acceptance and inter-subjective recognizance of individual property arise when benefits are to be reaped most widely. While the acclamation of capitalist landlords' property as legitimate may not come readily, the transition from peasant holdings to petty commodity producers' farms does not have to pose the same kind of difficulty: the social acceptance of property rights would be most readily forthcoming in the case of land that is divided up among direct producers who all command resources sufficient to control their own labour. Legal change bringing forth such circumstances, will have the greatest measure of success.

What petty commodity production represents in terms of specific ideology and political behaviour is much debated and usually explained in structural terms. The two genetic factors which were discussed above, namely, the establishment of individual property and the state's ratification of the outcome of the class struggle in favour of petty commodity production, may illuminate another facet of this specificity. The first allows the development of a fiction of equality where every household is an owner, and therefore an equal participant in the market. Hence a 'simple market society'

(Macpherson, 1962) is upheld, the defence of which encourages petty commodity producers to justify their seemingly irrational attachment to their independent status. This status becomes an effective obstacle to the development of capitalist relations, has its own peculiar pattern of accumulation, and has political and ideological effects on the national unit which are different from either peasant or capitalist agriculture. The second factor, i.e. the involvement of the state in the genesis of petty commodity production, determines the evolution of a curious interdependence and a continuing relationship between the two parties. State policies ensure that farmers enjoy reasonable economic health and seek to orientate them. On their part, perhaps more than other social groups, farmers expect as their right, and agitate for, favourable political intervention. In Turkish history since the 1950s these two factors and their effects have been felt acutely and politicians have ignored the strength of petty commodity producers' ideology at their peril.

Notes

1. See for example, Tekin, 1934; Boran, 1945. Also see the following village studies all in *Sosyoloji Dergisi*: Göknil, 1943; Ülken, et al.,1950; Demirkıran, 1952.
2. Commercialisation started during the nineteenth century in the coastal areas; first the Aegean, then the Black Sea and the Mediterranean.
3. For overviews see, Kanbolat, 1963; a report on research conducted by members of the Faculty of Political Science in Ankara, 1954; Tanyol, 1958-59. For ethnography of specific villages see, Kurhan, 'Eskitaşlı köyü monografisi', 1955-56; Yörükan and Cebe, 'Catak köyü araştırması', 1955-6; and Tütengil,1955-6.
4. Stirling, 1965 provides an excellent description of such a village community.
5. I am referring to the literature on clientelism. See, for example, Gellner and Waterbury, 1977.
6. For a description of such reciprocity in the Turkish context see Sirman, 1988.
7. The debate and additional articles can now be found in Hilton, 1976.
8. Yalman, 1971; for a more recent account see Akcay, 1985.
9. For two analyses of the same event with different emphases, see Birtek and Keyder, 1975; and Keyder and Pamuk, 1984-85.
10. The standard left interpretation is that the legislation was a failure although 433, 117 families received land through it in the 1947-1972 period; Taraklı, 1976, p.117.

11. Based on 1950 and 1963 agricultural censuses. Türkiye Cumhuriyeti, D.İ.E., 1956, 1965.
12. For the full argument see Keyder, 1987.
13. Barkan, 1980; also Gerber, 1987, whose argument is similar to mine.
14. Calculated from T.C.D.İ.E. *İstatik Yıllıkları*, various years.

13

Studies in Rural Transformation in Turkey 1950-1990

Bahattin Akşit

Autobiography and Rural Transformation

My first encounter with the world was through a village socio-cultural milieu. I was born, in 1945, into a village located in the interior Aegean region of Western Turkey. However, my first encounter with the idea of rural transformation, and its success or failure, was in 1955-56, when I was a fourth-year student in the only elementary school of my village. This was not through 'modernisation theory', nor the various versions of 'underdevelopment theory', but through a short story by a Turkish writer, A. Nesin, a master humorist of the contemporary Turkish transformation; a spontaneous 'culture critique', not the academic formulations to which I am now professionally committed (Wolf, 1982; Worsley, 1984; Giddens, 1984; Sahlins, 1985; Akşit, 1985).

I describe the scene, and those present, as I remember it.

My oldest father's brother's son, a teacher trained in the village institutes, *köy enstitüleri*, during early 1940s; my oldest brother, trained in a vocational technical school and the army, during the middle 1940s, and just back from Korean War; my second oldest father's brother's son, a second year university student at the medical school in Istanbul; and my older brother, a first year university student at the forestry engineering faculty in Istanbul are, all together, repairing our radio in our newly constructed tile-roofed house - one of the few tile-roofed houses in a village of 300 households, in Denizili, Western Turkey. My father, a rural religious leader, *imam (hoca)*, educated in a *medrese*, during the 1920s, continuing the *medrese* education tradition of his father and older brother, was also in the room; together with my mother, and an illiterate daughter of an elementary schoolteacher who also had a formal Muslim education.

At one point, I started reading aloud to those present in the room, and especially to my parents, a story titled *Medeniyetin Yedek Parçası* (Spare Part of Civilisation) from a book, *Yedek Parça* by Aziz Nesin (1955), which had been brought to the village by one of my older brothers or cousins. The story, briefly, is as follows. A certain Hamit Ağa used to cultivate his eighty decares of land with a pair of oxen. However, under pressure, from his son, recently back from his two-year service in the army as a driver, from his daughter and her husband - both village institute graduate teachers - and `finally from his wife, in a rat race with the neighbours, he bought a tractor. He sold his pair of oxen, and got a loan from the bank. Before he could save up to pay the first instalment, however, a part of the machine broke in a tractor race. The search for the spare part cost him ten decares of his land. Fuel plus the instalment cost some more decares of land. Then another part of the tractor broke. The spiral of the search for spare parts and selling pieces of land ended with Hamit Ağa selling most of his land, and then destroying the machine and liberating himself from the oppression of the 'civilisation machine', *medeniyet makinası*. The story ended with Hamit Ağa telling his adventure in the village coffee house. All of us in the room, and especially my parents, burst out laughing. To this day, I remember this episode and the tension built into it very vividly.

Towards the middle of the 1950s, 40 thousand tractors, 2 million wooden ploughs and 950 thousand iron ploughs were owned by 2.5 million peasant households cultivating 200 million decares of land. Ours, being a mountainous forest village, had very little prospect of acquiring tractors till the middle of the 1970s, when the total tractor stock of Turkish agriculture had jumped to 200,000. Why, then, was there such tension in the story, turning into laughter? Frankly, I do not know. What I know is that this puzzle fed my curiosity about rural transformation in Turkey. However, despite my birth into a village and thirty years of research, my understanding of this transformation is still partial. What follows is a short story of the transmutation of theoretical frameworks used in the course of thirty years of research on the structure and transformation of Turkish villages. Unfortunately, I can answer only a few of the questions that it raises.

Modernisation in the Villages in the 1950s

The 1858 Land Edict, my grandfather's decision to split from a tribal nomadic (*yörük*) community by settling in our present village, and to get interested in religious (*medrese*) education all happened in the nineteenth century. The Ottoman state had embarked upon a thorough reorganisation of military, administrative, juridical and educational systems with a programme of 'modernisation from above' (Trimberger, 1978). The Ottoman system was becoming peripheralised within the world system (Keyder, 1987). A secular educational system was first consolidated at the centre, and later extended towards the periphery. The Islamic educational system was thus undergoing reform and modernisation. These changes parallelled the expansion of modern science, and of communications systems (Gilsenan, 1982; Akşit, 1985 and 1991; Mardin, 1989). In this paper, my aim is not to detail the history of modernisation in Turkey before the 1950s. The point is that during the hundred years preceding the arrival of commodities and tractors in a remote village of Western Turkey, private ownership and formal education, both Islamic and secular, had been consolidated. The elementary school was established in my village in the middle 1930s, which was when my family shifted from religious to purely secular education.

As argued by Keyder (1983a), the consolidation of small land ownership was not a linear evolution but a cyclical one, in the hundred years preceding 1950. However, the cyclical course of alternation between small land ownership and large land ownership might not have been due only to the Kondratief cycles in the world economy, as argued by Keyder; but also to the domestic cycles of the households as described by Stirling (1965) in two Central Anatolian villages. The combination of the two cycles might, together with other factors at community, region and state levels, explain the unevenness and inequality in land and power distributions in the villages in 1950s and in the decades preceding it.

As in many countries, agricultural surveys and censuses in Turkey are not very reliable. However, I believe that the data obtained from these surveys can give us some idea of the number of village households in rural Turkey, the total amount of the cultivated area and some estimate of the land distribution at regional and national levels. For example, on the basis of the 1952 Agricultural Sample Survey by the State Institute of Statistics (D.İ.E., 1965, p.91), it can be calculated that, in the beginning of 1950s, 62 per cent of the 2,527,000 village households owned or farmed less than 50 decares of land each (the average being 23 decares); their share accounts for only 19 per cent of the 194 million decares of total cultivated land that was estimated on the basis of the sample. While the village households owning and/or farming 200 decares or more of the land (the average being 553 decares) was only 6 per cent of the total number of village households, their estimated share in total cultivated lands was 41 per cent of the total (D.İ.E., 1965). This rather high inequality in land distribution was paralleled by the inequalities in power and prestige (Makal, 1950 and 1954; Stirling, 1965; Akşit 1988).

The transition to multi-party democracy, the commercialisation of agriculture, and the transformation of village households into commodity producers has greatly increased in the forty years since the Second World War. Curiously, the establishment of the Democrat Party (DP) in 1946, by some prominent MPs, among whom were some well-known large land owners, is consequent upon a dispute within the ruling Republican Peoples Party (RPP) over some articles of Land Reform Law of 1945. After its establishment, the new party organised opposition to the secular, etatist, bureaucratic, modern–isation-from-above policies of RPP, and it was predicted by the secular intelligentsia that landlords, merchants and sheikhs were going to take control of the country. Contrary to these fears, and in conformity with villagers' hopes, the changes were in the direction of the preservation of newly-won rights of private ownership in land, the disintegration of landlordism and the beginnings of the emergence of well-to-do farmers from among the ranks of the villagers, with small and medium size land ownership. After its accession to power by winning the 1950 elections, the DP did not carry out the programme of land reform, which the founders of the party had opposed. Nevertheless, DP governments did not halt the distribution by the Land Reform Commission of 24 million decares of state lands to landless and small-land-owning peasants. (Taraklı, 1976). What is more important is the DP's tacit encouragement of unofficial land reclamations. Through these reclamations a further 85 million decares of state lands were appropriated by middle and large size land owners, some of whom became tractor owners. The number of tractor-owning farmers increased from 16,000 at the beginning of 1950s, to 40,000 at the end of 1950s (D.İ.E.; Margulies, 1985).

Parallel with these developments, agricultural credits to modernising farmers were increased. The area of irrigated lands was expanded. The transportation network was improved so that the regional markets became more and more integrated. The secular academic middle schools, vocational technical schools, teacher training schools, and half-secular half-Islamic İmam-hatip schools had reached the villages. So had the mass media (Akşit, 1991, Mardin, 1989). All these factors contributed to further integration of the villages with towns and cities, and thereby opened the way for rural to urban migration and the consequent heterogenisation of the cities along the following lines; '*hemşehrilik*' (belonging to the same place) '*gecekondu*', (squatter housing), occupation, income, lifestyle, ethnicity, religious commitment, class and political party affiliation (Akşit, 1985). Although a pluralistic democracy has not yet been fully consolidated in Turkey, its beginnings lay in the1950s, with the explosion of rural to urban migration.

At this point I give another reminiscence from 1956-7, the last year before I went to high school in Denizili town. A prominent Democrat Party MP, a medical doctor from a nearby town, where my father had had his *medrese* education in close association with the MP's father and uncles, had arrived in the village for election propaganda. A boy, a few years older than me, the son of a previous *muhtar*, had covered himself with flags of the opposition party, the RPP, and challenged the revered MP. To my surprise, the MP's reaction was very mild; he merely suggested that one flag was enough to signify party affiliation. This was democracy, I reckoned, and I admired his democratic posture, although my sympathies were with the RPP, perhaps because of my older brothers' opinions. However, I was surprised a second time a few years later, when I read in the newspapers that the same MP, whom I had admired for his democracy, was the head of a commission to prosecute opposition leaders.

Some Debates on Rural Transformation in the 1960s

On the basis of 1963 Agricultural Census (D.İ.E., 1965), it was estimated that the number of land-owning and farming households increased from 2,527,000 in 1952 to 3,100,000 in 1963. The level of inequality and unevenness in land distribution, from 1952 to 1963, remained more or less the same. Yet, those owning and/or farming less than 50 decares of land, increased from 1,570,000 (62%) in 1952 to 2,132,000 (69%) in 1963, while their share in total cultivated land also increased from 19 per cent to 25 per cent. The number of those cultivating more than 200 decares of land decreased from 146,000 (6%) in 1952 to 116,000 (3.7%) in 1963; while their share in total cultivated land also decreased from 41 per cent to 28 per cent (SIS, 1965 and 1973; Margulies, 1985; Akşit, 1988a).

Stirling (1965, pp. 133-147), combined the domestic cycle of the households with what he called the cycle of wealth to suggest one possible source of the differentiation in land ownership/cultivation, wealth and power of households and lineages. In order to highlight inter-village variations, by taking into account only population and land ratios, he developed two village models. In the 'land in plenty' village, as the sons of the household head grow and get married, the amount of cultivated land and wealth, and household power and prestige increase, bringing the patriarchal household head into the top circle of the influential and powerful in his village. When the head of the household dies, the household is split among his sons, and the cycle starts all over again, giving rise to fluctuations in upward and downward mobility of households. This was a stage in the social history of many villages which lasted to the 1950s. By this time, due to a decrease in death rates and an increase in the number of households in the villages, the land that could be reclaimed had reached its limits. His second model is the village with 'land shortage'. In this type of village, the households get poorer at the end of each domestic cycle due to the division of land among heirs, unless there is massive seasonal or permanent migration, or technological innovation. Did these developments also contribute to differentiation and polarisation in the villages? Almost certainly not.

In the 1960s, Kıray was active in formulating a research programme which hypothesised land and class polarisation through such processes as commercialisation, cash crop production, mechanisation, and credit usage (Kıray, 1968). These processes were seen to operate in villages characterised by large land ownership, where polarisation was going to take place between the large land owner and share croppers. Similar developments would by implication have taken place in a large number of villages where land ownership was much more evenly distributed, if differential access to credit, modern technology, credit-debt relationships with merchants or usurers had persisted and expanded during 1960s and 1970s. The class polarisation in 'large land ownership' villages through the transformation of the feudal landlord into an agro-industrial capitalist and of share-croppers into wage workers was argued by Kıray on the basis of data collected from an irrigated cotton producing village in Adana, a province in the south-eastern corner of the Mediterranean coast of Anatolia (Kıray, 1968; Hinderink and Kıray, 1970). The 'small land ownership' villages were undergoing changes, but were not yet differentiated and polarised. The usury relationships between merchants in towns and cash-crop producing farmers in the villages were depicted by Kıray (1968) as mechanisms of 'depeasantisation' and polarisation. Massive rural to urban migrations during the second half of the 1950s and 1960s were sure evidence of 'depeasantisation'. The question was whether these processes of depeasantisation were accompanied by the processes of differentiation among the villagers in terms of acquisition and use of modern agricultural technology and inputs, marketing of the produce, employment of wage labour leading to differential land ownership, 'capital' accumulation and stratification along class lines.

In order to investigate these and related questions, I entered the field of rural sociology in 1966. In that academic year, with a group of other second-year students on a course taught by Kıray at METU, I surveyed two cereal producing villages in interior Anatolia, near Ankara. The findings of the research revealed that in villages, households had been integrated to some degree with the regional and national markets, thereby increasing the proportion of marketed products as well as the share of extra-household and extra-village produced goods in total household consumption. In each village 8-10 tractors had been bought by relatively large land owning farmers. National education, communication and transport systems were established in the villages, integrating them with Ankara. Clearly, there was a differentiation among villagers in terms of the amount of the land farmed, tractor ownership, integration to urban centres, wealth and power (Akşit, 1967). Yet this differentiation did not amount to the predicted class differentiation and polarisation.

Expecting to find more evidence to support the prediction of capitalist differentiation, I went to Antalya in the summer of 1966, and selected two cotton producing villages, one dominated by large land ownership and the other by small land ownership. The large land ownership village had been settled during the 1940s by a semi-nomadic tribal group, *yörük*. The head of the group, *aşiret reisi*, was transformed into a village landlord, *ağa*, while the other members of the community became sharecropping and small land owning peasants in the course of settling permanently in their former winter encampment. The fields were acquired by clearing the bush. During the 1950s and the first half of the 1960s, they had undergone a second transformation. The landlord had become an agricultural capitalist, cultivating cotton on 5,000 decares of irrigated land, using 11 tractors, and employing permanent as well as seasonal workers. The sharecropping and small land owning peasants had continued to reside in the village, cultivating cereals in non-irrigated lands, using ox-drawn ploughs. In 1966, they bitterly complained to me that they had been displaced from the irrigated lands by the landlord and that they lacked even the ready cash to search for jobs in the city, let alone to defend their rights on the irrigated lands against the powerful and influential landlord (Akşit, 1967). However, the landlord was not powerful enough to evict the peasants from the village for a successful 'enclosure' of their land, as was the case in one of the Adana villages studied by Hinderink and Kıray (1970).

Before the 1950s, the households in the small land owning village were producing cereals mainly for subsistence, and sesame as a cash crop. The individuals and households were differentiated by gender, age, prestige, lineage size and power similar to the dimensions depicted by Stirling's first model. However, the production and marketing of sesame as a cash crop during the first half of the present century led to some capital accumulation by some of the relatively larger landowning villagers, who became merchant-grocers, *bakkals*. These local merchants acted as intermediary links between regional, national, and international markets and the village households. In the course of the 1950s and 1960s most of the households shifted to cotton production as a cash crop. The relatively large land owning *bakkals* invested their accumulated capital in tractors and trucks. A few other households which happened to possess relatively more land also bought tractors and trucks. Land that was not already occupied and farmed by the increasing number of oxen or horse-drawn ploughs was occupied and farmed by the new tractor owners. The size of land farmed by these tractor owners increased to 400-500 decares of land by 1966. Some of these lands were reported to have been bought from other villagers. These rich farmers, who appeared to me as capitalist farmers at that time (Akşit, 1967), employed tractor drivers with long-term contracts. They also employed, for hoeing and cotton picking, short-term workers from within the village and seasonal migrants from outside. Below this top group of modern 'capitalist' farmers, a stratum of farmers cultivated their medium-sized lands with shared or hired tractors. They employed only short-term seasonal workers for hoeing and cotton picking. They achieved some capital accumulation, aiming to buy tractors in the coming years. The third stratum consisted of farmers owning smaller amounts of land, hiring others' labour when needed and also hiring their labour out when their own work was not pressing. Their income from wages was not essential for their livelihood. The fourth stratum of households owned either very small amounts of land or none at all, at the time of the interview; or their fathers being alive, they had not, yet, inherited any land. Wage labour was their main source of income. As I observed at that time, these young workers were informally organised into small groups of work gangs hoeing and cotton picking (Akşit, 1967, 1985).

The findings of Kıray's and my own research carried out within a capitalist transformation perspective was generalised beyond the case study villages by Avcıoğlu (1968). This view was opposed by a different argument, emerging from an analysis of 1952 and 1963 agricultural censuses; and a debate, within the Turkish left, on whether Turkish agriculture is dominated by feudal and semi-feudal relationships or by capitalist relationships (Boratav, 1969-1972; Seddon and Margulies, 1984; Aydın, 1986). Boratav argued that Turkish agriculture was dominated by petty commodity producers, who made up 75-80 per cent of all farms and households, and that merchant capital agriculture in its various forms had developed on this basis.

One of the convictions that emerged from my own village studies and the research by others during 1960s was that the strategic influences coming to villages were from towns and cities. Hence my research interest shifted to middle-sized cities during late 1960s and the first half of the 1970s. My MA and PhD research was not on the villages but on change and cleavage in towns and cities (Akşit, 1971, 1985).

Research on Paths of Rural Transformation During the 1970s

The D.İ.E. Agricultural Census of 1970, revealed little change in land distribution since the 1963 census. The number of households and/or farms remained, more or less, the same. (Çınar and Silier, 1979; Varlier, 1978; Akşit, 1988a).

The argument which asserted the dominance of small commodity producers in Turkish agriculture gained greater prominence during the 1970s. Varlier (1978) and Çınar-Silier (1979), using census and other survey results at the macro level, emphasised the persistence of inequality in land distribution, a small increase in the percentage of small land owners and/or cultivators, and a slight tendency towards land concentration. These macro-level findings were complemented by Keyder, Akşit and others' findings on paths of rural transformation (Akşit and Keyder, 1981; Akşit, 1985; Keyder, 1983b).

The research undertaken with Keyder and other members of the research team provided me with re-visits to the villages in Antalya province; and new research on villages in Adana, Dıyarbakır, Ankara, Çankırı and Uşak. The major encounter for me during this research was my re-visit, in 1979, to the two villages in Antalya Province. In 1966, the large mechanised capitalist cotton farm, and the non-mechanised cereal producing sharecroppers and peasants coexisted in the same village. In 1979 the cereal-producing peasants were transformed not into wage workers but into small and medium land owning farmers cultivating cotton in irrigated lands, with approximately eighty tractors, all bought during the thirteen years which had elapsed since the time of the first visit (Akşit, 1985). A third crucial transformation has taken place in the social history of the village. The Turkish Irrigation Department constructed a dam to irrigate formerly dry cereal land, and make possible the cultivation of cotton by the peasants. This was complemented by the primary commodities boom in early 1970s. The land reform discourses of governments after the 1971 military intervention encouraged the peasants' entrenchment on the lands they had been cultivating. The democratic competition between parties in the middle of the 1970s for votes further enhanced the transformation of medium peasants into commercial farmers. Finally, the election of a medium commercial farmer as the village *muhtar*, displacing the landlord's headman, uprooted the almost customary political domination of the landlord-capitalist. He was dead by 1979, and had left the farm to three university educated sons. All these events and circumstances not only interrupted the possible enclosure moves of the landlord to evict the peasants, but also enhanced the processes of transformation of subsistence-producing peasants into commodity-producing modern farmers.

The other cotton producing village in Antalya province also displayed, in 1979, the interruption of class polarisation and land concentration. The heads of households of the top group of capital accumulating, land enlarging and tractor/truck buying farmers were dead by 1979. Almost as if to illustrate Stirling's model of the dispersion of land, wealth, and power at the end of the domestic cycle, the top group of farmers were not there any more. At the bottom of the stratification hierarchy there were also some developments reducing class polarisation. The introduction of labour-intensive greenhouse gardening made small farmers less dependent on wage work. So the outcome of the transformations of the 1970s was differentiation, but not polarisation, of the village 'commodity' farmers. The accumulation potential of various strata in a cotton village in Söke, during the first half of the 1980s, is masterfully analysed by Sirman (1988).

Together with some other members of the research team, I travelled to Adana province to look for villages dominated by capitalist farms. Kıray and Hinderink's village, dominated by a large capitalist farm, was there; but in the village there had settled some 600 households, all migrants from south-eastern Anatolia. Another factory-farm in Adana province, very close to Kıray and Hinderink's village, demonstrated the workings of capitalist farms producing cotton and cereals as cash crops (Akşit 1985; Sirman, 1988). Further east in Dıyarbakır, we studied two villages where peasants producing for an overlord as sharecroppers had been transformed into peasants raising animals and participating in seasonal migratory labour for subsistence. These landless peasants coexisted in the same village with capitalist farms. Technology had brought tenant farmers from other provinces, and wage workers to man tractors and other machinery (Akçay, 1985, 1987, Akşit, 1985).

To find other types of villages with different paths of

transformation it was necessary to travel into the interior provinces of Anatolia. In a subdistrict of Ankara province, Polatlı, we studied a village where commercial wheat production and sheep raising have been main economic activities. In this village, the production of wheat by using tractors, mainly for market, was combined with the outmigration of some of the households into urban areas and the sale of their lands to those remaining in the village. This combination resulted in the emergence of a village structure, similar to cotton producing villages in coastal Antalya, consisting of more or less evenly distributed land owning family farmers engaged in commercial agriculture (Keyder, 1983b; Akşit, 1985).

In an interior Aegean province, Uşak, we studied a village with smaller lands not as fertile as those discussed so far. The households of the village were engaged in seasonal employment in the cotton producing villages of the coastal Aegean region during the 1940s and 1950s. During the 1960s and 1970s they stopped seasonal migration and diversified their economic activities in the village. In addition to the production of some cereals and garden vegetables for market, they started to grow poplar trees, and to raise bees commercially. The young women in the households also started to weave rugs and embroider clothes for city merchants. In another province in the interior Anatolia, Çankırı, we found a similar village, most of whose adult population was in the large cities and abroad sending remittances to elderly parents and to their own children living with their grandparents. There were also those in the village who bought tractors to cultivate cash crops such as lentils. If more households engaged in cash crop production emerge, the village might be transformed to one of the previous types. If, however, outmigration of adult population continues then the village might decline into a deserted ghost village.

I am usually asked why we described only three or four paths, or types, of transformation in rural Turkey. My answer is that such typologies are not intended to be logically tight and exhaustive, but to provide heuristic models for research. For example, Barrington-Moore, Jr. (1966) proposed only three paths of transformation from agrarian to modern industrial societies. His typology takes us beyond the histories of single countries and helps us to understand the liberal- democratic path of England, France and America in contrast to the authoritarian and labour-repressive regimes of Germany, Japan and Italy; whilst these two paths are, themselves, contrasted with the peasant revolutions in Russia and China. Turkish transformation and the experiences of many other countries do not exactly fit Barrington-Moore' s paths. Yet the typology is very useful in thinking about and carrying out research (Trimberger, 1978). Similarly, the experiences of many villages do not exactly fit into the paths of rural transformation we have formulated, yet our model is useful. For example, my own native village has a lot of similarities to the diversified village in Uşak. But in order to describe the extent of diversification in my own village, I must add the following activities to those in Uşak the following : cloth weaving with 70 power looms, owned and operated by young male household heads in putting-out arrangements with city merchants; raising cows in many households leading to the marketing of, in total, one ton of milk a day; ten large chicken farms; raising cucumbers for pickling and export in putting-out arrangements with city merchants.

Concluding Notes: Rural Transformation in the 1980s

1980 Agricultural Census data, collected by the interviewers of the State Institute of Statistics (D.İ.E., 1980), indicate that the percentage of land owned by those households owning more than 200 decares of land started to increase after two decades of decline. This percentage decreased from 41 per cent in 1952 to 28 per cent in 1963 and, finally, to the lowest level of 25.5 per cent in 1970. In 1980, however, it increased to a level of 35 per cent. Similarly, the percentages of households and/or farms cultivating more than 200 decares were respectively as follows: 5.8, 3.7, 3.1, and 6.1 per cent; indicating a decrease from 1952 to 1970 and then an increase in 1980. The number of households cultivating 227 million decares of land increased from 3.08 million in 1970 to 3.65 million in 1980. Although there is an increase in the amount of reported land area, in reality, the amount of land cultivated remained, more or less, the same; while half a million new households entered agriculture as new units. It is interesting to note that while there are significant decreases in the percentage of the number of smaller farmers and the percentage of the area they cultivate, there are definite increases in the percentages of middle and larger farmers and the areas they cultivate (D.İ.E., 1980; Akçay, 1985; Akşit, 1988). In a rural society where population increase and inheritance practices normally lead to fragmentation, such a development cannot be explained without the tendencies of land concentration concomitant with seasonal and permanent migration to urban areas.

Given the observations above, I attempt, (in the year 1990) a critical assessment of arguments about small commodity production, especially in its variants formulated by myself in late 1970s and early 1980s (Akşit, 1985), and by Keyder (1983b; 1988). I disagree with Keyder' s thesis of the entrenchment of small commodity production throughout Turkish agriculture during 1950s once and for all, except in eastern and south-eastern Anatolia. I believe that the 1960s and the first half of the 1970s were as crucial as the 1950s for the entrenchment of small commodity production and the defeat of landlordism; and for the subordination of merchant capital to industrial capital. I further believe that during the 1980s small farmers faced, and will continue to face, pressures of so-called structural adjustment measures, such as adverse terms of trade, and the withdrawal of price supports which have been in effect from the 1930s to 1980 (Gürkan and Kasnakoğlu, 1986; Boratav and Yalman, 1989). Moreover capitalist farms are not restricted to south-eastern Anatolia. This region' s large landlordism as the main path to capitalist farming is overemphasised by Keyder. Research shows that this region's experiences of transformation (Akşit, 1985 and 1990; Akçay, 1985 and 1987; Ertürk, 1987; Taraklı, 1976) are similar in many ways to those of other regions (Mediterranean, Aegean, Marmara and Central Anatolia) where capitalist farms exist alongside modern family farms. Furthermore, as argued by Hann (1984) for the East Black Sea coast, and by Sirman (1988) for Söke, and by myself for Antalya, small commodity producers or family farmers have been highly differentiated within, as well as between, the villages, forcing us to revise an emphasis on paths of transformation occuring solely at the village community level. Rural Turkey has left the tightly organised village community of peasants behind; fortunately, the highly atomised mass of family farmers with an ethos of 'amoral familism' (Banfield, 1963) is not widespread. The paths of transformation travelled by 40,000 villages and 3.5 million village households have been bewilderingly divergent and, it seems, the spectrum will continue to widen. This divergence is a fertile ground for research, and also, hopefully, for democracy.

| 14 |

Impact of External Migration on Rural Turkey

Nermin Abadan-Unat

The Turkish newspaper *Milliyet* reported a conversation between two Turkish migrants in Essen, waiting for a green traffic light who had lowered their car windows to talk (*Millyet*, 18/5/1990). 'Is there anything in your fax machine today?', 'No, nothing. Do you think something happened to my mother?' Both migrants had fax machines in their central Anatolian village homes. Now that Turkey has achieved a remarkable record in extending its telecommunication network to the smallest villages, the international telephone link, particularly with Federal Germany, is almost always blocked. Since regular daily contact with home had become a real need, a fax machine is the most convenient means to escape overloaded lines.

Nothing could illustrate better the real and deep changes that have taken place in recent years in rural Turkey. As Kıray rightly pointed out, 'Migration today is not simply an accidental movement to gain cash for a single expenditure such as buying an ox or saving enough for the bride price, it is the start of a new form of life!' (Kiray, 1976, p.210).

Turkish migration to Europe started timidly in the late 1950s, began to be sponsored by the State in the 1960s, and reached its summit in the early 1970s. Recruitment came to an end abruptly in 1973; but the European guestworker syndrome certainly did not end. It only changed character: from a temporary export of excessive manpower, it turned into a lifelong 'commuter/citizen' phenomenon, which brings a great number of indirect consequences and structural changes. Most participants of the first wave of Turkish migration, representing a true example of the Ravenstein two-step migratory model (a move first to the nearest small town and then to the larger city), emerged predominantly from urban communities. The second massive wave came mostly through a one-step move directly from rural communities to the cities of the West.

Available data confirm this change. While 53 per cent of the Turkish migrants in the Federal Republic of Germany in 1962 came from Thrace and Istanbul, in the peak years 1971-3 the share of migrants from urban centres fell to 27 per cent in 1971, and 21 per cent in 1973. In 1973, the proportion of migrants from northern Anatolia rose to 41 per cent from eastern and southern Anatolia, which at the beginning had sent no migrants, to 8 per cent each.[1]

One reason among others for the high number of rural migrants in Europe, particularly in Federal Germany, is the creation of the project known as Village Development Co-operatives. This scheme was launched by the Ministry for Village Affairs in 1962, and was intended to promote rural development via the contributions of prospective migrants. The idea was that all persons who founded such a co-operative and contributed financially a certain sum, pledging to continue this payment while abroad, were assured jobs after return, and shares in the enterprise to be created. In return, all members of these VDCs were granted priority to migrate. This scheme was increasingly used solely as a mechanism to jump the official emigration queue, which after 1965 exceeded one million. Members of these co-operatives, once abroad, did not fulfil their membership obligations, so that most VDCs had very limited resources to promote development. The scheme was phased out after 1969. The practice of sending migrants through the channel of the VDCs was encouraged by politicians of various parties, seeking electoral support by mediating for potential migrants. Another way used frequently by politicians was to obtain special status for a given community, based on the justification of natural disasters such as drought, flood or earthquake. In such cases, applicants bypassed the official waiting lists. Some potential migrants with relatives in priority areas moved to that area, and obtained a second residence certificate, thus increasing their chances of selection (Martin, 1991, p.29).

Besides these exceptional forms of recruitment, structural changes led first to internal, and later to external, migration. With the introduction of modern agricultural technology, cash cropping and new varieties of crops, the former tenant farmers were deprived of their position as sharecroppers in large and landowning areas and had to migrate to obtain urban employment. Urban industrial and administrative jobs, however, could not readily absorb all these migrants. Consequently many had to acquire marginal jobs, in the so-called informal economies, ready to move again for more secure jobs when and where they emerged. It is mainly these populations who have been pulled by the demand for labour in Western Europe. Rural to urban migration then, together with international migration, is the mechanism through which millions turned into uprooted populations and became 'outsiders'.

Monographs such as Yasa's research on the impact of migration on Ankara province (1979, p.17) confirm this trend. Both Yasa and later Kozak's research on Erzurum (1979), indicate that a great majority of migrants of these provinces came from villages. Yasa's survey gives 508 out of 605 male and 54 out of 65 female respondents coming directly from villages. A longitudinal survey covering a period of four years on returnees, carried out by Hönekopp from the German Employment Bureau, indicates that 44 per cent of the returnees he studied came from villages and small towns of up to 10,000 inhabitants. The distribution of these returnees according to their region of residence indicates that 23.5 per cent came from the Black Sea, 21.6 per cent from the Marmara, 17.1 per cent from the Aegean, 13.1 per cent from north central Anatolia, 10.4 per cent from south central Anatolia, 7.7 per cent from the Mediterranean and 6.5 per cent from eastern Anatolia (Hönekopp, 1990, Table 1).

Next to officially recruited workers, a considerable number of irregular, officially illegal migrants also went abroad under the label of 'tourists'. The survey Keleş, Penninx, Van Renselaar, Van Velzen, Yenisey and I carried out in Boğazlıyan (province of Yozgat), in 1974, indicated *inter alia* that 42.4 per cent of migrants abroad and 42.5 per cent of returnees had travelled abroad as 'tourists', and later looked for a job without any formal contract or work permit (Abadan-Unat, 1975, p.180, Table 5.2.2.1). Studies on Turkish migrants living in Sweden and Belgium revealed that in certain cases the process of chain migration - meaning the mediation of one person in favour of relatives and neighbours - resulted in a heavy concentration of migrants from one single community such as Kulu, province of Konya (in the case of Sweden) and Emirdağ province of Afyon (in the case of Belgium). In these last cases, the proportion of persons with a rural background was high.

After the end of recruitment in 1973, many migrants, particularly those who were employed illegally and did not benefit from social security coverage, decided to return. During these years various European countries launched policies to encourage their return. There were two types of return: officially encouraged and financed returns and individually motivated returns. Three major waves can be observed. First, early returns in the mid-1970s of predominantly unemployed, illegal migrants; second, returns in the late 1970s, mostly by male migrants who had preferred to stay alone abroad; and third, officially encouraged organised family returns in 1983/84, sponsored by the German and French governments using financial incentives. The second half of the 1980s also registered individually motivated returns, though on a lower scale. These movements make it possible to follow the changes which have taken place both for the returnees and for those left behind. The bridge between outsiders and insiders is in itself an important source of change, particularly in rural areas.

What have been the major implications of Turkish migration for rural structure? Among many changes in rural life I outline some areas where migration seems to play an important role.

Migration, Landownership and Depeasantisation

One dramatic change which migration, internal or external, causes, occurs in attitudes to the ownership of land, the value of landowning, and the intentions of villagers for land usage.

For those migrants who own some land, the change does not lie in a lack of interest in landownership. On the contrary, a considerable amount of new acquisition also takes place. Observers in Boğazlıyan report that some migrants have adopted a multi-faceted investment pattern. They have placed most of their savings in non-agricultural areas, buying shops or houses in urban areas, but they have also purchased farmland if the opportunity has presented itself. Apparently old proverbs such as 'Even a bad field gives more than a good brother' still retain their value. In explanation of their behaviour, these migrants asserted that although they do not intend to work as farmers, land provides security. Gitmez found in his survey that in three provinces, namely Bursa, Afyon and Kırşehir, a total of 26.6 per cent of investments went for the acquisition of a house or flat, 12 per cent for land, 10.3 per cent for a building plot.[2]

Migrants made considerable use of their right to import tractors. These they used for different purposes; leasing them, using them for transport of animals and persons, and eventually selling them for profit. In some cases the acquisition of a tractor served as a mark of prestige for the owner.

Similarly migrants also invested heavily in livestock. The attraction of such spending is that whatever work may be entailed can be performed by women left behind in the village, and that home consumption deriving from animals means appreciable cash savings. However migration also caused a growing unwillingness to perform traditional household duties. Women increasingly became, through the impact of remittances, convinced consumers. The Boğazlıyan study revealed that in those households where remittances arrived regularly and women were able to decide independently about the allocation of work, tasks such as herding, weeding, harvesting were turned over to hired workers from outside Yozgat. Thus in some cases external migration might lead to a new form of internal migration (Gitmez, 1983, p.198, Table 6.27). Illegal migrants, who abroad performed the most tiresome, prestigeless and dangerous jobs without benefiting from minimum wages and social security, were mostly unable to acquire land and were obliged to opt for some kind of marginal activity in urban areas. Such a situation was particular bitter for those farmers who, anticipating regular employment, had sold property to finance the voyage abroad.

Economic and Technological Changes

Since the major incentive for going abroad was the hope of securing new opportunities, the drive to save as much as possible was intense. This trend has been particularly high among rural migrants for whom a stay abroad was looked upon as a kind of prolonged, compulsory military service, during which one adopts a very frugal mode of life and saves in order to 'guarantee one's future'. Various empirical research (Abadan,1964; Kozak,1979; Yasa,1979; Kemiksiz,1989) indicates that single migrants were spending approximately one-third of their wages, and saving the remainder.

These savings were invested in several ways. Land was acquired, both as an 'investment in agriculture', in case of a return to the village of origin, and for a speculation in urban building plots. These undertakings created in the mind of the urban migrant a relevant change. They came to see their savings as capital, which might be used for different objectives. Thus the migrant worker of yesterday - without espousing the status and outlook of an industrial worker - transformed himself to a 'bourgeois/proletarian' (Penninx and van Velzen, 1975, p.286).

Rural migrants also invested heavily, for a while in shares in 'Workers' Companies', and in family owned enterprises, such as restaurants, petrol stations and the like (Abadan, 1972, p.3). Matching their investments new migrant families abroad, returnees and family members at home, acquired new habits of consumption, and the use of technological innovations. Turkey's telecommunication system has undergone a major improvement during the last ten years.[3] Almost every village in Turkey now has private telephone subscribers; the use of phone cards is now popular. Access to international communications channels has become a real need - direct oral contact with those members of the family who live abroad has replaced letter writing. This explains why the installation of a fax machine - although not common - is not an exception. The use of tape recorder cassettes for private letters is also extensive, and provides the illiterate or semi-literate members of the migrant's family with precious information. Cassettes are also widely used for religious sermons and political messages.

Among the items in most demand which migrants bring home, are TV sets, refrigerators and more recently VCR. A video recording of weddings has become almost a must nowadays.

Since the beginning of migration the acquisition of a car has been a major goal. Migrants of rural background wanted to achieve two things: first to operate a taxicab in the nearby town and to impress the home village with a symbol of their personal achievement. First they chose old, expensive cars - such as the Mercedes the novelist Adalet Ağaoğlu describes so marvellously in her novel *The Delicate Rose of My Imagination.* Later migrants opted for large station wagons, which permitted them to bring along huge quantities of gifts and goods. In some cases rural migrants have also imported pornographic tapes, to be shown in closed sessions to male audiences in village coffeehouses. Migration also partly affected the build-up of transportation and communications infrastructure. Special supplementary flights are put on for the *gurbetçiler* on the eve of religious or national holidays.

The concept of distance has changed. Stirling reports that before 1948, it took around ten hours by ox cart or donkey to cover the thirty kilometres to Kayseri from the village he lived in; and in the 1930s men walked for two weeks to find work in Ankara. Today Turkish workers are employed on five continents. Peasant women in *şalvar* and men with traditional baggy trousers are boarding planes for Stockholm, Sydney, Berlin. For them the sphere in which one earns one's bread has grown to a global scale.

Changes in House Building

For the migrants to save in order to improve the existing house or to build a house, or buy a flat, have remained to the present day top priorities. Keleş and Yasa report that approximately two-thirds of those migrants they investigated, invested around 63 per cent of their savings in home building (Kelso, 1975, p.289-90; Yasa, 1979, p.49). Unlike the old adobe or stone houses, the '*Almanya evleri*' distinguished themselves by their bright colours, often emulating the rainbow. These houses serve also to accentuate new patterns of social stratification in many villages. Villagers almost always choose the outskirts of the village for their new houses.

Although these houses have more rooms, thus permitting also more privacy, the household members sometimes continue to use only one room. Freedom of consumption does not always mean the liberty of choosing a different way of living. The other rooms are left for display - conspicuous consumption being the most convincing evidence of accomplished upward mobility. Migrants and their family members are anxious to acquire within their communities an image reflecting their newly gained affluence and prestige. This involves also purchasing new style furniture. Traditional handicrafts such as rug and kilim weaving for home needs, have almost completely vanished. These handicrafts are now flourishing in the Konya, Kayseri, Gaziantep areas for the hand-made market, mostly organised and financed by metropolitan entrepreneurs.The products are mostly sold in Istanbul, İzmir, and Antalya, and are aimed at foreign tourists' tastes. The migrants of rural background prefer to buy tapestries manufactured in Europe, often depicting Mecca. One can find such a wall carpet, even showing the Last Supper, in some Muslim homes.

Iron or wooden beds are among the first things migrant families buy after money becomes more abundant. Usually they are first occupied by the head of the household and his wife. Next come refrigerators and vacuum cleaners (Yenisey, 1975, pp.360-1). Together with investment in houses in villages and flats in small towns, the construction process has also changed. While previously villagers would build their houses with the collective help of neighbours, nowadays they use a qualified labour force. This represents of course the increase of GNP, but indirectly can also be related to the migratory process. In Boğazlıyan after 1968, labour and construction materials were secured from outside the district (Penninx and van Velzen, 1975, pp.280-1). Thus where external migration has among other factors induced large scale house construction, similar to the situation in agriculture, it has also partly led to some extent to internal migration.

Changes in Consumption

In villages where migrants have returned or where families with migrant owners are living, credit purchases are declining significantly. Bills are no longer paid only once a year, at harvest time. More meat, vegetables and fruits are consumed in village homes. In the past breakfast consisted of soup; today people take bread and cheese with tea.

Sources of energy have also changed. While in the past natural energy such as dried dung (*tezek*) was used predominantly, nowadays gas, electricity and bottled paraffin have replaced it. Similarly, more people eat around a table instead of sitting on the floor around a *sini* (large tray). Yasa (1979, p.139) reports that in the villages of Ankara, 23 per cent of the migrants were eating at the table, against only 7 per cent of the local population . The use of individual plates has also spread. Yasa reports that 29 per cent of the migrants, who previously ate from one common plate, have switched over to individual plates. Another 21 per cent admitted that they use different plates with guests, but continue to eat the traditional way when alone.

Changes in Values and Opinions

Differences between the evaluation of global issues by migrants and by non-migrants also serve as a measure of attitudinal change. Yasa established a self-weighting scale in regard to the most important foreign news and applied it to migrants and non-migrants. Although the Arab-Israel and Vietnam wars, and the landing on the moon were at the time of the survey the most important items in the news, the respondents gave other topics priority. The energy crisis in Turkey (36% migrants, 53% non-migrants), and the end of recruitment of workers by foreign countries (34% for migrants, 20% for non-migrants) came first and second. Both migrants and non-migrants displayed a rather restricted interest towards the Arab-Israel and Vietnam wars. (6% for migrants, 2% for non-migrants).

Attitudes toward fatalism and other-worldiness also show changes. Of non-migrants 86 per cent agreed with the proposition that a person's fate is predetermined at birth, but only 70 per cent of migrants. Similarly faith in other-worldiness - belief that real happiness can only be realised 'beyond' - found only 57 per cent approval with migrants, and 90 per cent with non-migrants (Yasa, 1979, pp.137, 138, 145). Of course one may also argue that perhaps these differences in attitudes existed before the departure of the migrants and were one factor in their decision to migrate.

Changes in the Family, Sex-Roles and the Status of Women

Empirical research on structural change within family life in general indicates that migration has led to a variety of fragmented family types. According to Kudat, twelve combinations can be deduced from three basic situations: (a) father working abroad, (b) mother working abroad, (c) both parents working abroad (Kudat, 1975; cf. Abadan-Unat,1977).

The two major reasons for this fragmentation have been, first, the regulatory policies of European host countries discouraging family reunion, and second, the strong desire to increase savings. Thus the families involved in the migratory movement accepted employment abroad, tried to secure employment for the marriage partner, and tended to leave dependants in the home country. As a result, family disintegration or fragmentation was the dominant pattern until the early 1970s. This pattern changed considerably after the end of recruitment in 1973 and particularly after child allowance allocation was increased for those children living with their parents abroad.

Thus after 1975 the exodus of rural women increased greatly. There, unprepared for life in industrial surroundings, some entered the labour market to the extent existing laws and regulations permitted them to work. Work in an industrial setting forced them to acquire a more precise sense of time than they were accustomed to, and to adopt values related to work discipline.

Marriage also changed. For example, a growing number among the younger generation refused to accept without objection pre-arranged marriages. Attitudes differ. Some younger migrants do not any longer follow blindly their fathers' choice, thus they contest the patriarchal authority. Others, particularly those living in closely interrelated ethnic enclaves, still carry on the endogamy rule. Some also continue to pay a bride price, which their larger financial resources enable them to meet (Kleff 1984, p.212; *Hürriyet*, 20/3/1981).

Yasa's survey, which was carried out in the mid 1970s contains interesting opinions relating to the freedom of action recognised for rural women. According to his findings, 14 per cent of the returnees did not object to their wives moving around in the village without their heads covered. Similarly, returnees approved to some degree mixed marriages, meaning marriages with foreigners. The rate of favourable responses in this regard was 8 per cent for sons, 3 per cent for daughters (Yasa, 1979, p.110). These attitudes may have changed recently for returnees due to the growth of fundamentalist ideology, both abroad and at home.

In a few instances, Turkish migrant married couples of rural background also faced reversal of role patterns. Such situations were not solved smoothly. An earning woman in Germany, for example, married a village man, who then had to wait a year before being allowed to enter Germany, and then on the condition that he did not have a work permit. In such cases, the transfer from plain peasant wife/mother to the principal breadwinner led to deep attitudinal changes. In many cases serious marital conflicts about expectations in regard to the duties of the wife, the care of children and the responsibility for household chores led to a dissolution of marriage (Nauck, 1985, pp.256-9).

However in cases without serious conflicts, particularly among returnees, recent research has shown that the migratory process did create some lasting changes. Kemiksiz (1989, p.187) states that, in 1988 among female returnees in Ankara, 58 per cent wanted to share the decision-making process with their husbands, 62 per cent were in favour of women working outside the home, 94 per cent condemned polygamy, and 80 per cent were in favour of asking the opinion of their children in intra-family matters. The great value and importance attached to education was also reflected in an almost egalitarian preference for university education of boys (68%) and girls (66%). Nevertheless the traditional role model for women, namely to be a mother and a homemaker, remained on a high pedestal. For the overwhelming majority this status appeared to be the primary goal and the only way to achieve happiness.

In sum, it can be said that the impact of migration on rural women appears to be relatively limited , particularly in cases of late reunion with the husband, and of no paid employment after reunion abroad. The general orientation of these women appears to be rather conservative, particularly among women living in ethnic enclaves with strong social control. By contrast, rural women who are left at home with permission to live alone with their children, apart from their husband's parents, have changed more radically. These women, during long periods of separation, acquired a relatively high degree of personal independence. They have been obliged during the absence of their husbands to assume new responsibilities and new tasks - running the farm, transactions at the bank or the post office to cash remittances, selecting places and types of schools for the children, leasing land, supervising house construction, organising social functions such as engagements and weddings (Abadan-Unat, 1988, pp.49-51).

The majority of returned migrant women have not displayed any strong motivation to develop further their new knowledge and experiences acquired abroad. It is also questionable whether such a learning process abroad has been beneficial. Although female returnees are clearly showing a certain degree of determination to shed traditional attitudes, the prevailing social controls, which since the adoption of compulsory religious education are constantly gaining ground, forces them to repress these aspirations. Thus the display and use of new consumption habits and the modernisation of the household constitute the major changes.

Changes in Political Attitudes

Migrant workers abroad, urban as well as those of rural origin, have been subject to depoliticisation. They were until recently excluded from the electoral process both at home and abroad. Sweden started to revise this policy by granting foreigners in 1975 the right to participate at local elections. Since then Norway, Denmark, the Netherlands and the Swiss canton Neuchâtel have also extended the right to participate in local elections. The length of stay required can be quite long; in the case of Switzerland, it is is 15 years. Published statistics do not provide evidence for the political behaviour of rural migrants from Turkey in these elections.

However there is some information on the participation rate in Turkish associations abroad. In the beginning these associations served as surrogate trade unions, but later acquired clear-cut political colours. These associations started to recruit members from well-organised networks, establishing a link with various regions in Turkey. Among the most important and energetic associations are those developing among specific ethnic or religious groups. These associations appear to function as interest groups, attracting members from specific minorities - Islamic sects, Islamic splinter groups, Kurds, and so on - channelling their need for belonging into a special ethno-religious identity. Extreme rightist, leftist and fundamentalist political parties at home, who are anxious to obtain financial and moral support from abroad, eagerly build up their networks with these bases. For rural migrants adherence to fundamentalist groups appears to have a special attraction (Gitmez and Wilpert, 1987, p.110, n. 7).

For returning rural migrants, political parties promoting private enterprise and conservative ideas, such as the Anavatan Partisi (Motherland Party), the Doğru Yol Partisi (True Path Party), and to some extent the Refah Partisi (Reform Party), seem to exercise an appeal. However returning migrants do not constitute in Turkey a noticeably distinct pressure group. The political parties do not look on them as active or influential; their existence passes unnoticed during electoral campaigns. The real target for all political parties remains the migrant groups abroad. Political leaders use all kinds of communication channels in order to obtain their support. This support translates itself into influencing their family members and their networks in Turkey.

Turkish citizens residing six months and longer abroad have been given the right since November 1987 to vote at any border crossing. But their political participation has been very low. At the general elections of 1989 a total of only 49,800 votes were cast, although the voting booths were set up at all airport entries and frontier posts six weeks prior to the elections. One might conclude by saying that rural migrants abroad are subject to an extreme degree of depoliticisation, which affects also their involvement in national affairs. This tendency can also be estimated by establishing the ratio of newspaper reading among migrants and the family members at home. This second group even in rural areas, pays more attention to political events than the returnees. Of course, the overwhelming role is played by television.

Social Mobility and Social Stratification

Although there is insufficient fieldwork carried out on social stratification, one might still state that the impact of migration on some rural communities has been a kind of social earthquake. While in the traditional rural community the ruling principle has been equilibrium and order, rural communities which were substantially involved in external migration are very different.

People living in such communities have acquired a different outlook on the world and their own life chances. Although different interpretations have emerged, it seems quite appropriate to say, in Schiffauer's words, that rural migrants have replaced their spatial outlook on the world with a time-related historical one. For some, history brings progress and development, for others decline (Schiffauer, 1991, p.365). At home they were peasants, abroad they became unskilled or semi-skilled industrial workers. Although their place in the hierarchy of jobs incorporated in the global market system forced them to perform jobs which the national workers were no longer willing to perform, at home these migrants looked upon themselves as 'achievers'. Yasa (1979, pp.82-3) tried to measure this mobility by applying a self-weighting scale. Accordingly 23 per cent of the returned villagers identified themselves with the upper-middle class, 50 per cent with the middle strata; only 9 per cent classified themselves under the label 'poor. Even if one cannot speak of a sharp polarisation between the '*Alamanyalı*' (those from Germany, even after their return from that country) and the indigenous, a major division has taken place. The majority of rural migrants consider themselves as belonging to the 'haves'. They look down on manual work, often even on agricultural tasks, they aim at self-employment and want to lead a comfortable, stress-free type of life basically by profiting from various rent-securing schemes. However, exposure to a different life style has not imbued these migrants with the desire to become innovators in their own community. Thus for most a frictionless co-existence emerges once the migrants of yesterday opt to return to their roots. Actually most of the rural migrants prefer to buy a home in the nearest small town, while retaining their land in the village of their origin.

Conclusion

External migration has caused in rural Turkey a chain reaction of social change; changes in the economy, in technological innovation, in telecommunication and transport, and finally to some extent in social stratification and political participation. It has produced individuals who, even if they totally rejected the alien, dominant culture of the host country, has espoused the orientation of individuals who act on their own.

External and internal migration together have also caused structural changes such as an acceleration in the exodus to urban areas. It has incited additional internal migration to satisfy new local demands for a qualified work force in construction and agricultural tasks.

At the individual level external migration has been instrumental in rural Turkey in giving birth to a different type of '*gurbetçi*'. Although these migrants adopted mostly a antipathetic attitude towards the population of the host country by rejecting the dominant culture, they still represent persons with a different outlook to world affairs. For them one of the remedies against the lack of opportunities and employment at home is the alternative of seeking one's daily bread elsewhere.

The rural migrant to Europe, who is named '*Alamanyalı*' irrespective of where he has been, is a new type in Turkish society. But the hopes and expectations planners attached to the experiences of these migrants have not been realised. Contrary to predictions, the experiences and new knowledge of these migrants have served only marginally in the development of Turkey's economy and society. But these people have gained a different dimension in empathy; they are able to imagine themselves on all the five continents of the earth. In order to gain prestige after having toiled over the years, they are investing both in lucrative as well as prestige objects such as houses, land, tractors, automobiles, modern furnished flats, and small businesses. For them, education also has become an area of investment; they consider social mobility for their children as the fulfilment of their own dreams.

Migration has left its impact also on the migrant's family, as Kıray (1976, p.224) stated so well 'The separate-house-in-the-village syndrome, has to be considered as one of the most important functional changes in the role of women, brought by migration in Turkey, as no law of the republican era could bring in change on such a scale!'. Rural migrants of today are more consumers than producers, more passive than active citizens, yet they have introduced a new life style into a large number of Turkish villages. Even those who do not assume the role of innovator, are instrumental in producing change.

Notes

1. Figures for 1962 from Abadan, 1964, p.26; figures for 1971-3 from R. Penninx and Van Renselaar, 1975, p.17. Table 1.2.4.
2. A survey carried out by Ali S. Gitmez and Czarina Wilpert revealed that in Berlin over 100 families from a single village from Erzincan had migrated - some 550 people; similarly 140 families (about 1,050 people) came from six villages of Urfa. See A.S. Gitmez and C. Wilpert, 1987, p.95 and Rex, J., et al., 1987.
3. The number of telephones per 100 persons was 2.90 in 1980, grew to 5.07 in 1985 and reached 15.27 in 1991. See special edition *İletişim Zirvesi Gazetesi*, May 13, 1992, p.3.

List of References

In a few cases it has not been possible to discover publishers and places of some publications. (Turkish Government Publications are under Türkiye Cumhuriyeti).

Abadan, N. *Batı Almanya'daki Türk İşçileri ve Sorunları.* Ankara: D.P.T. Yayını, 1964.

____. 'Le non-retour à l'industrie, trait dominant de la chaîne migratoire turque', *Sociologie du Travail*, 3, 1972.

Abadan-Unat, N. 'Implications of Migration on Emancipation and Pseudo-Emancipation', *International Migration Review*, 11, 1977.

___. 'The Socio-Economic Aspects of Return Migration in Turkey', *European Journal of International Migration and Ethnic Relations*, 3, 1988.

___., Keles, R., et al. *Migration and Development.* Ankara: Ankara University, 1975.

___. et al. *Turkish Workers in Europe, 1960-1975.* Leiden: E.J.Brill, 1976.

Akçay, A. 'Traditional Large Land Ownership and its Transformation in Two Southeast Anatolian Villages'. M.Sc. Thesis, Department of Sociology, Middle East Technical University. Ankara: 1985.

____. 'Türkiye Tarımında Büyük Topraklı İşletmelerin Oluşum Süreçleri Üzerine Notlar' 11, Tez Kitap Dizisi, 7, M.E.T.U., 1987.

Akşit, B. *'Türkiye'de Azgelişmiş Kapitalizm ve Köylere Girişi'.* Ankara: Orta Doğu Teknik Üniversitesi Öğrenci Birliği Yayınları, 1967.

____. 'Two Turkish Towns: A Study of Social Change, Class Structure, Commercial Involution and Industrial Underdevelopment'. M.A. Thesis, Department of Sociology, University of Chicago, 1971.

____. *Köy, Kasaba ve Kentlerde Toplumsal Değişme* Ankara: Turhan Kitabevi, 1985.

____. 'Kırsal Dönüşüm ve Köy Araştırmaları: 1960-1980', in *Türkiye'de*

Tarımsal Yapılar. Ed. by Pamuk, Ş. and Toprak, Z. Ankara: Yurt Yayınları/T.S.B.D. Yayınları, 1988.

____. 'Küçük Meta Üretimi, Sosyo-Kültürel Değişme ve Güneydoğu Anadolu Sulama/Kalkınma Projeleri', *Toplum ve Bilim*, 48/49, 1990.

____. 'Islamic Education in Late-Ottoman Medreses and Republican Imam-Hatip Schools', in *Islam in Modern Turkey*. Ed. by Tapper, R. London: Taurus 1991.

____. and Keyder, Ç. 'Kırsal Dönüşüm Tipolojisi', *Yeni İmece*, 1, 1981.

Akşit, B.T. 'Adut solunum yolu enfeksiyonları Sivas ve Van illerinde yapılan odak grup görüşmeleri'. Paper presented for the ARI Working Group. Ankara: Hacettepe University, March, 1989.

__ and Akşit, B. 'Social determinants of infant and child mortality in Turkey', *Social Science and Medicine*, 28(6), 1989.

Aksoy, A. et al. *Trabzon 89*. Trabzon: Küzey Gazeteciler, 1989.

Andrews, P.A. Ed. *Ethnic Groups in the Republic of Turkey*. Wiesbaden: Otto Harassowitz, 1989.

Ardener, E.W. '"Remote areas" - some Theoretical Considerations', in *The Voice of Prophecy*. Ed. by Chapman, M. Oxford: Basil Blackwell, 1989.

Arıcanlı, T. 'Property, land and labor in nineteenth century Anatolia', in *Landholding and Commercial Agriculture in the Ottoman Middle East*. Ed. by Keyder, Ç. and Tabak, F. Albany: State University of New York, 1991.

Aston, T.H. and Philpin, C.H.E. Eds. *The Brenner Debate: Agrarian Class Structure and Economic Development in Pre-Industrial Europe*. Cambridge: C.U.P., 1985.

Avcıoğlu, D. *Türkiye'nin Düzeni*. Ankara: Bilgi Yayınevi, 1969.

Ayata, S. *Kapitalizm ve Kücük Üreticilik: Turkiye'de Halı Dokumacılığı*. Ankara: Yurt Yayınları, 1987.

Aydın, Z. *Underdevelopment and Rural Structures in South-eastern Turkey: The household economy in Gisgis and Kalhana*. London: Ithaca, 1986.

____. 'Turkish Agrarian Debate', *New Perspectives on Turkey*, 1, 1987.

Banaji, J. 'A summary of selected parts of Kautsky's *Agrarfrage*', *Economy and Society*, February 1976.

Banfield, C. *The Moral Basis of a Backward Society*. Chicago: University of Chicago, 1963.

Barkan, O.L. 'Türk toprak hukukunda tanzimat ve 1274 (1858) tarihli arazi kanunnamesi', in *Türkiye'de Toprak Meselesi*, Istanbul, 1980.

Barrett, M. *Women's Oppression Today: The Marxist/ Feminist Encounter*. London: Verso, 1980.

Beck, L. *The Qashqa'i of Iran*. New Haven, 1986.

Beneria, L. *Women and Development: The Sexual Division of Labor in Rural Societies*. New York: Praeger, 1982.

___. and Sen, G. 'Accumulation, Reproduction and Women's Role in Economic Development' in *Women's Work: Development and Division of Labor by Gender*. Ed. by Leacock, E. and Safa, H.I. Massachusetts: Bergin and Garvey, 1986.

Benninghaus, R. 'The Laz: an example of multiple identification', in *Ethnic Groups in the Republic of Turkey*. Ed. by Andrews, P.A. Wiesbaden: Otto Harassowitz, 1989.

Berger, J. *Pig Earth*. New York: Pantheon Books, 1979.

Berkes, N. 'Two Facets of the Kemalist Revolution', *Muslim World*, LXIV-4, 1974.

Berman, P., Kendell, C. and Bhattacharyya, K. 'The household production of health: Putting people at the centre of health improvement'. Paper presented at a Workshop on Mother's Education and Child Survival. Ahmedabad: India, January, 1989.

Bernstein, H. 'Capitalism and petty bourgeois production: class relations and divisions of labour', *Journal of Peasant Studies*, 15, 2, 1988.

Bertan, M. and Guriş, D. *Türkiye de Çocuk Sağlığının Durumu*. Ankara: Hacettepe University, Department of Public Health, 1989.

Beşikçi, İ. *Doğu Anadolu'nun Düzeni*. Ankara: E. Yayiinları, 1970.

___. *Devletlerarası Sömürge Kürdistan*. 1990.

Birge, J.K. *The Bektashi Order of Dervishes*. London: Luzac, 1937, reprinted 1965.

Birtek, F. and Keyder Ç. 'Agriculture and the state. An inquiry into agricultural differentiation and political alliances: the case of Turkey, *Journal of Peasant Studies*, 2, 4, 1975.

Black-Michaud, J. *Sheep and Land: The Economics of Power in a Tribal Society*. Cambridge: C.U.P., 1986.

Blaschke, J. 'Einleitung: Zwischen staatlicher Planung und autonomer Organisation-Bruchstellen der Entwicklungs-politik' in *Bruchstellen: Industrialisierung und Planung in der Dritten Welt*. Ed. by Berliner Institut für Vergleichende Sozialforschung. Frankfurt\Main: 1981.

Boran, B.S. *Toplumsal Yapı Araştırmaları*, Ankara, Türk Kurumu,1945.

Boratav, K. *Gelir Dağılımı*. Istanbul: Gerçek Yayınevi, 1969-1972.

___. 'Türkiye Tarımının 1960' lardaki Yapısı ile ilgili Bazı Gözlemler', *Siyasal Bilgiler Fak. Dergisi*, 27, 3, 1973.

___. *Türkiye İktisat Tarihi: 1908-1985*. Istanbul: Gerçek Yayınevi, 1988.

___. and Yalman, G. 'A Study on the Political Economy of Structural Adjustment: Workers and Peasants During a Major Reorientation of Economic Policies Turkey 1980-1987'. Research paper Ankara: Türk Sosyal Bilimler Derneği, 1989.

Boserup, E. *Women's Role in Economic Development*. London: George Allen and Unwin, 1970.

Bryer, A.A.M. *The Empire of Trebizond and the Pontos*. London: Variorum Reprints, 1980.

____. and Winfield, D. *The Byzantine Monuments and Topography of the Pontos*. Washington: Dumbarton Oaks, 1985.

Bulutay, T., Tezel, Y. and Yıldırım, N. *Türkiye Milli Geliri (1923-48)*. Ankara: S.B.F., 1974.

Bumke, P.J. 'The Kurdish Alevis - boundaries and perceptions', in *Ethnic Groups in the Republic of Turkey*. Ed. by Andrews, P.A. Wiesbaden: Otto Harrassowitz, 1989.

Caplan, L. *Studies in Religious Fundamentalism*. London: Macmillan, 1987.

Charachidzé, G. 'Le Systéme réligieux de la Géorgie païenne: Analyse structurale d'une civilisation'. Ph.D.Thesis, Paris, 1968.

Çinar, M. and Silier, O. *Türkiye Tarımında İşletmeler Arası Farklılaşma*. Istanbul: Boğaziçi Üniversitesi, 1979.

Cleland, J. G. 'Maternal education, health seeking behaviour and child survival'. Paper presented at a workshop on Mother's Education and Child Survival. Ahmedabad, India: January, 1989.

Collier, J.F. and Yanagisako, S.J. Eds. *Gender and Kinship: Essays Toward a Unified Analysis*. Stanford: Stanford U.P., 1987.

Cousins, M. 'Material Arguments and Feminism', *m/f: a feminist journal*, 2, 1978.

Croll, E.J. 'Rural Production and Reproduction: Socialist Development Experiences', in *Women's Work: Development and Division of Labor by Gender*. Ed. by Leacock, E. and Safa, H.I. Massachusetts: Bergin and Garvey, 1986.

Delaney, C. 'The Meaning of Paternity and the Virgin Birth'. *Man*, 21, 3, 1986.

____. 'Seeds of Honor, Fields of Shame', in *Honor and Shame and the Unity of the Mediterranean*. Ed. by Gilmore, D. Washington: American Anthropological Association, 1987.

____. 'Participant-Observation: The Razor's Edge', *Dialectical Anthropology*, 13:3 August, 1989.

____. *The Seed and The Soil: Gender and Cosmology in Turkish Village Society*. Berkeley: University of California Press, 1991.

Demirkıran, S. 'Bağlum köyünde köylü işletmesi anketi', *Sosyoloji Dergisi*, 7, 1952.

Dodd, C. H. *The Crisis of Turkish Democracy*. North Humberside: The Eothen Press, 1983.

Doh, R. *Die sozio-ökonomischen Faktoren der internen Migration in der Türkei*. München: 1985.

Duben, A. 'Household Formation in Late Ottoman Istanbul', *International Journal of Middle East Studies*, 22, 4, 1990.

____. and Behar, C. *Istanbul Households: Marriage, Family and Fertility, 1880-1940*. Cambridge: C.U.P., 1990.

Dubisch, J. Ed. *Gender and Power in Rural Greece*. Princeton: Princeton

University Press, 1986.

Edholm, F., Harris, O. and Young, K. 'Conceptualizing Women', *Critique of Anthropology*, 1977.

Elson, D. *Male Bias in the Development Process*. Manchester: Manchester University Press, 1991.

Engels, F. *The Origin of the Family, Private Property and the State*. 1884. New York: Pathfinder Press, 1972.

Erder, T. *The Making of Industrial Bursa: Economic Activity and Population in a Turkish City 1835-1975*. Ph.D. Thesis, Princeton: Princeton University, 1976.

Ertürk, Y. 'The Impact of Market Forces on Rural Households in Southeastern Turkey', *METU Journal of Human Science*, 2, 1987.

Evans-Pritchard, E.E. *The Position of Women in Primitive Societies and Other Essays in Social Anthropology*. London: Faber and Faber, 1965.

Even, H., Yeşilyaprak, K., Elwert, G. and Stauth G. *Sozio-ökonomische Differenzierung und Arbeitsmigration in der ländlichen Türkei*. Saarbrücken: Fort Lauderdale, 1984.

Evers, H., Clauss W. and Wong D. 'Subsistence Reproduction: A Framework for Analysis', in *Households and the World Economy*. Ed. by. Smith J., Wallerstein I. and Evans H. Beverley Hills: Sage Publications, 1984.

Faculty of Political Science. See Siyasal Bilgiler Fakültesi.

Finkel, A. and Sirman, N. Eds. *Turkish State, Turkish Society*. London: Routledge, 1990.

Fischer, M. and Finkelstein, A. 'Social Knowledge Representation: a Case Study', in *Using Computers in Qualitative Research*. Ed. by Fielding, N.G. and Raymond, M.L. London: Sage, 1991.

Folch-Lyon, E. and Trost, J.F. 'Conducting focus group sessions', *Studies in Family Planning*, 12, 1981.

Fortes, M. *Kinship and the Social Order*. London: Routledge, 1969.

Frankenberg, R. 'The beginning of Anthropology: The challenge of the New Africa to the sociological study of small-scale social processes'. Tokyo: Proceedings of the VIIIth International Congress of Anthropological and Ethnological Sciences, 2, 1968.

Friedl, E. *Women and Men: an anthropologist's view*. New York: 1975.

____. 'The Position of Women: Appearance and Reality', in *Gender and Power in Rural Greece*. Ed. by Dubisch, J. Princeton: Princeton University Press, 1986.

Friedman, H. 'Household production and national economy: concepts for the analysis of agrarian formations', *Journal of Peasant Studies*, 7, 4, 1980.

Geiger, B. et al. Eds. *Peoples and Languages of the Caucasus*. The Hague: Mouton, 1959.

Gellner, E. *Saints of the Atlas*. London: Weidenfeld & Nicholson, 1969.

____. *Muslim Society*. Cambridge: C.U.P.,1981.
____. *Nations and Nationalism*. Oxford: Blackwell, 1983.
____. and Waterbury, J. Eds. *Patrons and Clients in Mediterranean Societies*. London: Duckworth, 1977.
Gerber, H. *Social Origins of the Modern Middle East*. Boulder: Lynne Reinner, 1987.
Gerholm, T. and Lithman, G. Eds. *The New Islamic Presence in Western Europe*. London: Mansell, 1988.
Giddens, A. *The Constitution of Society*. Cambridge: Polity Press, 1984.
Gilman C.P. *Woman and Economics*. Boston: Harper and Row, 1899, 2nd ed. 1966.
Gilsenan, M. *Recognizing Islam*. London: Croom Helm, 1982.
Gitmez, A. *Dışgöç ve Dönenler: Beklenenler, Gerçekleşenler*. Istanbul: Alan Publishing, 1983.
__. and Wilpert, C. 'A Micro-Society or an Ethnic Community, Social Organization and Ethnicity amongst Turkish Migrants in Berlin', *Immigrant Associations in Europe*. Ed. by Rex, J., Joly, D. and Wilpert, C. Aldershot: Gower, 1987.
Gökalp, A. *Têtes rouges et bouches noires*. Paris: 1980.
____. 'Alevisme Nomade: des communitaires de statut à l'identité communitaire', in *Ethnic Groups in the Republic of Turkey*. Ed. by Andrews, P.A. Wiesbaden: Otto Harrossowitz, 1989.
Gökalp, Z. *Türkçülüğün Esasları*. Ankara: Milli İçtimaiyat Kitabhanesi, 1923.
Göknil, N. 'Bilecik bölgesi Kasımlar köyü'. *Sosyoloji Dergisi*, 2, 1943.
Goldschmidt-Clermont, L. *Economic Evaluation of Unpaid Household Work: Africa, Asia, Latin America and Oceania*. Geneva: ILO, 1987.
Göloğlu, M. *Anadolu'nun Milli Devleti, Pontos*. Ankara: Göloğlu Yayınları, 1973.
Goody, J. *Production and Reproduction*. Cambridge: C.U.P., 1976.
____. *The Oriental, the Ancient, and the Primitive*. Cambridge: C.U.P., 1990.
Güneş-Ayata, A. 'Class and Clientelism in the Republican People's Party', in *Turkish State: Turkish Society*. Ed. by Finkel, A. and Sirman, N. London: Routledge, 1990.
Gürkan, A. and Kasnakoğlu, H. 'Tarımın Türk Ekonomisinin Gelişimine Katkısı: Bugün ve Yarın', 1985-6 Enka Bilim ve Sanat Ödülleri, Istanbul: 1986.
Hale, W. *Aspects of Modern Turkey*. Epping: Bowker, 1976.
Hale, W.M. *The Political and Economic Development of Modern Turkey*. London: Croom Helm, 1981.
Hann, C. M. 'Rural Transformation on the East Black Sea Coast of Turkey; a note on Keyder', *Journal of Peasant Studies*, 12, 4, 1985.

____. *Tea and the Domestication of the Turkish State,* Occasional Papers in Modern Turkish Studies 1. Huntingdon: The Eothen Press, 1990.

Hardon, A. P. 'The use of modern pharmaceuticals in a Filipino village: Doctors' prescription and self-medication', *Social Science and Medicine*, 25, 1987.

Helman, C. *Culture, Health and Illness.* Bristol: John Wright and Sons, 1986.

Herzfeld, M. *Anthropology Through the Looking-Glass: Critical Ethnography in the Margins of Europe.* Cambridge: C.U.P., 1987.

Hill, P. *Development Economics on Trial.* Cambridge: C.U.P., 1986.

Hilton, R. 'Introduction', in *The Transition from Feudalism to Capitalism.* Ed. by Sweezy, P. et al. London: N.L.B., 1976.

Hinderink, J. and Kiray, M. *Social Stratification as an Obstacle to Development.* New York: Praeger, 1970.

Hirschman, A. *Getting Ahead Collectively: Grassroots Experiences in Latin America.* New York: Pergamon Press, 1984.

Höneko, E. 'Zur beruflichen und sozialen Re-integration Türkischer Arbeitsmigranten im Zeitverlauf', *Mitteilungen zur Arbeitsmarkt und Berufsforschung*, 1, Nürnberg: 1990.

Igun, U.A. 'Stages in health seeking: A descriptive model', *Social Science and Medicine*, 13A, 1978.

İnan, H. 'Peasants, commercialization and legitimation of state power in sixteenth century Anatolia', in *Landholding and Commercial Agriculture in the Middle East.* Ed. by Keyder, Ç. and Tabok, F. Albany: S.U.N.Y., 1991.

İncirlioğlu, E.O. 'Gender Relations and Rural Transformation: Two Central Anatolian Villages'. Ph.D.Thesis, University of Florida: 1991.

____. 'The Struggle for Reality'. Unpublished Ms., M.E.S.A. Conference Paper, Portland: 1992.

Kabeer, N. and Joekes, S. 'Researching the Household: Methodological and Empirical Issues', *IDS Bulletin*, 22, 1, University of Sussex: 1991.

Kahn, J. 'From peasants to petty commodity production in Southeast Asia', *Bulletin of Concerned Asian Scholars*, 1, 1982.

Kanbolat, Y. *Türkiye Ziraatinde Bünye Değışikliği.* Ankara: 1963.

Kandiyoti, D. *Women in Rural Production Systems: problems and policies.* UNESCO: 1985.

Kantorowicz, E. *Die Zwei Körper des Königs.* München: dtv, 1990.

Karpat, K. *The Gecekondu: Rural Migration and Urbanization.* Cambridge: C.U.P., 1976.

Kağıtcıbaşı, Ç. *Çocuğun Değeri: Türkiye de Değerler ve Doğurganlık.* Istanbul: Bosphorus University, 1981.

Keleş, R. 'The Building of a House as an Investment: Right or Wrong', in *Migration and Development.* Ed. by Abadan-Unat, N., Ankara: 1975.

____. and Yavuz, F. *Yerel Yönetimler.* 2nd edition. Ankara: Turhan

Kitabevi, 1989.

Kemiksiz, N. 'Yurtdışına İşçi Göçü ve bu olgunun dönen işçilerin siyasal tutum ve davranışları üzerindeki etki'. Ph.D. Thesis. Ankara: Ankara University, 1989.

Keyder, Ç. *Definition of a Peripheral Economy, Turkey 1923-1929*. Cambridge: C.U.P., 1981.

____. 'The cycle of sharecropping and the consolidation of small peasant ownership in Turkey', *Journal of Peasant Studies*, 10, 2-3, 1983a.

____. 'Paths of Rural Transformation in Turkey', *Journal of Peasant Studies*, 11, 1, 1983b.

___. 'Die Agrarstruktur', *Türkei zwischen Militärdiktatur und Demokratie*. Ed. by Seven, O. Hamburg: 1984.

____. *State and Class in Turkey*. London: Verso, 1987.

____. and Pamuk, Ş. '1945 Ciftciyi Topraklandırma Kanunu üzerine tezler', *Yapıt*, 7, December/January 1984-5.

Kiray, M. 'Values, Social Stratification and Development', *Journal of Social Issues*, 24, 2, 1968.

___. 'The New Role of Mothers: Changing Intrafamilial Relationships in a Small Town in Turkey', *Mediterrannean Family Structures*. Ed. by Peristiany, J.G. Cambridge: C.U.P., 1976.

Kleff, H.-G. *Vom Bauern zum Industriearbeiter, Zur lektiven Lebensgeschichte der Arbeitsmigranten aus der Türkei*. Ingelheim: Manthano Verlag, 1985.

Köker, A. F. *Herausbildung der strukturellen Heterogenität in einer unterentwickelten Gesellschaftsformation am Beispiel der Türkei*. Frankfurt\Main: Fischer, 1980.

Kolars, J.F. *Tradition, Season and Change in a Turkish Village*. Chicago: University of Chicago Press, 1963.

Kozak, İ. E. *Yurtiçi ve Yurd Dışına İşgücü Akımı acısından Erzurum ilinin Nüfus İşgücü, İstihdam Meseleleleri ve Dönen İşçiler*. Erzurum: Atatürk University, 1979.

Kroeger, A. 'Anthropologies and socio-medical health care research in developing countries', *Social Science and Medicine*, 17, 1983.

Kudat, A. *Stability and Change in the Turkish Family at Home and Abroad*. Berlin: Wissensschaftszentrum, 1975.

Kurhan, Y. 'Eskitaşlı köyü monografisi', *Sosyoloji Dergisi*, 10-11, 1955-56.

Lenin, V.I. *Development of Capitalism in Russia*, Volume 3 of *Collected Works*. Moscow: Foreign Languages Publishing House, 1964.

Leopold U. *Sozio-ökonomische Ursachen der Migration türkischer Arbeitskräfte*. Bremen: Veröffentlichungen aus dem Übersee-Museum Bremen, Reihe D, 4, 1978.

Lerner D. *The Passing of Traditional Society: Modernizing the Middle East*. London: Collier Macmillan, 1964.

Leslie, J. 'Time costs and time savings to women of the child survival revolution'. International Center for Research on Women, 1987.

Levine, N. 'Differential child care in three Tibetan communities: Beyond son preference', *Population and Development Review*, 13, 1987.

Lewis, G. *Turkey*. London: Benn, 1957.

Luzbetak, L. J. 'Marriage and the Family in Caucasia: a Contribution to the Study of North Caucasian Ethnology and Customary Law', *Studia Instituti Anthropos*, 3, Vienna: 1951.

McCarthy, J. 'Foundations of the Turkish Republic: social and economic change', *Middle Eastern Studies*, 19, 2, 1983.

MacEoin, D. and Al-Shahi, A., Eds. *Islam in the Modern World*. London: Croom Helm, 1983.

Macpherson, C.B. *The Political Theory of Possessive Individualism*. Oxford: O.U.P., 1962.

Magnarella, P. J. 'The Assimilation of Georgians in Turkey. A Case Study', *The Muslim World*, 66, 1976.

Makal, M. *Bizim Köy*. Istanbul: Varlık, 1950.

____. *A Village in Anatolia*. London: Vallentine Mitchell, 1954.

Mardin, Ş. *Religion and Social Change in Modern Turkey: The Case of Bediüzzaman Said Nursi*. Albany: S.U.N.Y., 1989.

Margulies, R. 'Small Family Farming and Transformation of Turkish Agriculture: 1950-65'. PhD. Thesis, University of East Anglia, 1985.

Martin, P.L. *The Unfinished Story: Turkish Labour Migration to Western Europe*. Geneva: ILO, 1991.

Meeker, M. 'The Black Sea Turks: A Study of Honor, Descent, and Marriage'. Ph.D. Thesis. University of Chicago, 1970.

____. 'Meaning and Society in the Near East: Examples from the Black Sea Turks and the Levantine Arabs', *International Journal of Middle Eastern Studies*, 7, 2 and 3, 1970.

____. 'The Black Sea Turks: Some Aspects of their Ethnic and Cultural Background', *International Journal of Middle Eastern Studies*, 2, 4, 1971.

Meillassoux, C. *Maidens, meal and money: capitalism and the domestic community*. Cambridge: C.U.P., 1981.

Melikoff, I. 'Le problème Kızılbaş', *Turcica*, 6, 1975.

Molyneux, M. 'Mobilization Without Emancipation? Women's Interests, the State, and the Revolution in Nicaragua', *Feminist Studies*, 11, 2, 1985.

Moore, B. *Social Origins of Dictatorship and Democracy, Lord and Peasant in the Making of the Modern World*. London: Penguin, 1967.

Moore, H. *Feminisim and Anthropology*. Minneapolis: University of Minnesota Press, 1988.

Morvaridi, B. 'The Process of Agrarian Transition: Household Production and Reproduction in a Sugar Beet Growing Region of Turkey'. Ph.D. Thesis, University of Kent at Canterbury, 1987.

__. 'Modern Agricultural Inputs and Sharecropping Arrangements', Oxford Agrarian Studies, XVII, 1988.

__. 'The Strategies of Households in the Production of Cash/Food Crops', in *Political, Social and Economic Perspectives on the International Food System*. Ed. by Marsden, T. and Little, J. Aldershot: Gower, 1990.

__. 'Agrarian Reform and Land Use Policy in Turkey: Implications for the South East Anatolian Irrigation Project', *Land Use Policy*, 7, 1990.

__. 'Cash Crop Production and the Process of Transformation', *Development and Change*, 21, 4, 1990.

__. 'Gender Relations in Agriculture: Women in Turkey', *Economic Development and Cultural Change*, April, 1992.

__. 'Is Sustainable Development More than a Concept?', in *Sustainable Development and Environmental Policy*. Ed. by Kitchen, R. Discussion Paper, Special Issue, Bradford, D.P.P.C., 23, 1992.

__. 'Land Degradation in the Communal Areas of Rural Zimbabwe: Implications for Structural Adjustment Policy', in *Sustainable Development and Environmental Policy*. Ed. by Kitchen, R. Discussion Paper, Special Issue, Bradford, D.P.P.C., 23, 1992.

__. 'Resettlement, Demographic Change and Resource Use', in *The Political, Social and Economic Development of Northern Cyprus*. Ed. by Dodd, C.H. Huntingdon: The Eothen Press, 1993.

__. 'Agriculture and the Environment', in *The Political, Social and Economic Development of Northern Cyprus*. Ed. by Dodd, C.H. Huntingdon: The Eothen Press, 1993.

Mülayim, Z. G. *Assessment of Rural Landlessness in Turkey*. Ankara: FAO: National Assessments of Rural Landlessness, Final Report, 1985.

Nasr, S. H. *Ideals and Realities of Islam*. London: George Allen & Unwin, 1966, reprinted 1985.

Nauck, B.B. *Arbeitsmigration und Familienstruktur*. Frankfurt: Campus Verlag, 1985.

Nesin, A. *Yedek Parca*. 1955.

Nicolas, M. *Croyances et pratiques populaires turques concernant la naissance*,.Paris: Publications Orientalistes de France, 1972.

Norton, J. 'Bektashis in Turkey', in *Islam in the Modern World*, Ed. by MacEoin, D. and Al-Shahi, A. 1983.

Olson, E.A. 'Anthropological and Sociological Studies of Turkey: an American Perspective', *The Turkish Studies Association Bulletin*, 10, 2, 1986.

Overholt, C., Anderson, M.B., Cloud, K. and Austin, J.E. *Gender Roles in Development Projects: A Case Book*. West Hartford, Connecticut:

Kumarian Press, 1984.

Paleczek, G. 'Der Wandel der traditionellen Wirtschaft (Subsistenz- und marktanteilige Produktion) in einem westanatolischen Muhacirdorf'. 3 Vols. Ph.D.Thesis, Vienna, 1984.

___. 'Der Wandel der traditionellen Wirtschaft in einem anatolischen Dorf.', *Wiener Beiträge zur Ethnologie und Anthropologie*, 4, Vienna, 1987(a).

___. 'Der Wandel der bäuerlichen Lebensbedingungen in der Türkei' in *Jahrbuch zur Geschichte und Gesellschaft des Vorderen und Mittleren Orients, 1985/1986. Thema: Gesellschaft und Politik in der Türkei*. Ed. by Blaschke, J. Berlin: 1987(b).

___. *Analyse der Modernisierungsversuche in der türkischen Landwirtschaft als Entscheidungshilfe für die Österreichische Wirtschaft Bericht des Forschungsprojektes Nr.2639*. Vienna: 1988.

___. 'Modernisierungsstrategien und Probleme der türkischen Landwirtschaft', *Journal für Entwicklungspolitik*, 5, 1, 1989(a).

___. 'Turkish Families in Transition: Some Remarks on Household Composition in Rural Turkey', in *Kinship, Social Change and Evolution*. Ed. by. Gingrich, A., Haas, S., and Paleczek, G. Vienna: Wiener Beiträge zur Ethnologie und Anthropologie, 6, 1989(b).

Pamuk, Ş. 'War, state economic policies and resistance by agricultural producers in Turkey, 1939-1945', *New Perspectives on Turkey*, 2, 1, 1988.

Parry, J. and Bloch, M. Eds. *Money and the Morality of Exchange*. Cambridge: C.U.P., 1989.

Patrick, D. and Scamber, G. *Sociology as Allied to Medicine*. Bailliere Tindall, 1984.

Pelto, P. J. and Pelto, G.H. *Anthropological Research: The Structure of Inquiry*, (2nd edition). Cambridge: C.U.P., 1978.

Penninx, R., and Van Renselaar, H. 'Evolution of Turkish Migration before and during the current European recession', in *Migration and Development*. Ed. by Abadan-Unat, N. et al. Ankara: Ankara University, 1975.

___. and Van Velzen, L. 'Investment in Housing', in *Migration and Development*. Ed. by Abadan-Unat, N. et al. Ankara: Ankara University, 1975.

Pflanz, M. 'Relations between social scientists, physicians, and medical organizations in health research', *Social Science and Medicine*, 1975.

Picken, L.E.R. *Folk Musical Instruments of Turkey*. Oxford: O.U.P., 1975.

Ragnar, N. 'Being an Alevi Muslim in South Western Anatolia and in Norway: the impact of migration on a heterodox Turkish community', in *The New Islamic Presence in Western Europe*. Ed. by Gerholm, T. and Lithman, G. London: Mansell, 1988.

Republic of Turkey. See Türkiye Cumhuriyeti.

Redclift, N. 'The Contested Domain: Gender, Accumulation and the Labour Process, in *Beyond Employment*. Ed. by Redclift, N. and Enzomingione, E. Oxford: Basil Blackwell, 1985.

Rex, J., Joly, D. and Wilpert, C., Eds. *Immigrant Association in Europe*. Aldershot: Gower, 1987.

Rogers, B. *The Domestication of Women: Discrimination in Developing Societies*. London: Tavistock, 1980.

Rouget, G. *Music and Trance: A Theory of the Relations between Music and Possession*. Chicago: University of Chicago Press, 1985.

Sahlins, M. 'On the Sociology of Primitive Exchange', in *The Relevance of Models for Social Anthropology*. Ed. by Banton, M. London: 1965.

___. *Islands of History*. Chicago: University of Chicago Press, 1985.

Schick, I. and Tonak, E. Eds. *Turkey in Transition*. Oxford: O.U.P., 1987.

Schiffauer, W. *Die Bauern von Subay. Das Leben in einem türkischen Dorf*. Stuttgart: Klett-Cotta, 1987.

___. *Die Migranten aus Subay. Türken in Deutschland: Eine Ethnographie*. Stuttgart: Klett-Cotta, 1991.

Schirmer, A. 'Zum Problem der Ballungsräume im Orient: Industrielle Wachstumskerne als Entlastungsstrategien am Beispiel Istanbuls', *Orient*, 18, 4, 1977.

Scrimshaw, S.C.M. 'Combining quantitative and qualitative methods in the study of intrahousehold resource allocation', *Food and Nutrition Bulletin*, 1989.

__. and Hurdato, E. 'Training manual for use with rapid assessment procedures for nutrition and primary health care: Anthropological approaches to improving programme effectiveness'. Unpublished ms., 1989.

Scrimshaw, S.M. 'Infant mortality and behaviour in the regulation of family size', *Population and Development Review*, 4, 1978.

Seccombe, W. 'The Housewife and her Labor under Capitalism', *New Left Review*, 83, 1974.

Seddon, D. and Margulies, R. 'The Politics of the Agrarian Question in Turkey: Review of a debate', *Journal of Peasant Studies*, 11, 1984.

Sen, G. *Development, Crisis and Alternative Visions*. Earth Publication, 1988.

Senghaas, D. 'Vorwort: Elemente einer Theorie des peripheren Kapitalismus', in *Peripherer Kapitalismus: Analysen über Abhängigkeit und Unterentwicklung*, Ed. by Senghaas, D. Frankfurt \ Main: 2nd ed., 1977.

Sharma, U. *Women, Work and Property in North-West India*. London: Tavistock, 1980.

Shorter, F. C. and Macura, M. *Trends in Fertility and Mortality in*

Turkey: 1935-1975. Washington, D.C.: National Academy Press, 1982.

Simons, J. 'Cultural dimensions of the other's contribution to child survival'. Paper presented at a Workshop on Mother's Education and Child Survival. Ahmedabad, India, January, 1989.

Sirman, A. N. 'Peasants and Family Farms: the Position of Households in Cotton Production in Western Turkey'. Ph.d. Thesis, University of London, 1988(a).

Sirman, N. 'Pamuk Üretiminde Aile İşletmeleri', in *Türkiye'de Tarimsal Yapılar*. Ed. by Pamuk, S. and Toprak, Z. Ankara: Yurt Yayınları/TSBD Yayınları, 1988(b).

__. 'Köy Kadınının Aile ve Evlilik Güçlenme Mucadelesi', in *Kadın Başı Acısından: 1980'ler Türkiyesinde Kadınlar*. Ed. by Tekeli, S. Istanbul: İletişim Yayınları, 1990(a).

___. 'Köy Ünitisinin Tanımlanması', *Toplum ve Bilim*, 48/49 (Winter, Summer), Ankara: 1990(b).

___. 'State, Village and Gender in Western Turkey', in *Turkish State, Turkish Society*, Ed. by Finkel, A. and Sirman, N. London: Routledge, 1990(c).

Siyasal Bilgiler Fäkültesi, *Turkye'de Zirai Makinalaşma*. Ankara: Ankara University, 1954.

Smith, C. 'Does a commodity economy enrich the few while ruining the masses?', *Journal of Peasant Studies*, 12, 1, 1984.

Smith, J. and Wallerstein, I. Eds. *Creating and Transforming Households: The Constraints of the World-Economy*. Cambridge: C.U.P., 1992.

Spradley, J. P. *The Ethnographic Interview*. New York: Holt, Rinehart and Winston, 1979.

State Institute of Statistics. See Türkiye Cumhuriyeti.

Stewig, R. 'Bursa: Nordwestanatolien: Strukturwandel einer orientalischen Stadt unter dem Einfluß der Industrialisierung', *Schriften des Geographischen Instituts der Universität Kiel*, 32, 1970.

Stirling, P. 'The Social Structure of Turkish Peasant Communities'. D.Phil. Thesis, Oxford: 1951.

___. 'The Domestic Cycle and the Distribution of Power in Turkish Villages', in *Mediterranean Countrymen*. Ed. by Pitt-Rivers, J. The Hague: Mouton, 1963.

___. *Turkish Village*. London: Weidenfeld and Nicolson, 1965.

___. 'Impartiality and Personal Morality', in *Contributions to Mediterranean Sociology*. Ed. by Peristiany, J. G. The Hague: Mouton, 1968.

___. 'Cause, Knowledge and Change: Turkish Village Revisited', in *Choice and Change: Essays in honour of Lucy Mair*. Ed. by Davis, J. London: Athlone Press, 1974.

___. 'Social Change and Social Control in Republican Turkey', *Papers and Discussions: Türkiye İş Bankası International Symposium on Atatürk*. Ankara: Cultural Publications, Türkiye İş Bankası, 1984.

Stokes, M.H. *The Arabesk Debate: Music and Musicians in Modern Turkey*. Oxford: O.U.P., 1992.

Strathern, M. *The Gender of the Gift*. Berkeley: University of California Press, 1988.

Szyliowicz, J.S. *Political Change in Rural Turkey*. The Hague: Mouton, 1966.

Tachau, F. 'The Political Culture of Kemalist Turkey', in *Atatürk and the Modernization of Turkey*. Ed. by Landau, J. Boulder: Westview Press, 1984.

Talım, M. *Structural and Management Problems of Farms in Turkey*. Rome, 1985.

Tambiah, S. J. 'Bridewealth and Dowry Revisited: the Position of Women in Sub-Saharan Africa and North India', *Current Anthropology*, 30, 4, 1989.

Tanyol, C. 'Traktör giren 50 köyde ictimai değişmelerin kontrolu', *Sosyoloji Dergisi*, 13-14, 1958-59.

Tapper, R. *Pasture and Politics: Economics, conflict and ritual among Shahsevan nomads of northwestern Iran*. London: Academic Press, 1979.

____. and Tapper, N. '"Thank God we're secular!" Aspects of fundamentalism in a Turkish Town', in *Aspects of Relgious Fundamentalism*. Ed. by Caplan, L. London: 1987.

Taraklı, D. *Çiftçiyi Topraklandırma Kanunu ve Sonuçları*. Ankara: ODTÜ Yayınları, 1976.

Tekeli, İ. 'Osmanlı İmparatorlugundan günümüze nüfusun zorunlu yer değistirmesi ve iskan sorunu', *Toplum ve Bilim*, 1990.

Tekin, İ.H. *Türkiye Köy İktisadiyatı*. Ankara: 1934.

Thornburg, M.W., Spray, G. and Soule, G. *Turkey: An Economic Appraisal*. New York: Twentieth Century Fund, 1949. Turkish edition: *Türkiye'de Bugünkü Ekonomik Durumun Tenkidi*. Ankara: 1950.

Timur, S. *Türkiye'de Aile Yapısı*. Ankara: Hacettepe Üniversitesi Yayınları, 1972.

Todd, E. *The Explanation of Ideology. Family Structures and Social Systems*. Oxford: Basil Blackwell, 1985.

Trimberger, A.K. *Revolution from Above: Military Bureaucrats and Development in Japan, Turkey, Egypt and Peru*. New Jersey: Transaction Books, 1978.

Türkiye Cumhuriyeti.

Devlet İstatisik Enstitüsü. *İstatistik Yıllığı 1951*. Ankara: 1952.

____. *Ziraat Sayımı Neticeleri*. Ankara: 1956.

____. *1963 Genel Tarım Sayımı Örneklme Sonuçları*. Ankara: 1965.

____. *Türkiye'de Toplumsal ve Ekonomik Gelişmenin 50 Yıl*. Ankara:

1973.

____. *Turkiye Milli Geliri 1948-72*. Ankara: 1978.

____. *Genel Tarım Sayımı 1980*. Ankara: 1980.

____. *İstatistık Yıllığı 1985*. Ankara: 1986.

____. *İstatistik Yıllığı 1986*, Ankara: 1987.

____. *Genel Nufüs Sayımı 1990*. Ankara: 1991.

Devlet Planlama Teşkilatı, *Türk Aile Yapısı*. Ankara: DPT 2165, 1989.

Tunçbilek, E. Ed. *Infant Mortality in Turkey: Basic Factors*. Ankara: Hacettepe University, Institute of Population Studies, 1988.

Turhan, M. *Kültür Değişmeleri: Sosyal Psikolojik Bakımdan bir Tetkik*. Istanbul: Edebiyat Fakultesi Yayınları 479, Istanbul University, 1951.

__. Ed. *The Turkish Economy*. Istanbul: 1982.

Türk Sanayicileri ve İs Adamları Derneği, Ed. *The Turkish Economy*, Istanbul: 1988.

Tütengil, C.O. 'Keciler köyü incelemesi', *Sosyoloji Dergisi*, 10-11, 1955-56.

Ülken, H.Z., Kösemihal, N.S. and Tanyol, C. 'Karataş köyü monografisi', *Sosyoloji Dergisi*, 6, 1950.

Üner, S. *Effects of Migration on the Rural Economy of Turkey*. Rome: FAO. Employment and Manpower Planning Studies, 1980.

UNICEF. 'Control of ARIs: Status Report 1986-1988'. Ankara: UNICEF, 1988.

Union of Turkish Chambers and Exchange. *Turkey Economy*. Ankara: 1992.

Vandergeest, P. 'Commercialisation and Commoditisation: a dialogue between perspectives', *Sociologia Ruralis*, 28, 1, 1988.

Varlier, O. *Türkiye Tarımında Yapısal Değişme, Teknoloji ve Toprak Bölüşümü*. Ankara: DPT Yayını, 1978.

Vryonis, S. *The Decline of Medieval Hellenism in Asia Minor and the Process of Islamization from the Eleventh through the Fifteenth Century*. London: University of California Press, 1971.

Werle, R. *'Modell' Turkei. Ein Land wird kaputtsaniert*. Hamburg: Junius, 1983.

Whitehead, A. 'Effects of Technological Change on Rural Women: A Review of Analysis and Concepts', in *Technology and Rural Women: Conceptual and Empirical Issues*. Ed. by Ahmed, I. London: Allen & Unwin, 1985.

Wolf, E. *Europe and People Without History*. Berkeley: University of California Press, 1982.

World Bank. *World Development Report 1986*. New York: O.U.P., 1986.

World Bank. *Agricultural Mechanisation*. Washington, 1987.

Worsley, P. *The Three Worlds: Culture and Development*. London: Weidenfeld and Nicolson, 1984.

Yalçın, L. 'Aşireti Kadın', in *Kadin Başı Acısından: 1980'ler*

Türkiye'sinde Kadınlar. Ed. by Tekeli, S. Istanbul: İletişim Yayınları, 1990.

Yalçın-Heckmann, L. *Tribe and Kinship among the Kurds*. Frankfurt\Main: 1991.

Yalman, N. 'Islamic Reform and the Mystic Tradition in Eastern Turkey', *Archives Européennes de Sociologie*, 10, 1969.

___. 'On land disputes in Eastern Turkey', in *Islam and its Cultural Divergence*. Ed.by Tikku, G.L. Illinois: 1971.

Yasa, İ. *Yurda Dönen İşçiler ve Toplumsal Değişme*. Ankara: 1979.

Yazıcı, H. *Fındıklı*. Fındıklı: Karadeniz Matbaası, 1984.

Yörükan, T. and Cebe, T. 'Çatak köyü araştırması', *Sosyoloji Dergisi*, 10-11, 1955-56.

Yenisey, Leyla. 'The Social Effects of Migrant Labour on the District Left Behind. Observations on two Villages of Boğazlıyan', in *Migration and Development* by N. Abadan, Keles, R. et.al. Ankara: Ankara University, 1975.

Yücel, Y. 'Fatih'in Trabzon'u Fethi Öncesinde Osmanlı-Trabzon-Akkoyunlu İlişkileri', *Belleten* 49, 1985.